NONPROFIT ESSENTIALS
Managing Technology

Date Due

NONPROFIT ESSENTIALS
Managing Technology

Jeannette Woodward

WILEY

John Wiley & Sons, Inc.

For general information on our other products and services, or technical support, please contact our Customer Care Department within the United States at 800-762-2974, outside the United States at 317-572-3993 or fax 317-572-4002.

Wiley also publishes its books in a variety of electronic formats. Some content that appears in print may not be available in electronic books.

For more information about Wiley products, visit our Web site at *www.wiley.com.*

Library of Congress Cataloging-in-Publication Data:
Woodward, Jeannette A.
    Nonprofit essentials : managing technology / Jeannette Woodward.
        p. cm.
    Includes index.
    ISBN-13: 978-0-471-73838-1 (pbk.)
    ISBN-10: 0-471-73838-7 (pbk.)
    1. Office practice—Automation. 2. Nonprofit organizations—Management. 3. Information technology—Management. I. Title.
    HF5548.2.W648 2006
    004.068—dc22

ISBN-10: 0-471-73838-7

ISBN-13: 978-0-471-73838-1

Printed in the United States of America

10 9 8 7 6 5 4 3 2 1

To Laura, Chris, Lowell, and John with much love.

The AFP Fund Development Series

The AFP Fund Development Series is intended to provide fund development professionals and volunteers, including board members (and others interested in the nonprofit sector), with top-quality publications that help advance philanthropy as voluntary action for the public good. Our goal is to provide practical, timely guidance and information on fundraising, charitable giving, and related subjects. The Association of Fundraising Professionals(AFP) and Wiley each bring to this innovative collaboration unique and important resources that result in a whole greater than the sum of its parts. For information on other books in the series, please visit: http://www.afpnet.org

The Association of Fundraising Professionals

The Association of Fundraising Professionals (AFP) represents 26,000 members in more than 170 chapters throughout the world, working to advance philanthropy through advocacy, research, education, and certification programs. The association fosters development and growth of fundraising professionals and promotes high ethical standards in the fundraising profession. For more information or to join the world's largest association of fundraising professionals, visit www.afpnet.org.

2004-2005 AFP Publishing Advisory Committee

Acknowledgments

It takes very special people to devote themselves to the service of others through participation in a nonprofit organization. I have been fortunate in working with some extraordinary leaders of mission-based organizations. Whether Syd Miller, who has saved countless dogs through her work in the local Pet Connection, or the volunteer librarians who bring a love for books to the farthest, windswept corners of Wyoming, they have all served as inspiring examples. I am also grateful to my son-in-law, John McBride, for his technical expertise and to the other members of my family for their enthusiastic support and encouragement.

About the Author

Jeannette Woodward is a founder and principal of the Wind River Nonprofit and Educational Consulting group. She is also a nonprofit board member, volunteer, and battle-scarred veteran of bake sales, wine tastings, and rubber duck races too numerous to mention.

Before becoming involved in the Wind River Nonprofit and Educational Consulting Group, Woodward was a library administrator with many years' experience in public and academic libraries. It was her responsibility to supervise the library's technical staff and plan for the development of a variety of computer systems. She was also instrumental in obtaining grant funds for technology and assisting other libraries and nonprofits to obtain technology resources.

As an active member of many community groups, she realized that nonprofits experience even more computer crises than comparable, for-profit business organizations. Vital projects like fundraising campaigns are not as effective as they should be because of inadequate information. Since a group's mission should guide its use of technology, she decided a book that addressed the unique needs of these organizations was badly needed.

Woodward's books published by the American Library Association, *Creating the Customer-Driven Library* (2004) and *Countdown to a New Library* (2000), include chapters on technology planning and management. She has also written a number of journal articles dealing with technology and is the author of a chapter in the *Annual Review of Information Science and Technology* (American Society for Information Science, 1996). Among her other publications is the college writing textbook *Writing Research Papers: Investigating Resources in Cyberspace* (McGraw-Hill, 1999).

Woodward holds a masters degree in library and information science from Rutgers University with further study in higher educational administration at North Carolina State University. She is the mother of two children: Laura, a social psychologist, and Christopher, an attorney who is presently working on the Pacific island of Saipan.

Contents

Preface

In recent years, successful nonprofit organizations have used computers to become more effective in nearly every way. They have learned how to enhance the productivity of both staff and volunteers, so they can achieve more with limited resources. Because competition for funding dollars has become so aggressive, organizations that have ignored the computer revolution or use computers as expensive typewriters are at a serious disadvantage.

What makes some organizations successful while others flounder, losing membership lists in hard drive crashes or going over budget because of computer-generated errors? The answer is neither more generous funding nor more high-tech expertise. Successful nonprofits have learned to manage technology. That means that computers and software programs have been absorbed so completely into the missions and goals of these organizations that they are inseparable from them. Technology isn't a frill or a toy. It is a tool used by all group members to achieve their shared vision.

Purpose

This book is intended to help nonprofit leaders become not only more effective as administrators, marketers, researchers, and fundraisers, but also more responsible custodians of limited funds. When every penny counts, computers can help to make it possible for small, committed groups to perform the routine tasks that once required a small army to accomplish. Technology in nonprofits is most useful when it frees both human hands and human imagination.

Where once technology costs were so high as to be beyond the reach of all but large organizations, even the smallest nonprofit can now design and implement a basic technology plan. There is no question, however, that technology isn't always a faithful servant. As many groups can attest, failed technology can actually interfere with an organization's effectiveness. Instead of easing the workload of staff and volunteers, freeing their time for more meaningful work, technology becomes a handicap and a source of conflict. This is not usually the result of equipment failure but, like so many other organizational breakdowns, more the result of human failings like the unwillingness to learn, to share information, and to cooperate.

Overview of the Content

Failures happen when technology is someone else's responsibility, when group members view the computer system as some other member's brainchild that exists chiefly to complicate their lives. This tends to occur when technology is imposed from on high. One or more members of the organization become a sort of technical elite and seek to impose their plan on the organization.

Although this book will describe some of the "nuts and bolts" of setting up computer systems, its real emphasis will be on people rather than on machines. It is not intended for computer pros but for people who care deeply about their organizations and will do what it takes to help them succeed. Everyone can use technology effectively no matter what his or her level of technical sophistication. It's great to have computer gurus among our ranks, and we have much to learn from them. However, the real secret to success lies not in high-tech achievements but in incorporating basic computer literacy into the goals of our organizations.

Technology Brings Change

Computers, when used effectively, tend to move an organization toward greater structure, since responsibilities must be formally assigned. Unlike business enterprises, a formal division of labor is difficult for nonprofits that depend heavily on large numbers of volunteers who each contribute a few hours of their time. Effective use of computers depends on developing habits, and this is difficult when so much time elapses between work periods. This means that written instructions are needed to standardize procedures, another difficult adjustment for organizations accustomed to "flying by the seat of their pants." Routine and uniformity are essential, not because of a power-seeking individual's whim, but because that's the way computers work. Thus, changes in the organization are essential, but they must arise from the common consent of the group, not from the command of an elite group.

Audience

This book is intended for all mission-based organizations. In other words, it may be useful to both staff and volunteers of charitable, faith-based, advocacy, professional, and even government-funded organizations like schools and libraries.

A special need, however, exists for a book that can speak specifically to smaller and midsize nonprofits that may employ few paid staff members and carry out much of their work with volunteer labor. For such organizations, there is a lack of professional literature to guide their forays into technology planning. Policies and practices that work well for businesses with technology departments and full-time staff are often impractical where any computer may be used by a dozen or more volunteers and where no technical support staff is immediately available to deal with crises. This book, therefore, is intended to make the basics of technical planning intelligible and even enjoyable to board members, administrators, and volunteers who have found the subject intimidating in the past. All these organizations depend on a special kind of synergy that enables ordinary people using limited resources to move mountains.

NONPROFIT ESSENTIALS
Managing Technology

CHAPTER 1

Getting Started with Technology

After reading this chapter, you will be able to:

- Decide exactly what it is you want to get from technology.
- Measure both the cost and the rewards of technology.
- Perform a technology assessment.
- Understand the basic components of a technology plan.

The Impact of Computers

In just a few years, computers have become a part of nearly every aspect of modern life. In fact, they have transformed every sector of our society. At first, only larger organizations could afford the high cost of hardware and software. In recent years, however, costs have fallen to the point that most individuals and organizations have some kind of computer access. As time goes on, it becomes increasingly clear that the effective use of technology is one of the most important determinants of success for any organization. It is no longer possible for most public, commercial, or mission-based endeavors to be competitive with inadequate technology planning and implementation.

Learning from the Business World

It is no exaggeration to say that computers have revolutionized the business world. Business organizations have embraced computers because they can readily see technology's impact on that universal measure of success, the bottom line. Unlike nonprofit organizations, businesses routinely measure both cost and profit. The impact of automation can, therefore, be calculated in dollars and cents, allowing any business to know precisely what technology is worth. Hard-pressed nonprofits have no such clear measure to guide their planning.

By definition, nonprofits are unable to use profitability as a measure of success. In addition, they find it more difficult to measure cost than do business enterprises. Cost, as calculated by nonprofits, involves not only the expenditure of funds but also the use of other resources. How, for example, does one calculate the cost of volunteer labor? Even though no paycheck is involved, it must be considered a cost. If those volunteer hours were not needed to perform a given task, they might be devoted to some other project. That means that if technology can reduce the number of volunteer hours needed to perform routine tasks and free individuals to perform other duties, the result is increased productivity. Although nonprofit productivity can be compared to profitability in the business world, this is rarely done.

In order for nonprofit organizations to make effective use of technology, they must develop methods for evaluating costs and benefits. To do so, it is necessary to focus on both the investment of the organization's resources and the projected returns on those investments. Before embarking on a technology program, nonprofits must decide exactly what it is they want computers to do for them (the return they expect on their investment). Where can the biggest gains be realized with the smallest outlay of resources? Which functions and projects lend themselves most readily to automation and do not place unrealistic demands on staff and volunteers?

Planning for Technology

In many nonprofit organizations, technology enters the picture almost by accident. A used computer is offered and accepted. It often happens that a newly formed nonprofit is initially grateful for almost any donation. Group members may find it convenient to donate their old computers when they purchase new ones for their personal use. Before anyone is aware of what's happening, the organization is loaded down with piles of equipment that no one quite knows what to do with.

About the time that the second computer is offered, give some careful thought to the role of computers in your organization. A technology plan is the first essential step and should be hammered out before your organization begins accumulating equipment or investing in a computer system. What does your group really plan to do with computers in the near future? A generation of technology has a very short life. Computers purchased today are obsolete in three years, so vague long-term plans are not useful at this point. What can computerization do for your organization now? Next week? Six months from now? Of course, planning must extend further into the future but emphasis should be on the concrete.

Assigning Responsibility for Technology

The key to a successful technology program is the involvement of a diverse group of talented people. Technology should never be the responsibility of one individual, and effective planning requires buy-in by both decision makers and the general membership. A technology team should be selected soon after the first computer arrives. This should be a small group of possibly four or five computer-literate group members. If possible, it should consist of a board member, an administrator, and representatives of different committees, departments, or other groups within the organization.

At least one of the members of the "tech team" should meet the definition of "technology advocate." Technology advocates possess a level of computer sophistication that is beyond what would normally be considered basic computer literacy. They may or may not be computer professionals but they have enough experience to provide leadership in making computer-related decisions. Other members of the team can represent the board, staff, committees, and volunteer groups. Together, they possess a clear understanding of the needs of the organization and occupy respected leadership roles.

Technology Planning Takes Time

Although most of the members of the tech team need not be highly skilled computer users, it is important that members understand that this will be a demanding job and will require real commitment. As time goes on, their work may become less intensive, but in the beginning they must be prepared to work closely together, meeting weekly or even more frequently. In addition, they should be prepared to spend time researching technology issues and consulting colleagues in other organizations. It is they who will be guiding their organization's technical development and doing much of the planning.

Each tech team member should have clearly defined responsibilities both to the tech team and to the group he or she represents. In a sense, belonging to the tech team is an educational experience. At each meeting members share their research or question invited guests about their technology options. Even though members may begin with average computer skills, they soon acquire the information needed to make important technology-related decisions. This means that members who frequently miss meetings will not acquire this knowledge base and will not be prepared to participate in the decision-making process. For this reason, many tech teams limit the number of meetings their members can miss without forfeiting membership.

Performing a Technology Assessment

Before a group can create such a plan, however, they must assess the resources that are already available. What funding, equipment, and expertise can be counted on? What resources could be made available with a little effort? Your initial response may be that you have no resources. While it is true that a new or very small organization probably has a small budget and very little equipment, those are not the only considerations. Every nonprofit has access to a combination of human and material resources. Which of these could be contributed to an automation project? Here are some questions to get you started:

- What is your organization's annual budget? How much money can be set aside annually to purchase and maintain a computer system?

- Does the organization employ paid staff members? Could any staff time be made available for computer maintenance and other computer-related activities?

- Do you have any volunteers who possess special computer skills?

- How would you describe the average computer skill level of your group members?

- What proportion of your staff and volunteers use computers on a daily basis (either their own, their employer's, or the nonprofit's)?

- Do you have at least a few group members who have the skills to install computer equipment and perform simple maintenance functions?

- If the answer to the last question is a resounding "No," would you say that your group is going to need a lot of preparation or training to use computers effectively?

- How many computers does your organization now own?

- How old is each of the computers?

- Are the computers linked to one another in a network?

- Are you able to access the Internet? If so, must computers use the same dial-up phone line used by telephones, do they have their own phone line, or do they connect to the Internet via a high-speed data line?

In addition to answering these general questions, it is a good idea to create an inventory of both hardware and software currently owned by your organization (see Exhibit 1.1). The TechSoup website (www.techsoup.org) offers a word-processor-based software assessment worksheet, but it is easy to create your own.

LEARN MORE ABOUT

Technology Assessments

- Discover Npower, which provides technology assessment and planning tools, at www.npower.org.

- Consider using the Nonprofit Organizational Assessment Tool available at www.uwex.edu/li/learner/assessment.htm.

- Find a variety of useful articles at TechSoup, a great resource for nonprofits at www.TechSoup.org.

Focusing on Individuals

Once you have answered these questions and completed the inventory, you have the basis of your "technology assessment." This summary of your resources will become your guide for future planning. Pay special attention to the abilities and interests of your group members. Many nonprofit administrators contend that this is the single most important determinant of a successful technology program. It may be a good idea to survey group members to learn about their computer skills and interests.

Each nonprofit organization tends to attract its own unique group of supporters, but there are some generalizations that can be made. People who are still in the workforce usually have access both to computers and computer training. The older the individuals, the less likely it is that they have enjoyed these advantages. Some administrators mistakenly assume that older retirees are unable to learn to use computers. In reality, most senior volunteers enjoy learning new things and can become proficient computer users if they are fully trained. Such training, however, is a commitment involving the expenditure of some of the organization's resources. Although the costs of creating a computer-literate staff and volunteer corps are high, training is the key component that will largely determine the success of all future automation projects.

EXHIBIT 1.1

Taking a Hardware and Software Inventory

Carefully examine each computer. On your equipment inventory worksheet list:

Brand

Model

Serial number

Monitor type

Processor type and speed

RAM (random access memory)

Hard disk capacity

Available hard disk space

Other drives (CD, DVD, floppy)

Operating system

Modem or network card (if any)

USB ports

Other equipment, including printers, switches, and scanners

On your inventory worksheet list the major software packages owned, include:

Program title

Version number

Number of computers on which software can legally be installed

Number of simultaneous users legally permitted to use the software

Identifying Talented Members

To achieve this goal, you will need leaders who possess the enthusiasm and mentoring ability to bring along reluctant members. Are there individuals in the group who have teaching or training experience? In other words, are there some members who can keep reminding the tech team of the human side of technology planning? They are the ones who will become the mentors and trainers as your technology plan is implemented.

As mentioned earlier, the cost of computer equipment has gone down sharply, and new hardware and software is often available in the form of corporate donations. In fact, the cost of the nuts and bolts side of technology actually constitutes a relatively small part of the total investment (about 30%). Costs associated with people resources are actually considerably higher. Do not forget that time devoted to training staff and volunteers must also be treated as a cost. Computerization will not be successful if a large portion of your membership cannot use the system effectively.

Matching Personalities with Responsibilities

Within your organization, there may also be individuals who enjoy working alone more than they enjoy working with people. If they have an interest in technology, there are many roles that they can productively fill, but they are not the ones who will be bringing the group along. Too often, it is these people who are chosen to lead technology projects. Although they may create highly functional computer applications, they tend to do this in isolation, and so technology does not become infused into the organization itself. They make decisions independently, responding to an agenda that is not really shared by the group. One of the hallmarks of successful organizations is that they treasure their members and find ways to bring out individual talents while minimizing the impact of negative characteristics. It is never too early to begin assessing those talents and taking note of interpersonal skills. It is also a good idea to develop a set of written policies for volunteers that clarify rights and responsibilities (see Exhibit 1.2).

EXHIBIT 1.2

Policies Governing Volunteers

While employers inquire into the qualifications and work records of applicants, nonprofits are usually grateful for any volunteer who offers assistance. Similarly, nonprofits may have no written rules governing volunteer ethics, screening, evaluation, and termination. Written personnel policies are necessary to create a safe, fair, and productive environment. Each policy should include the following information:

- Policy name, date of approval, and revision dates
- Purpose of the policy
- Persons covered under policy
- Persons responsible for administering the policy

The following are some common personnel policies intended to protect nonprofits and manage risk:

Volunteer Screening Policy

- May require volunteers to complete a personal information form
- May state that volunteer employment will be terminated for lying on form
- May require that all volunteers or those in high-risk positions provide character references
- May specify situations in which the organization may request a police check

Professional Conduct or Professional Standards Policy

- Emphasizes position of trust and accountability held by volunteers
- Establishes standards of integrity and ethical conduct

continued on next page

- Describes unacceptable behavior
- Emphasizes volunteer's obligation to preserve and protect the property, assets, and goodwill of the organization
- Requires compliance with established professional, legal, and ethical standards.

Safety Policy

- Expresses organization's commitment to safe and secure environment.
- Describes volunteers' responsibility for the safety of program participants and others
- Asserts the right of volunteers to be informed of any hazardous material, practice, or process they may encounter

Risk Management Policy

- Identifies different types of risks
- Distinguishes risks to the organization from risks to individuals
- Specifies insurance requirements for certain tasks and positions

Recruitment Policy

- Lists the characteristics of desirable volunteers
- Lists special qualifications and requirements for volunteer assignments
- Describes how volunteers will be selected for different assignments
- Specifies the conditions under which volunteer applicants may be rejected
- Emphasizes the importance of meeting the personal needs of volunteers

Discrimination Policy

- Defines discrimination
- States organization's position on discrimination
- Emphasizes need for broad representation of majority and minority populations

Evaluation Policy

- Describes how volunteers are evaluated and by whom

- Sets out basis for evaluation

- Describes methods for resolving conflict between volunteers and their supervisors

- Describes follow-up to unsatisfactory evaluation

Termination Policy

- Specifies conditions under which volunteer employment can be terminated.

- Describes dismissal procedures, including verbal and written warnings, suspension, and permanent dismissal

- Lists reasons for immediate dismissal, including client abuse, immoral or indecent conduct, criminal actions, conviction for crime related to volunteer duties, acts that endanger the lives and property of others, possession of unauthorized firearms, and possession of or use of alcohol or illegal drugs

- May list work infractions that can result in termination such as missing meetings, failing to work scheduled shifts, and failing to perform assigned tasks

- May list unacceptable behavior toward customers, clients, staff, and volunteers

Confidentiality Policy

- Describes what records and other information are considered confidential

- Specifies who may have access to confidential information

- Describes penalty for divulging confidential information to unauthorized persons or organizations

- Describes where and for how long personal records will be kept

- Describes the information that can be given out in references for those seeking other paid or volunteer employment or applying for credit

continued on next page

Children and Young Adults Policy

- Emphasizes the vulnerability of children and young adults
- States conditions under which volunteers may be alone with children and young adults
- Describes situations in which written parental consent is required
- Specifies the conditions under which children may be transported
- Describes limits on physical contact

Assessing Current Computer Use

Next, consider how your organization is currently using computers. Consider not only computers owned by your organization but personally owned computers used at least occasionally to support your nonprofit. Do at least some members:

- Maintain a list of members in a word processing program, database, or spreadsheet?
- Record contributions in a computer program?
- Use a computer program to schedule volunteers and/or record their hours?
- Search the World Wide Web for grants and other funding possibilities?
- Send out a newsletter that has been created with a word processing or publishing program?
- Communicate with one another by email?
- Maintain a website?
- Use a computer program for bookkeeping?

These are only a few of the possible ways you can use computers to make your organization more effective.

Where Do You Begin?

Previous experience with computers is an important part of your technology assessment. Even if members use technology for little more than email, you have some place to begin. It is also important to know whether the group has some shared experience on which to base decisions. You might think in terms of giving your organization a grade for effective use, like the ones on student report cards. Is your organization an A+ computer user or does it rate only a D− ?

If we were to concoct some sort of recipe for a successful computer project, we would begin with one large part enthusiastic computer users. Next, we would add another essential ingredient—excellent communication among group members. The recipe should include a few especially good communicators who can make sure that everyone is kept informed of developments and changes. To this mixture must be added technical support, whether from computer-sophisticated volunteers, family members, local businesses, or training professionals. In other words, help must be available to make more complex technical decisions and to "fix what's broke."

Take a good look at both your organization and your community. If you gave your organization a low grade for computer use in the question above, ask why this is the case. Were you trying to do too much? Did group members refuse to get

 TIPS & TECHNIQUES

Barriers to Effective Use of Technology

- Staff and volunteer reluctance

- Lack of computer or network literacy

- Lack of "buy-in" from decision makers

- Inadequate training

- Absence of appropriate and continuing technical support

- High staff and volunteer turnover rate

onboard? What does this experience tell you about the human resources that will be at the core of your technology plan? Could it be that there's been a mismatch between the projects selected for computerization and the people responsible for carrying out those projects? Only when all these human elements are understood can you begin adding the nuts and bolts to your recipe.

Choosing Your First Technology Project

It is difficult for an organization that has little or no experience with technology to plan effectively. When required to produce a technology plan by a funding agency, an inexperienced nonprofit is likely to copy a document off the Internet or borrow one from another organization. This is a mistake, since you may then be committed to a plan that is totally unsuited to your own needs. Instead, it is a good idea to begin with one small and not too demanding project. Once a project has been carried through to completion, group leaders have a better understanding of how technology fits into their goals, and they have had an opportunity to assess the computer skills of their members. It is only with such experiential knowledge that it is possible to produce a realistic technology plan. Such a project should not be too ambitious. Grandiose plans are not only unnecessary but can also destroy the confidence and enthusiasm of your group members.

Measuring Results

As this first project takes shape and evolves, it is important to take stock and evaluate its impact on the organization. This brings up the question: "How do you measure success and how do you weigh the positive results of a project against its cost?" Costs are not merely measured in monetary terms. In the "Starting Small" box (page 15), the cost of equipment and software was minimal. Much more significant was the time that the staff and volunteers devoted to planning the contributor database, collecting the information, attending workshops, and entering data. This was time, whether paid or donated, that might have been spent on other activities. In other words, it was necessary to consider what did not get done because of the project. The group was wise to choose a project that had a potentially large return.

IN THE REAL WORLD

Starting Small

One small but highly successful nonprofit decided that it would focus on only one project before developing a more comprehensive technology plan. Realizing that many group members felt hesitant about using computers, it was decided that what was needed most was a resounding success. The project chosen would consist only of creating a simple but accurate database of contributors and potential contributors. However, every single member of the organization would participate. Each was responsible for verifying existing information and for identifying a given number of possible donors. Each attended workshops to learn to use the database and followed written instructions for entering information. It was not until group members felt satisfied that they had a firm grip on the contributors' database that they returned to their technology plan and considered future computer development. As might be expected, it was discovered that this was far from the most efficient way of creating a database and errors were not uncommon. However, in the end the project resulted not only in a useful resource but in a group of enthusiastic, computer-literate volunteers as well.

By improving the quality of the information available on contributors, the organization was able to be more effective in its fundraising efforts. Since considerable attention was paid to training, group members emerged from the project with new skills that could be used later for other projects.

Comparing Alternate Projects

While the group was trying to decide on their first computer project, a number of voices were raised in support of projection equipment and PowerPoint software. You've undoubtedly attended programs at which the speaker accompanied his or her presentation with a variety of colorful slides. These are usually produced with Microsoft's PowerPoint software program loaded on a laptop computer. A special projector, controlled by the program presenter, is connected to the laptop. Audiences usually pay more attention when they have something to look at, and nervous presenters are more comfortable because the advancing slides act as cues, triggering their memories and preventing them from losing their places. Speakers also feel more relaxed because the eyes of the audience are busy taking in the slides and are not watching their every move.

As part of their fundraising activities, members of this small nonprofit group make a lot of presentations to local clubs, government agencies, and other organizations. PowerPoint capability was the first thing some members thought of when asked to choose a computer application. Others in the group supported the contributor database described above. Which should they choose: the contributor database or PowerPoint presentations? The best way to make such a decision is to analyze the costs and benefits involved in each.

Analyzing the Cost of the Database Project

Let's begin with equipment costs. To build and maintain the contributor database, the group must obtain at least one desktop computer. The database they have in mind will make no unusual demands on a computer like special sound or video cards. It should, however, be equipped with a CD "burner" (a CD-ROM drive that can both read from and write to a disk), so the database can be backed up easily. Such a computer equipped with a monitor can be purchased for approximately $600.00 to $800.00.

The group will also need a printer to produce lists of contributors' phone numbers and other needed information for use by fundraising volunteers. Although printer costs range from one hundred to several thousand dollars, a lower end printer will meet their needs. Let's say that a satisfactory printer can be purchased for about $300.00. An expense that is not often considered is the cost of printer toner cartridges. For printers in this price range, toner cartridges cost about $35.00 each, and it is usually necessary to have one cartridge for black text and another for color printing. Let's say that since the group will be doing only occasional printing, the annual cost of cartridges will be about $100.00 a year. No phone line or Internet connection is needed so total hardware costs for the database project will be about $1,000.

Analyzing the Cost of the Presentation Project

To produce and project PowerPoint slides, it will be necessary to obtain both a laptop computer and a video projector. These are two very expensive pieces of equipment. Equipment prices are changing rapidly, but the cost of a laptop computer usually runs about twice the cost of a desktop computer. We will, therefore, estimate the cost of the laptop at about $1,200. Prices for video projectors have remained high because their market is relatively small. Home users purchase laptops in large numbers, but they do not purchase projection equipment. Cost is based mainly on the brightness of the lamp and, at this writing, a medium-quality projector can be purchased for about $1,500.

A printer will also be needed to produce the handouts that are usually distributed to audiences, so we'll add another $300.00 and, assuming the same printing volume as above, we will add an additional $100.00 for toner cartridges. This brings the equipment total for PowerPoint capability to $3,100.00. Although it is possible to produce PowerPoint presentations without access to the Internet, most users copy their visual images from the Web. If the group does not have an Internet connection, they will have to produce their own images or do without. Images can also be created with digital cameras, but since neither a camera nor an Internet connection is absolutely essential, we will not include them in this cost estimate.

Software costs in this particular example are actually identical. The group has learned that it is eligible for a donation of the Microsoft Office suite. The professional edition includes, in addition to a word processor and several other modules, both PowerPoint and Access, an excellent database program. If, however, only the standard version of Microsoft Office were available through donation, the cost would be calculated differently. PowerPoint would still be included, but since the standard edition does not include a database program, it would have to be purchased separately.

Additional Costs

Hardware and software are not the only costs. How many people will have to be trained to use both hardware and software? Since this is the first project, training is an important part of it. This will be a good opportunity to get everyone involved in computerization, and so extensive training will be required for the whole group. Whether you bring in a professional trainer or use your own staff and volunteers, training is a big investment. It requires substantial time that could be spent on other activities.

Most people find it easier to master PowerPoint than learn to use a database program effectively. On the other hand, equipment setup is the most difficult part of using presentation software. While the desktop computer is always available and never requires special setup procedures, both the laptop and the projector must be reconnected each time they are used. Volunteers insist that there seem to be dozens of cords, including an AC power cord for each piece of equipment, cables to connect them, a power strip and extension cord, a mouse for the laptop, and a remote control device to advance the slides. To feel secure when an audience is waiting for the program to begin, volunteers must practice setup procedures again and again before the big event. Otherwise, they may become flustered and confused. It would probably be reasonable to say then that the complexity of the database is roughly equivalent to the difficulty involved in PowerPoint setup procedures. Training costs and the related time and energy involved in learning to use both programs will, therefore, be similar.

Identifying the Benefits of the Database Project

Now that the group has estimated both monetary and human costs of both projects, they are ready to focus on the benefits of each. In the end, a computer-literate staff and volunteer corps may be the most important long-term result of both projects, but let's focus on more immediate gains. Both projects are intended to help the group with their fundraising efforts. That will make it easier to compare the two, since we can then ask which project is more effective in achieving fundraising goals. Of course, answering this question requires guesswork, but yours is not the only organization making technology decisions. There are many other nonprofits in your locality and at least some have participated in similar computerization projects. What was their experience? What worked for them, and what did not?

One local nonprofit created a database for donor information similar to the one being considered. This meant that when the organization conducted a fundraising drive, it had the names, addresses, phone numbers, and donation histories of everyone who had contributed in the past. The group also had similar information on prospects identified since the last drive. They could not really estimate how much additional revenue the database had generated. However, they thought that if they had to start from scratch each year, they would waste a huge amount of time assembling information and would still miss a lot of possible contributors. Knowing the amount of previous donations also meant that they could ask for a specific amount of money. Although this sister nonprofit could not assign a dollar amount, they knew that the database had significantly improved their ability to raise funds. When they considered what they had spent in terms of both time and money, it seemed well worth the investment.

Identifying the Benefits of Presentation Support

Another local nonprofit had purchased both a laptop computer and a video projector for their speaking engagements. A volunteer produced a PowerPoint program that members could take with them when invited to speak to groups. When approached about their experience, the group's contact person was somewhat less than enthusiastic. It was true that when members learned to use the equipment correctly, the PowerPoint slides enhanced the quality of their programs.

What they discovered, however, was that they had overestimated the number of presentations they really made. Someone from the group might be asked to speak to a local club about once every two months. They had also made occasional presentations to the city council and had twice held a public meeting at the library. Let's say, then, that the equipment was used 8 to 10 times that year. For the remainder of the time, it sat in a closet gathering dust. Although everyone had been trained on setup procedures, members soon forgot how to connect all those tangled cables. After an embarrassing experience in front of a restless audience, a speaker might avoid using PowerPoint again.

Had the ability to project PowerPoint slides made it possible for the group to raise more money? It was hard to say. Of course, their programs were more interesting, but it was really impossible to know the extent to which they contributed to their fundraising capability. Other groups, naturally, had different experiences to share, but the bottom line seemed to be that spending $3,000 for equipment that was used less than 10 times a year with no clear benefits did not seem to make sense (remember that the monetary costs of the PowerPoint project were much higher than the database project—$3,100 for projection equipment versus $1,000 for a

TIPS & TECHNIQUES

Making Technology Part of the Project

Here's a step-by-step procedure for planning a technology project:

- Identify a problem that needs attention.

- Decide exactly what needs improvement. In other words, what aspect of the program is not working as well as you would like?

- Decide what you want to happen. Identify desired outcomes. What should be different after the project is implemented?

- Identify the people who can make it happen.

- Decide how much you can spend.

- Divide the project into small pieces or segments.

- Assign responsibility for each segment.

---

desktop computer). It was, therefore, decided that the group's first computer project would be the contributor database. After this goal had been achieved and the database was in use, the group might consider PowerPoint again. However, they now knew that a number of organizations in their area owned the needed equipment, and it was usually sitting in a closet somewhere gathering dust. When it came time to implement a PowerPoint project, they would either borrow or rent the equipment as the need arose.

Creating a Written Technology Plan

Once the tech team has assessed its technology resources and focused on a practical starting point for its efforts, they are ready to begin making technology an integral part of their organization. They are ready to begin developing a formal plan that will guide their organization through the next several years. The plan will allow them to make wise purchases and channel their efforts into the most productive projects. Other good reasons for developing a technology plan are listed in Exhibit 1.3.

EXHIBIT 1.3

Why Do You Need a Technology Plan?

Although there are literally dozens of reasons why creating a technology plan is worth the effort, you may need some additional justification if your group seems somewhat reluctant. Here are just a few ways a technology plan can enhance the effectiveness of your organization:

- Saves money on technology because you buy only what you need.

- Provides a valuable a tool to help you accomplish your mission.

- Helps your organization obtain funding. Funders respond to organizations that take technology seriously.

- Encourages members to discover new ways to integrate technology into their work.

- Makes your nonprofit more productive. Planning ahead avoids mistakes.

- Allows you to anticipate equipment failure before it happens.

- Makes it possible to use staff time more effectively.

- Provides documentation of existing systems. This is invaluable when information is lost due to turnover.

In addition, the technology plan will be used to show funding agencies that the organization has assumed firm control of its technology program and can be trusted to make effective use of funds provided for this purpose.

Looking Ahead to the Future

While part of the plan will be quite concrete and specific, some intelligent "crystal gazing" will also be necessary, since it is difficult to look into the future and imagine what one's needs will be. In planning and completing that first project, the group learned a lot more about the skills of its members and the other resources at its command. This information will help them identify training needs and determine the pace of innovation. What are some logical next steps? One desktop computer

TIPS & TECHNIQUES

Five Keys to a Successful Technology Program

- Focus on stakeholders. You must have buy-in from the whole group.

- Limit dependence on consultants. It is your plan, not theirs.

- Emphasize diversity on the tech team. Involve volunteers, board members, administrators, staff, and even clients.

- Nurture a pro-technology culture within the organization.

- Emphasize continuity. The tech team's job is not finished when the technology plan is written.

may be sufficient to get started, but the staff will soon need more computers. No matter what an organization's focus, it is all but inevitable that it will need to expand its computer capability, but how rapidly? How much can the organization afford to spend and what does it hope to accomplish?

Gradually, ideas takes shape but now the group must consider the time factor. Over what period of time will the plan be implemented? Some experts advise three-year technology plans because the computer world changes so rapidly. Five-year plans are common because of the considerable effort involved in their development, but such plans should include provisions for reviews and updates within that period. Be sure to include completion dates for each phase of the plan. It is important that the group be able to assess progress and know whether or not they are on target. Of course, some parts of the plan will take more time to implement than anticipated, but the timeline should be specific enough to alert the group to problems and delays.

Developing Technology Leadership

People are really the most important element of any technology plan, so make sure you give at least as much attention to the human side of technology as to hardware and software matters. How will you develop technology leaders? What will it take to create a core of computer-literate decision makers and trainers? How will they be identified? What skills should they possess? What skills will they need to acquire? Remember that the trainers themselves must be trained.

Discovering Community Leadership Resources

An important part of the technology plan concerns interpersonal networking or developing relationships with key individuals and organizations. This becomes especially important when it comes to nurturing technology leaders. Does your local chamber of commerce provide technology workshops for the business community? Does the community college offer noncredit computer courses? Is there someone in the community who could be persuaded to provide pro bono training in a computer lab at the local high school? Consider what resources might be available outside your organization and how you might go about taking advantage of them.

Educational Opportunities for Leaders

Of course, your technology leaders will need to stay abreast of changes in technology, so an ongoing program should be developed to meet their needs. Are there conferences they should attend? Should the organization purchase a small collection of books, manuals, and magazines devoted to technology? All of these components should be melded together into a brief list of leadership objectives, including a timeline for achieving goals, and a budget to cover essential expenses.

For a technology program to be successful, nonprofit decision makers must actively support technology. This means that board members cannot be computer-phobes who regard technology as none of their concern. Leadership in any nonprofit comes from its board, so board members must be the first to receive support. Although they need not be highly sophisticated computer users, board members must fully understand what technology can and cannot do for their organization. This may mean working with a consultant or conducting special training sessions for board members. Exhibit 1.4 summarizes the elements that together make an effective technology plan.

LEARN MORE ABOUT

Online Resources for Board Members

- Find tools for building strong and effective boards from BoardSource at www.boardsource.org.

- Read the Board Development FAQ at www.allianceonline.org/FAQ/board_development.

- Take a look at the Board of Directors FAQ at www.nonprofits.org/npofaq/keywords/1a.html.

- Read about Building and Managing a Better Board at www.enterprisefoundation.org/model%20documents/1105-Building&ManagingBetterBoard.pdf.

- Get the Complete Toolkit for Boards at www.mapnp.org/library/boards/boards.htm.

EXHIBIT 1.4

Characteristics of a Good Technology Plan

- It is more like a roadmap than a wish list.

- It includes both the route and the destination.

- It includes recommendations on policy, professional development, and staffing.

- It is characterized by a holistic approach to planning.

- It assigns responsibilities.

- It addresses the decision-making process.

- It includes methods for evaluating success.

Identifying Training Needs

Once leaders have been identified and trained, how will other members of the organization become full participants? Will everyone be expected to use the computers or will system passwords be restricted to a smaller group of regulars. It may not be necessary for every single member of the group to be able to use every computer program. However, when the only volunteer who knows how to use the bookkeeping program moves away, chaos can ensue. Certainly, a significant portion of the membership must be fully trained. Once trained, they will need "brush-up" sessions to keep up their skills.

Planning an Effective Training Program

Most of this training will be done by group leaders. Occasionally, however, it is a good idea to bring in a professional from the outside who can "rev up" enthusiasm and bring the group information about recent developments. What about training materials? All computer users will need study materials for workshops. In addition, they will need manuals and written instructions near at hand when they are doing their work. This means that you will probably need a materials budget to cover photocopying, as well as commercial materials. You may also want to purchase some videos or DVDs that demonstrate basic Windows skills. Once again, these plans must be condensed into a set of objectives, accompanied by a timeline and a budget.

The Nuts and Bolts of Technology

It is only at this point that you can begin to consider the equipment side of your technology plan—specifically the computer system and its functions. By this time, used equipment is very likely being left on your doorstep, so donations should probably be the first issue to consider. Bear in mind that a three-year-old computer is at the end of its useful life. Of course, a three-year-old computer still runs (you hope) and an individual owner may want to keep it around the house for a while. However, it is useless as an integral part of your organization's computer system. It may not accommodate newer software and could endanger any records stored on it.

TIPS & TECHNIQUES

Getting Help for Technology Planning

If you feel ill-prepared to develop a technology plan, consider the following readily available sources of help.

- Your local business community.

- Family and friends of group members.

- Technical support staff in other nonprofits.

- Email discussion lists.

- Websites for nonprofits such as TechSoup.

- Community foundations.

- Nonprofit management centers.

- Interns from local colleges and universities

Establishing Hardware and Software Standards

On the average, hard drives "die" or become unreliable at about 4 years. You do not want to entrust valuable information about your organization to a hard drive that has a very good chance of self-destructing within the next year.

Most people do not remember how old their computers really are. They may have purchased discounted computers that were being discontinued, so the equipment was about a year old when purchased. It is also hard to keep track of time, and it may seem like only yesterday we purchased a computer when actually several years have elapsed. The best way to avoid obsolete computers is to maintain a set of standards. All computers maintained by your organization should meet certain minimum requirements that include speed, hard drive capacity, random access memory (RAM), and other basic considerations. Of course, such standards are quickly outdated, so a mechanism should be established to review requirements annually. The complete list of requirements need not go into the technology plan, but the mechanism for creating and reviewing it should definitely be included.

If you keep these written equipment requirements readily available, it becomes a great deal easier to reject unwanted donations without hurt feelings. If potential donors have lost track of the printed materials that came with their computer, you can explain to them that it is easy to click on "System Information" on their Windows menu. They might wish to print out the information displayed and bring the printout to you rather than the computer.

Try Before You Buy

Starting out with donated equipment can give your group members an opportunity to become comfortable with computers. By installing some simple application software, you begin to get an idea of what works best and how information can be effectively shared. Before making any purchases, however, this experience must be refined and realistic goals must be set. What computer applications can you reasonably expect staff and volunteers to master and which would most benefit your organization? Develop a timeline for implementing these applications, including purchasing needed hardware and software, developing procedures, training users, and entering data.

Donations of New Hardware and Software

What purchases will need to be made and what can be obtained through corporate donation? Elsewhere in this book we discuss sources of such donations. It may happen, for example, that one database program is available free or at a heavily discounted price. Will you choose this program or pay full price for another program that offers additional features? How will you make the decision? What considerations will be most important when choosing software? The same kinds of decisions must be made when selecting hardware. How will you measure the advantages of obtaining free or inexpensive hardware against the disadvantages? Your technology plan cannot include specifics, but it can spell out your priorities such as reliability, economy, and customer service.

Most of all, your technology plan must reflect your commitment, not to technology since that is merely a means to an end, but to maintaining accurate records

TIPS & TECHNIQUES

Implementing Your Technology Plan

Once your technology plan is written, do not file it away. Make it happen! Here are some suggestions:

- Remind yourself and others of the benefits the plan will bring.

- Evaluate your progress monthly.

- Break the plan down into "doable" components.

- Earmark funds as they become available. Do not let them slip away.

- Appoint an implementation manager.

- Implement the plan one item at a time, and take time to enjoy the results.

- Keep up the momentum.

and achieving your nonprofit's goals. This means taking charge of technology and not allowing it to develop a life of its own, possibly endangering your organization.

Summing It Up

Because computers are so inexpensive and so readily available, they commonly find their way to nonprofit organizations. A gaggle of computers, however, does not equal a technology program. When intelligently conceived and administered, technology can contribute significantly to your group's success. However, the focus must be on people, not machines. A computer is a tool like a pencil or a stapler. It can be of no use unless it is brought under the control of knowledgeable individuals who harness its power in a well-thought-out plan of action. Only when computers are fully integrated into your organization and their roles are carefully delineated can a technology program be truly effective.

CHAPTER 2

Technology Planning for the Small Organization

After reading this chapter, you will be able to:

- Better understand the strengths and weaknesses of your own organization.

- Accurately assess your organization's technology needs and the resources available.

- Implement an effective technology plan with a budget as small as $500.00 a year.

- Know when and when not to accept donations.

A Tale of Two Nonprofits

Nonprofit organizations come in many shapes and sizes. Although they are rarely large when compared to their counterparts in the business sector, they can range from a small town arts council to a multi-million-dollar national charity. How much technology is needed to meet the needs of each organization? How does each determine technical priorities? This chapter describes two imaginary organizations with very small budgets and informal organizational structures that are much like many of their counterparts across the country. The effectiveness of each of these organizations can be enhanced by the prudent use of technology, but each must be wary of pitfalls. Each must decide how much dependence it can place on technology given the human and fiscal resources available.

Where Does One Begin?

The Pleasantville Family Advocacy Association is raising funds to establish a small counseling center for at-risk families. At last, they have received official approval as a 501c3 organization, and a local social service agency has allowed them to use a small office. The board of directors, at their last meeting, decided the time has come to become better organized. One of their more technically sophisticated members convinced them that computerizing some of their routine tasks would increase productivity. Where, they wonder, should they begin? Although some might be tempted to purchase a computer or two and plunge into frenzied activity, there is a better way to get started.

The Anytown Arts Council is also considering the purchase of some computers, but it has been in operation longer than the Pleasantville group and has a somewhat larger budget to work with. A local businessman provides his storefront building to the council rent-free on the condition that they pay the cost of renovation and repairs. A few small grants have further stabilized the Arts Council, but members believe that it is time they put their activities on a more business-like footing.

How Can Technology Work for You?

There is no better time than the present for both small nonprofits to develop a simple plan for using computers to support their group missions. This means taking a good look at each organization's goals, resources, and budget. What kind of information would help them make better decisions? Which routine chores, now gobbling up staff and volunteer time, could be streamlined, thus freeing-up hours that could be better used to advance their goals? In other words, what tasks might lend themselves to computerization and what will it take to make it happen.

Taking the First Steps

The following is a simple step-by-step plan that both organizations will use to quick-start effective technology programs. In general, it is appropriate for most smaller organizations.

Step 1: Decide Who Will Do the Planning

Create a team to spearhead technology planning. In the last chapter, we discussed the composition and function of tech teams so our two nonprofits are ready to select members from their own groups. First, they will need to make sure that their leadership is well represented. Ideally, at least one team member should be on the board of directors and serve as liaison with the board. One should be the group's "technology advocate," a member who possesses above average knowledge of computers. Technology advocates need not be computer professionals, but it is important that they work with computers on a daily basis. Preferably, this person is already an active member.

Although the Arts group had no difficulty identifying someone who met this definition, there just did not seem to be anyone among the Pleasantville volunteers who had both time and sophisticated computer skills. To proceed with automation planning without leadership is a serious mistake, but it is not usually hard to identify a spouse, friend, or acquaintance willing to donate some time to the project. The other team members should own their own personal computers and understand basic applications like email and word processing.

At this point, both groups are led by volunteers and the Arts Council's lone administrative assistant performs mainly clerical duties. However, as soon as either group hires a director or other staff member with supervisory responsibilities, he or she should be included on the tech team. The success of a technology program depends on buy-in by everyone and should never be the province of just one constituency.

Step 2: Obtain Official Nonprofit Status

Fortunately, both of our nonprofits had no difficulty with this requirement; both have received approval as 501c3 organizations, and so they will be eligible for many corporate discounts and donations. However, even if yours is a publicly funded agency like a school or library, you may still be able to take advantage of these opportunities. You might want to consider starting a support group that qualifies as a separate nonprofit organization or making more effective use of an existing group like your parent-teacher association or friends of the library. Technology-focused companies are quite generous in their donations to nonprofits, and a wide variety of hardware and software is available at little or no cost.

Step 3: Decide on Two or Three Small but Significant Projects

Once our two groups have gotten their feet wet with a small computerization project as described in the last chapter, they will need to decide on their next steps. Technical savvy will grow and develop only if a group has some concrete projects to which they can devote their attention. The Pleasantville group is most interested in building its membership base. They would like to be more effective in attracting new members and better able to communicate with their existing members. Although this may sound simple, it could involve several computer applications. The team decides to limit its immediate plans to the following:

- Making it possible for everyone in the group to send and receive email. Email should be the first computer application selected by most nonprofits, since it can impact so many activities (see Exhibit 2.1).

- Using a simple database program to create mailing lists and keep track of members.

- Finding information on the World Wide Web about such topics as recruiting members, building a more effective organization, and even seeking grants.

The Importance of Email

Team members had a hard time narrowing down their list to these three, so they decided to create a "Back Burner" list. This list consists of future possibilities like a website that will be a more realistic goal when they have some experience with technology under their belts. It is useful to have an idea what you will be doing in the future because it helps you plan more effectively. Nevertheless, be careful to stay focused on your immediate needs. It always takes longer to computerize an activity than you anticipate, and do not forget the time needed for training.

The Arts Council, on the other hand, is most concerned about keeping better track of its money. Accustomed to operating out of a checkbook, members have discovered that their success with grants and other kinds of fundraising has created more complicated reporting requirements. Both foundations and government agencies insist that they account for every penny. Therefore, the group has decided that

EXHIBIT 2.1

Email: The Most Valuable Computer Application

When used effectively, email:

- Provides immediate, two-way communication.

- Keeps everyone in the organization informed.

- Distributes agendas, meeting notices, and minutes to group members.

- Shortens meetings by preparing participants ahead of time.

- Usually reaches decision makers directly, with no receptionist guarding the gate.

- Can be quickly forwarded to the person who can act.

- Encourages immediate response.

- Costs far less per unit than a letter or phone call.

- Gets time-sensitive information to many people in the same time needed to write one message.

- Helps members communicate with colleagues in other organizations.

- Allows members to request and receive help with marketing, fundraising, technology, policy issues, or legislation. Keeps volunteers informed of hours and policies.

- Makes it easy to publish and distribute an electronic newsletter.

- Alerts supporters to upcoming federal, state, and local legislation.

although it too needs to make better use of email, a simple accounting system is their most urgent need.

Step 4: Establish an Annual Budget

The Pleasantville Association decided that it can devote only $500.00 to its technology project, and it plans to spend $600.00 next year. This is not a lot of money, but it will give the tech team a budget to work with. It also represents a commitment from the organization to continue funding the technology project in the future. There are always costs associated with technology. As the project progresses, the group will become more and more dependent on computers. Vitally important information will be stored in them and must be kept safe. Even though small groups like the Pleasantville Association depend heavily on free, donated, and discounted hardware and software, they have nevertheless made a substantial investment, and their success will depend on safeguarding that investment. Even when the basic components of the computer system are in place, costs will continue to be incurred. Computers must be repaired or replaced, antivirus software subscriptions renewed, and supplies reordered. All too often a computer is seen as a toy, not a commitment.

The Anytown Arts Council's technology budget of $2,000 looks generous by comparison but again, much of the money must be devoted to safeguarding their system. Once the Arts Council's financial records are stored in computers, those computers' well-being is essential to the organization. If the records are lost or corrupted, the group may not be able to function. Bills will go unpaid or funds will be overspent long before the end of the budget cycle.

When we hear horror stories about nonprofits and their disastrous experiences with technology, failure to establish an ongoing budget is a common cause. These organizations may have made a one-time commitment to purchase hardware and software with no thought to the future. Once important functions depend on computers and vital data is stored, an organization's financial commitment to technology must increase, not disappear. While the program is in its formative stages, your organization should probably plan to increase spending each year. This is because you will be not only maintaining the system but expanding it. In fact, you might consider allocating the same percentage of the organization's budget to technology each year.

During hard times, administrators may sometimes think that technology spending is an easy place to make cuts. Although it is true that you may be able to coast for a short while with existing hardware and software, unless equipment is replaced regularly, you can expect computer "meltdowns" that endanger the future of the organization just as much as any funding crisis.

Step 5: Identify Additional Sources of Funding

As we've mentioned, technology is an area in which there are still many opportunities for external funding and in-kind donations. You might even want to seek funds for technology planning, since foundations and government agencies understand the importance of getting a good start. How will you obtain information about grants and in-kind donations? Who will write the applications and who will keep track of deadlines? Unless your organization has a system in place for identifying opportunities and acting on them, you will lose out on important resources that could make a world of difference to your program.

 LEARN MORE ABOUT

Online Opportunities for Grant Seekers

- Discover the Forum of Regional Associations of Grantmakers at www.rag.org.

- Look into CompassPoint for a wealth of nonprofit resources at www.supportcenter.org/sf.

- Discover the Nonprofit Resource Center at www.not-for-profit.org.

- Surf to the Charity Channel, which provides grant-seeking information at www.charitychannel.com.

- Investigate federal grants at www.grants.gov.

- Visit the Community Foundation Locator, which lists community foundations by name, region, state, or zip code, at www.community foundationlocator.org.

- Become familiar with the Foundation Center Grantmaker info at http://fdncenter.org/grantmaker/index.html.

Step 6: Take Stock of What You Have

This is the technology assessment we discussed in the last chapter. It is the part of the process during which you take a good look at what resources are already available. At first, it seemed that the Pleasantville Association was starting out with almost nothing. However, team members managed to come up with the following list:

- The use of a 12 by 16 foot office rent-free

- Access to a standard dial-up telephone line

- The services of some group members who, though they did not qualify as technology advocates, were experienced in setting up and maintaining their own personal computers

- The offer of three donated computers

- The willingness of several group members to use their own personal computers to help the group

When the Arts Council team took stock, they found that they had similar if somewhat more abundant resources. However, in one respect, they were in a much better position than the Pleasantville group. Among their active volunteers were several who possessed what might be called advanced computers skills. This wealth of human resources should have a greater impact on their technology planning than any other factor, including budget. Without readily available technical expertise, a group must plan conservatively. This does not mean that the Pleasantville Association cannot reap substantial rewards from technology, but they must adjust their plans to their abilities.

Step 7: Decide on Minimum Hardware Requirements

It is clear that with a budget of only $500.00, Pleasantville's team will have to depend primarily on donated hardware and software. The group will need to be sure that all equipment accepted for use with their computer system is compatible. This means that they will need to:

- Limit their acquisitions to computers that are no more than two years old, since it is generally accepted that computers have a three-year useful life. It is true that older computers can be upgraded, but equipment failures become common after the three-year mark.

- Limit their acquisitions to Windows-based computers. It is best not to mix Macs with PCs if you can avoid it. They are both good operating systems, but unexpected compatibility problems are inevitable. If your group does not have a technician available, it is best not to take chances. If your group has more Macintosh users, however, you may decide to stick with them and exclude PCs, but this is a more difficult road to travel.

- Make sure that all computers have the Windows XP operating system installed. Sometimes donated computers are wiped clean and arrive with no operating system. This means that you will have to install a new one. Donated copies of Windows XP are available to nonprofit organizations, and as long as the donated PC is not more than two years old, you should encounter no difficulties installing it.

- Decide how much you are willing to spend to make a used computer fully functional and compatible with your system. For example, it may be worth replacing a CD "burner," since they tend to be among the first hardware casualties. However, if you must upgrade the memory, install a network card, and replace the CD drive, your cost is nearing the $200.00 mark. Depending on the model, you can probably purchase a new computer/ monitor combination for $600.00, which comes with a warranty. Considering that the used computer has a much shorter useful life, it just is not worth the investment. Instead, you might want to place a $50.00 to $60.00 limit on expenditures for used equipment.

The Pleasantville team decides that two of the used computers offered to them meet their requirements. They will accept only these two and will have to decide how to gracefully reject the other offer. The Arts Council, too, will depend primarily on donated equipment. As we will soon be discovering, their plan will be somewhat more elaborate than Pleasantville's, and they will need to reduce their costs wherever possible.

Step 8: Decide How Computers Will Communicate with One Another

The Pleasantville group will store information about its members in a database software program that is loaded on one of those donated computers. How will new information be added to the database? At the moment, volunteers are updating membership information. Bob is seated at the database computer, efficiently calling

LEARN MORE ABOUT

Technology for Nonprofits

- Visit TechSoup, possibly the best site on the Web for nonprofit use of technology at www.techsoup.org.

- Find technology resources through TechFinder.org at www.techfinder.org.

- Stop by the Nonprofit Technology Enterprise Network at www.nten.org.

- Check out the Benton Foundation's Best Practices Toolkit at www. benton.org/publibrary/toolkits/stratcommtool.html.

- Investigate the Foundation Center Nonprofit Technology Resources at http://fdncenter.org/technology/tech_archive.html.

members, updating their contact information, and typing notes about their schedules into the database form. Susan is also updating information, but she is seated in front of the other donated computer. If the computers are not connected to one another in what is called a "local area network," Susan must handwrite her notes. Later when the database computer is free, she or someone else will have to copy the notes into the database. This is a lot of work and very inconvenient. However, there can be only one database. Otherwise, each computer would store different information.

Although the Pleasantville Association would like to be able to connect its computers to one another so all computer users can access the same database, a network is a complicated proposition. Volunteers with very good computer skills would be needed to set it up, maintain it, and troubleshoot problems as they occur. After giving it considerable thought, the tech team decides that they simply do not have enough members with the time or the skill to fill this role. Instead, they will develop a more efficient system for adding information to the database. Volunteers will handwrite information on specially-designed forms. One person will be responsible for collecting these forms and entering new information into the database in a consistent manner.

As mentioned earlier, the Arts Council has been in operation for several years now and has managed to attract a larger membership. Their tech team decides that since they have acquired several computers, linking them together is one of their highest priorities (see Exhibit 2.2), and with so much expertise within the group,

EXHIBIT 2.2

Networking Basics

When resources are available, it's usually desirable to link desktop computers together in a local area network (LAN) to share files, printers, and Internet access. Most LANs are either wired Ethernet or wireless.

An Ethernet LAN requires:

- Cabling (Wiring)
  - Can be installed by a professional for about $75.00 per computer
- Ethernet network interface card (cost approximately $30.00 each)
  - Many new computers come equipped with Ethernet cards
  - Ethernet card connects to Ethernet cabling
- Network hub
  - Links the computers together
  - Switching hubs (switches) offers better performance than standard hubs
- Network software
  - Windows operating system includes the software needed to create a network
  - Server software may be needed for larger networks
- Advantages
  - More reliable signal
  - Not affected by weather or other devices
- Disadvantages
  - Costly installation
  - Not portable
  - More difficult to add new hardware to network

continued on next page

A wireless LAN requires:

- Wireless network adapters (also known as wireless NICs or wireless network cards)
- Laptop computers usually include wireless adapters as a built-in feature
- Wireless router
  - Uses radio waves and/or microwaves to communicate between computers
- Access point
  - May be needed to join a wireless network to an existing wired network
- Wireless antenna
  - Increases the communication range of the wireless radio signals
- Network software
  - Included with Windows operating system
- Advantages
  - Offers mobility
  - Eliminates unsightly cables
  - Easy to add new hardware to network
- Disadvantages
  - Potential radio interference due to weather and other wireless devices.
  - Obstructions like walls can weaken signal

they should be able to achieve this goal. They will establish a small subcommittee, responsible to the tech team, to set up and manage the network. Subcommittee members will divide responsibility among themselves so that someone is always on call in case of network crashes or other emergencies.

Occasionally, a group includes a very vocal technology advocate, someone who possesses more sophisticated computer skills than other group members. Although it is great to have such a person on your team, remember that it is never safe to assign total responsibility for a computer system to one person. He or she may leave town, lose interest in the organization, or simply find that the job requires a greater time commitment than anticipated. This is why the Arts Council will make sure responsibilities are shared among several volunteers.

Although the human element is probably the first and most important consideration when deciding to network computers, a significant financial outlay will also be required. The next decision that must be made is whether to hardwire computers to communicate with one another or create a wireless network. We will discuss the pros and cons of both options in later chapters. After considerable research, the Anytown team decides on a wireless network. Installing the cabling needed for a hard-wired network is expensive and, since it must be done by service professionals, there are not many ways to reduce the cost. Besides, the Arts Council intends to expand its network in the near future, and wireless makes it much easier to add new computers and other equipment to the network.

Step 9: Decide How Your Computer System Will Access the Internet

Since one of the Pleasantville team's goals is to allow all group members to communicate with one another via email and find "how-to" information on the Web, their computers will have to connect to the Internet. The association pays the monthly bill for a telephone line installed in its donated office. The team considered upgrading to a high-speed connection like DSL or a cable modem, but that $500.00 budget would be entirely eaten up by monthly charges. They decide they will just have to use the standard 56K dial-up modems already installed in most computers. That means that either a telephone or a modem can be in use at any one time, but they cannot be used together. This will be inconvenient, so someday, when they get to those projects on the back burner like developing their own website, they will need to make other arrangements. For now, their one telephone line will serve their need.

Since the Arts Council is planning to install a local area network that can accommodate several volunteers working at the same time, it decides it must have a high-speed connection to the Internet that will allow several people to be online at the same time. The Arts Council will study the different options available in their area, including DSL, cable modem, and wireless access.

TIPS & TECHNIQUES

Opportunities for Nonprofits on the World Wide Web

Search the Web for:

- Access to all federal agencies

- Access to elected officials

- Up-to-date information about funding opportunities

- Advice from colleagues on technology development

- Demographic information for funding proposals

- Status of pending legislation

- Graphics for your organization's publications

- Model case statements

- Opportunities to exchange ideas with people you would otherwise probably never meet

- Access to international colleagues and experts

Since their budget is small, the tech team is looking for ways to obtain discounted service and/or share the cost of the line. A source of funding for telephone and other communications costs is the federal government's E-Rate program. You may want to find out whether your organization is eligible to participate in the E-Rate program or some other government-funded program that can reduce your communications charges. E-Rates are available to schools, libraries, and certain other organizations, but they come with a number of strings attached.

Step 10: How Will You Choose and Control Software?

Compatibility is just as important when you are considering software donations as hardware. You will want to choose a very small number of software programs and install the same programs on your organization's computers. File types created with one software program are often incompatible with other programs. That means that unless the same program resides on all your computers, one program will not be able to read a file created by another.

If some of your computers run only WordPerfect, and others are equipped with Microsoft Word, you can expect problems. Of course, some progress has been made translating files from one format to another. However, these "fixes" are rarely very successful. Even if the names of the programs are the same, they may be different versions. An older version of a software program is often unable to read files created by a newer version. Not only must your organization concern itself with whether its own computers can read the same files, but it must also consider anyone else who will be receiving files. For example, if you intend to submit grant proposals as electronic documents, then the grant-making agency must be able to read the file.

Businesses usually wipe their computers clean before donating them to non-profits, but private individuals may simply leave their personal software loaded. Not only are there legal restrictions on using software that comes on donated computers, but compatibility issues are just as troublesome. It is often best to assume that you will need to obtain new software for all new and donated computers (see Exhibit 2.3). To make sure that all your computers can share information, you would do well to obtain what's called a software "site license." This license gives you legal permission to install the same program on a specified number of computers. Microsoft and other software producers often make inexpensive site licenses for their software available to nonprofits on websites like "TechSoup" that will be discussed in more detail later.

Choosing Software

Consider the skills of staff and volunteers when selecting software. Too often, more sophisticated computer users choose software without regard to the limitations of their less skilled colleagues. There is ample evidence that when staff or volunteers find a computer program difficult and confusing, they avoid using it. When forced to use a program because they have no other options, they will make mistakes. It is best to choose programs that most members of the group can use effectively, even if they are less powerful than you might like.

Although good training is essential, *do not* assume that training alone will produce highly skilled computer users. Instead, take a good look at your pool of

EXHIBIT 2.3

Choosing Software

Many organizations purchase software that fails to meet their needs. Before purchasing any software program:

- Consider popularity. A popular program makes it easier to share files and get help from colleagues.

- Find out whether it's possible to share a site license with a parent body or another organization.

- Don't judge by the price. High price tags don't necessarily mean quality.

- Try out software before you buy it. Take advantage of demos and trial periods.

- Consider ease of use. You don't want to waste time learning a program or teaching others to use it.

- Ask how long the company has been in business. Is it large and stable enough to keep its promises and make good on its warranties?

- Find out whether the company provides free technical support for its software. If not, what is the cost of a typical phone call? Must you spend hours on "hold?"

- Find out if the program is updated regularly. When will updates be made available? Will you be eligible for free upgrades? If not, what will they cost?

- Ask if the program is sold in modules. Does the purchase price include all the modules you will need?

- Inquire into hidden maintenance fees or networking charges.

- Make sure the program is compatible with your equipment and your operating system.

- Ask for references, in other words names and telephone numbers of customers, for big purchases.

- Consider whether the program is compatible with your current procedures or will you need to change your procedures.

- Ask questions! Be sure you know what you are buying.

volunteers and make an honest evaluation of their skills. A training program will help address some of their weaknesses and instill good safety habits, However, volunteers whose skills are limited will not be able to master extremely complicated software programs.

For every program you install on your computers, someone, whether technician, administrative assistant, or volunteer, will have to learn enough to keep the program running. Each program will have its own idiosyncrasies and each will require time to install, update, and troubleshoot when it does not work correctly. To learn just one program well enough to deal with unexpected glitches and conflicts requires considerable time. When your technical support group must master a new but unnecessary program, it spreads their limited time thinner and makes the entire system more vulnerable to problems.

Step 11: Develop a Strategy for Attracting Computer-Literate Volunteers

It is clear to the Pleasantville planners that technology will be important to their success, and at present, they lack volunteers who possess the needed computer savvy. Of course, they need volunteers with a wide variety of skills, but what specific steps can they take to recruit volunteers who will work effectively with computers. One of their first ideas was to actively seek teen and college-age volunteers? However, to attract young people, they will need to change the culture of their organization. Many of their members are over 50 and tend to relate with young people as if they were their children or grandchildren. Schools are increasingly stressing the importance of community service and may even require that their students participate in such programs; so finding teen volunteers is not always the difficulty. If, however, teens are not treated as colleagues and given interesting and challenging responsibilities, they will look for other assignments.

Step 12: Plan a Computer Training Program

Once important information is stored in your nonprofit's computers, many people will need access to that information to do their work effectively. Computerization must not make it more difficult for group members to do their work or achieve their goals. This means that they will need to be trained to use the software programs chosen.

LEARN MORE ABOUT

Recruiting Teen Volunteers

- Read "A Springboard to Tomorrow: Creating Volunteer Programs for Young People that Encourage the Development of Skills" at www.nald.ca/fulltext/heritage/ComPartnE/springb1.htm.

- Visit "Volunteering for People Under 18" at www.serviceleader.org/new/volunteers/articles/2003/04/000047.php.

- Learn "20 Ways for Teenagers to Help Other People by Volunteering" www.bygpub.com/books/tg2rw/volunteer.htm.

- Discover "Family Volunteering: The Ties that Bind" at www.nald.ca/fulltext/heritage/ComPartnE/Family.htm.

- Read "Mentors Strengthen Student Community Service" at www .energizeinc.com/download/verserve.pdf.

In the previous section, we discussed the need for selecting software that can be used effectively by most of your group. Even though software was chosen with the skills of the group clearly in mind, training will still be needed. Will training consist entirely of learning to use specific programs or will it be necessary to provide basic Windows training as well?

Most volunteer groups include some advanced computer users and some with little or no computer experience. Nonprofit volunteer groups tend to be somewhat older and may include many people who completed their formal education before the advent of automation. This means that they were never taught to use computers in school and are largely self-taught. Although some may actually be afraid of computers, more have learned to use computers just for certain tasks such as email. They have taught themselves to do these few tasks without really understanding how computers work. This means that their skills cannot easily be transferred to new applications. On the other hand, people who use a computer at work every day are more likely to have learned to perform a variety of tasks and have experienced and resolved a wider range of problems.

Take a good look at the staff and volunteers who will be using your computer system. What will it take for them to use the system effectively? Do they require basic computer training or will you provide training only on the specific software programs they will be using? As a general rule, experienced computer users can be trained in larger group sessions, but novices need more personalized help. Inexperienced computer users might be given one-on-one training or receive instruction in groups of two, three, or four.

Who will provide training? Can the organization afford to bring in a professional trainer? Do any group members have experience as computer trainers? Let's face it: simply knowing how to use a computer does not qualify one to become a trainer. Later in the book, we will devote considerable time to the topic of training, but for now it is important to decide what organizational resources, both human and monetary, will need to be earmarked.

Some nonprofits begin with good intentions and plan several training sessions shortly after the computer system is installed. Soon after some volunteers leave and new ones join the group. Even experienced volunteers forget much of what they learned, and new arrivals receive only informal tips from other volunteers. Within a short period of time, much of what was taught in those first training sessions is lost. Security precautions are forgotten, and maintenance routines become irregular. Training must be an ongoing program. Everyone needs a refresher from time to time, and new volunteers need just as much support and guidance as those attending the early training sessions.

Step 13: Decide on the Role that Personally Owned Computers Will Play

Susan Smith, an active Pleasantville Association volunteer, owns a recent Windows-based computer, and she would like to be able to update mailing list information from home. This means that she would like to have access to the database containing the names and addresses of members. The data can be copied for her use, but does she have the appropriate program installed on her own computer and is the version compatible with the one installed on the association's own computers?

Even more important, there are confidentiality issues that must be considered. Is it really appropriate for Susan to have access to so much information about members?

If this were a database of donor information, the information would be even more personal. When an organization is very small and most members are operating out of their homes, there may be no choice. However, a database program allows you to print reports that include only selected information, while more confidential information can be omitted. It may be preferable to give Susan a printed list or report on which she can note corrections rather than a copy of the database file.

Mary, on the other hand, is the Anytown treasurer. She says she needs to concentrate when she uses the bookkeeping program and cannot do so with all the uproar at the group's office. If she has the same software program on her personal computer, it is possible to copy financial records and transfer them from one computer to another. However, Mary must purchase her own software. She may not copy the nonprofit's software onto her own personal computer. Depending on the nature of the software license, it is usually illegal to do so, and members must resist the temptation to make their own personal copies.

Personally owned computers can also spread viruses to the organization's own computers in email attachments and when files are copied and shared among computers. Make it a rule that volunteers who use their own computers will maintain current antivirus software subscriptions and update virus definitions on a regular basis. It is also a good idea to establish a goal of gradually eliminating dependence on personally owned computers.

Step 14: Decide How the Organization's Computers Will Be Protected

Personally owned computers are certainly not the only ones that are susceptible to viruses. Although most nonprofits make it a point to invest in antivirus software, the stories of virus-related hard drive crashes and data loss are, nevertheless, legion. This is usually because routine maintenance responsibilities have not been assigned. Even the small Pleasantville Association needs to create written procedures for maintaining computers and formally assign responsibility. Many organizations find it helpful to keep a clipboard beside each computer that holds a maintenance log. Maintenance routines include updating virus definitions, running virus scans, installing Windows Updates, and defragmenting hard drives, all of which must be performed frequently to keep computers operating safely and efficiently.

In the last few years, "spyware" has become as dangerous to computers as viruses. These are program routines that are unwittingly downloaded from the Internet without the user's knowledge or consent. They are intended to send information back to the individual or company that distributed them. Some of these programs called "adware" are merely intended to collect information about you for marketing purposes. Far more dangerous are the malicious programs that seek to steal your identity, sending back credit card numbers and other personal information. A number of excellent and often free software programs are available to search for this spyware and remove it from your computers. However, unless updates are downloaded and scans are run on a regular schedule, computers will remain vulnerable to attack.

As we learned, the Arts Council plans to install a DSL line or some other high-speed connection to the Internet. This means that their computers will be connected to the Internet for much longer periods. Whenever computers are turned on, the Internet will be available and so they are always vulnerable to attack. Do not imagine that just because no one has received a malicious email or surfed to a dangerous website, your computers are safe. As long as your line is open, danger can find you. This is why software programs called "firewalls" have been developed to wall off your computer from the outside world. They allow you to control both what information comes in and what information leaves your computers. Even the Pleasantville Association should install firewalls on all their computers, but the Arts Council, with its network and high-speed connection, is at much greater risk. Criminals conducting illicit businesses can take over distant computers, storing their records and operating their businesses from afar. This is how many child pornography operations are run, and the last thing your organization needs is a visit from the FBI.

Even without malicious invasions from the Internet, computers are vulnerable to all sorts of crises. Hard drives crash and all data stored on them can be lost. The Pleasantville group has chosen to store the master copy of its data on one computer. However, computers are machines and machines malfunction. There is a good chance that something will happen to this computer, ranging from an annoying system error to a full-scale meltdown. Since no organization can take such a chance, there must be procedures in place to rescue lost data, copy it to a new computer if necessary, and get back to work. This means that backup procedures are essential.

The group must think seriously about how much information it can afford to lose. If it can lose no more than one day's worth of changes and additions, then files must be backed up daily. During busy times like phon-a-thons and other fundraising activities when large quantities of data are being added, maybe more frequent backups are needed.

How will the backups be made? Will the data be copied to a CD? To a tape backup system? What about purchasing an extra external hard drive just for this purpose? Where should backup copies be kept? For the sake of simplicity, the Pleasantville volunteer responsible for making a CD backup might simply take the CD home, as long as he or she can locate it in an emergency. This would mean that if the group were to suffer an office break-in or fire, the data would be safe.

Step 15: Decide How and When Progress Will Be Evaluated and the Plan Will Be Updated

In the course of answering the questions above, you've created a preliminary technology plan. Bear in mind that your startup organization has very little experience on which to base a technology program and so you will need to revisit the plan at frequent intervals. You've given it your best shot but nonprofit leaders do not arrive equipped with crystal balls. Change can be rapid in small nonprofits as personnel changes and priorities are adjusted. That means your technology plan must change too. When will you revisit the plan? How will you decide whether your chosen projects are enhancing your productivity? How will you determine whether group members are participating fully in the program or whether additional training is needed? How will you select new projects? Include statements in your plan that commit the organization to reviewing it at specified intervals.

Putting It in Writing

Once all the above questions were discussed and tentative decisions made, the two groups had what might be called the skeletons or "bare bones" of their technology plans. Because funding agencies often require a technology plan, many nonprofits are tempted to throw together a plan that is strictly intended for looks. Such boilerplate plans begin with a lot of high-minded verbiage about lofty goals and then list some hardware and software the group plans to purchase. If the plan is created to accompany a grant proposal, it may simply paraphrase the wording of the grant guidelines or the proposal itself.

In fact, it must be admitted that the Arts Council Board had done just this short-ly after the group was organized. When faced with a requirement on a grant appli-cation, they simply searched for plans on the Internet, copied one that sounded vague enough to cover their activities, and voilà, they had a technology plan. That plan is probably buried in someone's file cabinet gathering dust and has not been seen since the grant application was submitted. In truth, it did not represent the group and so no attention was ever paid to its impressive sounding goals. When the board of directors recognized the need for a technology program, only one mem-ber remembered the wordy document and no one had any desire to resurrect it.

It is a good idea to get the basic components of your technology plan hammered out before encountering pressure from an outside agency. Do it when you can con-centrate on the actual needs of your organization, not on what someone else would like to see. Later, if your planning document must be reformatted for "public con-sumption," it is easy to make changes, but never substitute impressive verbiage for the strong, functional document you really need. In the case of the Arts Council, this generic technology plan may actually have delayed their development since there was less motivation to start all over. Nevertheless, the benefits of doing so will more than repay them for the effort expended.

Summing It Up

Watching a nonprofit organization grow and prosper is one of life's pleasures. Know-ing that our organizations have made a difference in people's lives is well worth the "blood, sweat, and tears" that may be required, and even the smallest nonprofits can achieve big goals when they learn to use their resources effectively. A technology program can make a significant contribution to achieving those goals if it is planned with care and is supported by continuing commitment. That commitment must come from both decision makers and the group as a whole. Technology will fail if it remains the province of one person or a small clique of "techies."

CHAPTER 3

Technology Planning for Midsized and Larger Organizations

After reading this chapter, you will be able to:

- Understand the basic elements of a local area network.
- Decide between different types of online connectivity.
- Understand different technical support options.
- Distinguish between up-to-date and "bleeding-edge" technology.
- Implement an effective technology plan for a midsized organization.

Organizational Growing Pains

Once an organization becomes established, it usually takes on a more solid identity, renting space or possibly building a permanent home. If all goes well, fundraising will become both more organized and more successful, resulting in more dependable budgeting. Policies and procedures gradually take the place of off-the-cuff management. In general, the organization comes to resemble a business rather than the club of enthusiasts of those early days. More people, both paid staff and volunteers, become involved, and communication becomes more difficult.

At this point, technology can make an enormous difference in the organization's ability to achieve its goals. However, at about the time a nonprofit makes the transition from a small, highly personal, and "hands-on" venture, it may encounter a technology crisis that shakes it to its very foundation.

Revisiting Pleasantville and Anytown

The Pleasantville Family Advocacy Association, which we met in the last chapter, has been doing very well. Generous contributions, as well as the support of the mental health community, has allowed the group to expand its services to include both a family counseling center and a shelter for the victims of domestic violence. The Anytown Arts Council has also been expanding. In addition to funding from various sources, it has received a sizeable bequest. Both groups now have a board of directors, several committees, and a large corps of volunteers. Anytown also has hired a small staff consisting of a director and one other paid employee.

Success has brought satisfaction, of course, but it has also been accompanied by stress and confusion. Such a large number of activities and participants require a more formal organizational structure and greater emphasis on efficiency. This is usually achieved only at the cost of a certain amount of frustration and some occasional disenchantment.

You may remember that the Pleasantville group started out with two donated computers that were not linked to one another. Soon they had enough money to purchase a heavily discounted new computer. That meant that the organization now owned three computers with different information on each. When volunteers needed to learn about contributors, they went to computer No. 1; when they wanted budget printouts, they had to wait until computer No. 2 was available. It was not long before they became frustrated with the situation and vociferously communicated their displeasure to the tech team. "What we need is a network," one of the members insisted when the team met to discuss the problem. However, the others wondered about the cost and the technical know-how needed.

Planning for Technological Change

The Pleasantville group lacked confidence when it came to computers, but they soon became adept at enlisting free technical help. To learn whether they were ready for a more sophisticated computer system, the tech team invited a local computer sales-man, who had been particularly helpful in the past, to meet with them. They also asked Roger, the husband of one of their members, to attend the meeting. Roger was not really an expert, but he had helped them deal with several small crises, and the team trusted him to understand their needs and their limitations. The team was wise to involve several people in the planning process. They might have asked Roger to simply make their decisions for them, but that would have been a mistake. Although he might know a lot more about computers than they did, they knew their organization.

Benchmarking

Before the tech team met with the computer vendor, Roger suggested that they take a good look at how their technical needs and resources had changed in the past few years. The business sector uses the term "benchmarking" for this process. Team members rate their organization on a series of questions intended to reveal both strengths and weaknesses. Your list may be somewhat different from the Pleasantville tech team's, but be sure that it provides your group with an opportunity to assess how your organization currently uses technology and how effective it has been. What are your strengths and what are your challenges? Include questions that will elicit suggestions for improving technology use to better support your mission. Here are some of the questions that Roger asked the tech team to consider:

The Technology Plan

- Does your organization have a technology plan?

- If you have such a plan, when was it last revised?

- Is the leadership of your organization solidly behind your technology plan?

- Are funds available to implement your technology plan? This includes money not only for hardware and software but also to cover "human costs" such as training, maintenance, and staff support.

- Are responsibilities for implementing the plan clearly assigned?

- Does your plan establish guidelines for hardware and software compatibility?

- Is there a process for regularly reviewing your plan and evaluating progress?

Decision Making

- Is managing technology taken seriously in your organization?

- Do you have a tech team that meets regularly?

- Are those responsible for technology empowered to make most routine decisions or must they seek authorization from leaders for every small expenditure?

- Is input sought from a number of sources before major technical decisions are made?

- Is your organization's mission a key consideration when making technology decisions?

Stability and Security

- If the individual in your organization who is most involved with your computer system resigned, would others be able to take over his or her responsibilities?

- If this individual left suddenly, would essential information be lost?

- Have procedures been written for most routine computer maintenance and Windows tasks?

- Has your organization developed a safety net of reliable computer support and technology expertise (for example, computer repair businesses, consultants, substitute systems administrators, and so on)?

- Do staff and volunteers have easy access to the hardware and software they need to do their jobs?

- Do staff and volunteers have desktop access to the Internet?

Computer Literacy

- Are all members of your organization trained in basic computer skills?

- Is there a plan in place for upgrading and refreshing staff and volunteer computer skills?

- Are there regular training sessions and/or workshops to acquaint staff and volunteers with new hardware and software?

- Is technical help readily available when staff and volunteers need it?

- Are staff and volunteers supportive of technology?

- Do staff and volunteers feel as if they are in control of technology?

Answering these questions together as a group really put things into perspective for the tech team. On the one hand, they realized that they had come a long way. They had put a lot of work into their small computer projects and could now reply in the affirmative to many of the questions. On the other hand, the questions made it clear that a network alone was not the answer to their problems. For example, what about that exasperating dial-up telephone line they all had to use? At least the association now had several phone lines, one of which was supposedly intended for Internet use. However, connecting to the Web continued to be a chore. It was clearly time to think about a faster, more reliable way to connect. The two subjects actually went together, Roger asserted. The team agreed that they would investigate the different types of communications options as part of their network planning.

Making Technology Decisions

Now it was finally time to meet with the local vendor who could suggest solutions to their problems. Never underestimate the amount of excellent advice that can be obtained from local computer sales personnel. The same is true of representatives of Internet service providers. Just bear in mind that they have a product to sell. Make sure that your budget limitations are clear from the very beginning, and beware the "sales pitch" that does not really answer your questions. Also be just a little suspicious of the over-enthusiastic vendor who wants to sell you cutting-edge technology. The "cutting edge" too often turns out to be the "bleeding edge." What you are looking for is a "work horse" network built on thoroughly tested components. You cannot afford mistakes, and your technical needs are not really so very sophisticated. Let large and affluent businesses experiment with high tech, and allow some time to elapse so you can learn from their successes and failures. Besides, a system that now bears an astronomical price tag will cost a lot less in six months, but it will do exactly the same thing and have roughly the same life expectancy. Your needs are not going to change that much in six months.

Network Basics

The Pleasantville tech team was meeting with the owner of a local business that regularly installed computer networks. Once everyone had a coffee cup in hand, the meeting began. First, the salesman quickly explained just what a network does. Most are more properly called local area networks (LANs); they link computers together so they can share files, printers, Internet access, and other resources. Staff members and volunteers can log on to the same program and see the same information no matter which computers they might be using. Computers may be wired together with coaxial cable or they may communicate over a wireless network. The big question is what the computer is connected to. It is possible to simply connect two computers to each other. Technically, that's all that's needed to create a local area network. More commonly, however, the computers in the network are not connected to one another but rather to a central server. That means that for two computers to share information, the data is passed from one computer to the server and then from the server to the second computer.

The Role of the Network Server

Roger entered the discussion at this point to emphasize that the group really needed a dedicated server to which all the other computers could be connected. He explained to the tech team that even though the server is usually just a powerful PC and can be used like the other computers, this was not a good idea. The term "dedicated" means that the server does nothing else but "serve." Roger's office had once tried to make do with a server that was also used as a regular PC workstation. Again and again, someone would inadvertently log off or shut down the server. Then, all the other computers on the network would go down as well. For this reason, Roger recommended that the server be off-limits to most computer users. Of course, it is more expensive to declare one computer off-limits, but Roger believed that a dedicated server was so much more reliable that it was well worth the added cost.

When individual computers are not connected to a LAN, files must be copied on floppy or CD Rom disks and reloaded on each separate computer. In a network, files that will need to be shared are loaded on the server. As each computer needs to use them, it calls for them. For example, a database record is sent from the server to the computer. After making changes and additions, the computer user saves the record to the server. To the user, the program looks just as it did when all information was stored locally. Now, however, just one backup will protect the work of many computer users. When one computer is unavailable, the same work can be performed on any of the others. When a new computer is added to the network, software can simply be copied from the server. When a computer breaks down, it is no longer a tragedy because it is interchangeable with all the others.

In a LAN, individual computers are not connected to the Internet. Instead, only the server or sometimes the "router" connects directly, preferably to one high-speed communications line. It is the function of the server to receive incoming web pages and messages and then route them to the correct computer. All the computers in the network can use the same line at the same time. A LAN also allows you to share peripheral equipment like printers so that one printer or one scanner can accommodate many computers. This can save quite a bit of money and allow you to purchase higher quality equipment than would be possible if you had to attach a printer to each computer. Fewer pieces of equipment mean fewer repair bills too.

Ethernet-based Networks

As you learned in the last chapter, wired networks are usually Ethernet-based. The Ethernet network card in each computer connects to an Ethernet cable. One disadvantage of a wired network is that cable should usually be installed by a licensed professional, just as other electrical wiring must be professionally installed. This can be expensive, costing approximately $75.00 per computer. Every wired computer must have a network interface card, in other words, a small piece of equipment that connects the computer to the cable. Many newer desktop computers come equipped with network cards but if you must buy them separately, they are usually quite inexpensive. The cards, slip into slots in the computer case and screw into place, an easy procedure for someone experienced with computers.

Wireless Networks

Increasingly, organizations are choosing to install wireless networks to reduce the complications created by all those cables. Smaller organizations may be housed in temporary facilities and may not wish to invest money for cabling infrastructure. Wireless networks eliminate many of those snakelike tangles on the floor that everyone is always tripping over. Another advantage of wireless networking is that you can connect most spaces, even conference rooms where computer connections are only occasionally needed, to your network. Wireless is also a good way to economically add on to an existing wired network.

The basic principle behind wireless networking is the use of radio waves or microwaves that communicate between computers. Many people find wireless terminology a little confusing. Technicians may talk unintelligibly about "Wi-Fi" and "Bluetooth," for example. These are actually standards that allow networking products to work together. By creating standards, different manufacturers are able to produce products that work with one another. Wi-Fi is actually the industry "802.11b" standard, and is an abbreviation for "wireless fidelity." The problem with wireless is that the signal gets weaker as computers are moved away from the source of the signal. Barriers like walls can slow or even halt communication. Another disadvantage of wireless is that it is affected by radio interference due to weather or other wireless devices.

Wireless Security Issues

Remember that computers can communicate with one another and with the Internet anywhere network signals are strong enough. This means that anyone with a laptop computer equipped with a wireless networking card can join your network. Group members can bring their laptops to a meeting and access the same information at the same time. Everyone can get to the Internet from either an office desktop computer or a personal computer. Your signal, however, may reach to the shop next door or be picked up by someone parked in a car outside your building. Perhaps you have been with your own teenager when he or she is cruising the neighborhood looking for an unsecured wireless connection to the Internet. Depending on the strength of the signal, it is possible to simply park one's car and connect.

Wired Equivalent Privacy (WEP) is a security protocol that comes included in all Wi-Fi certified products. It protects your data by encoding it while it is being transferred from one computer to another. For someone to get into your network, he or she must enter a long sequence of letters and/or numbers into their computer. This code or "key" is also entered for the wireless router, so unless visitors know the key, they cannot connect to the router or intercept transmitted data. Although WEP is very useful, it is not foolproof. Security is a very high priority when setting up a wireless network, and additional protection is needed.

Just as each wired computer needs an Ethernet network card, each wireless computer on a network needs a wireless networking card. Currently, these are somewhat more expensive than Ethernet cards. They are often built into new laptops, but they usually must be purchased separately for desktop computers. The Windows XP operating system includes built-in support for wireless networking.

It is the wireless router that connects directly to the Internet. Wireless routers are similar to traditional routers for wired networks in that they allow all your computers to share your Internet connection. They also act as firewalls. Many routers have built-in hubs that allow you to connect wired computers to a wireless network.

Alternatives to wireless routers are "access points" that allow wireless networks to join existing wired networks. One simply adds an access point to the network hub. One access point is usually sufficient for one or two offices, but if you want your whole facility to be accessible to the network, you will need to set up multiple access points and/or routers. Such equipment can make use of wireless antennae to increase the range of the wireless radio signal. Antennae can also be mounted on network computers to increase the range of wireless adapter cards.

Networking Macs and PCs Together

In the last chapter, we cautioned strongly against combining Macintosh computers with Windows-based PCs. We recommended staying with PCs unless you had some very technically sophisticated people on your staff or tech team. Once an organization becomes larger, it may want to consider combining the two types of computers. Many desktop publishers, publicists, and illustrators prefer the Mac's graphic capability, and some people just plain do not like Windows. If you have a knowledgeable technical staff, whether paid or volunteer, you may want to include both Macs and PCs in your network. Cross-platform networks can work fine, but they require some special software solutions that allow the two computers to "see" one another and decipher their file formats.

Using TCP/IP

For purposes of illustration, we will assume that you have an Ethernet network in place although a wireless configuration would utilize the same software solutions. One of the basic reasons for having a network is to allow all your computers to share an Internet connection whether dial-up, DSL, or cable modem. Fortunately, both Macs and PCs use TCP/IP, the language that networks use to communicate with the Internet. That means that hardware devices like modem routers, DSL/cable modem routers, and even some software-sharing tools will work with both kinds of computers.

Connecting Printers

When you connect your printer directly to the network (rather than an individual computer) using an Ethernet network interface card, you get around most compatibility problems. Once they are on the network, both Macs and PC's can usually access the same printer without any extra software or special configuration. If your printer did not come equipped with an Ethernet card, you can purchase one separately or purchase an external "print server" for about $200.00. If your printer is attached to any of your computers, it must support the PostScript printer language. In general, most high-end printers for PCs support PostScript, but less expensive home and home office PC printers may not. Nearly all Mac printers support PostScript.

Facilitating File Sharing

File sharing is somewhat more difficult because Macs and PCs essentially speak two different languages and require special software to allow them to make sense of one another's files. Special software is also needed when you wish to connect a printer directly to a Mac or PC. Your challenge will be to reduce your cost by purchasing as little software as possible. Your specific software solution will depend on whether you have mainly PC's with one or two Macs or the other way around.

PCMacLAN is a software program that runs on a PC, and allows it to "see and be seen" by a network of Macs. On the other hand, DAVE (Thursby Software) runs on Macs and allows them to see and be seen by a network of PCs. These are just two of the programs that can help your computers communicate with one another.

Sometimes, the real problem is not Mac/PC compatibility but different software programs or different versions of those programs. If you receive an email attachment that you cannot open, this may well be the problem. Two programs are sold by Dataviz, called Conversions Plus for PCs and MacLink Plus Deluxe for Macs. Both allow you to smoothly open and translate files created on either a PC or Mac.

Since there are many more PCs on the market than Macs, there are many software programs designed to run only on PCs. If you are in the position of having to run a Windows-based program on a Mac, you will need what is called Windows emulation software. Virtual PC (Connectix software) is one such program.

Once again, be sure that you have good technical support before you try to marry Macs with PCs. Small, unexpected problems tend to come up that require some technical expertise to troubleshoot.

Purchasing Technology

Once the tech team had clearly identified the organization's technical needs, it was time to make some essential purchases. The first thing they had to decide was whether to purchase hardware locally or from a national computer vendor. Here are some points they considered:

- Was it worth the savings offered by large discount vendors when computers and other equipment arrived unassembled in cardboard boxes?

- How much was it worth to have someone set up the network components and provide at least some preliminary explanations of how to use them? Setting up computer equipment is not really as difficult as it looks because cables and connections have been standardized. If something does not work, however, the vendor is better able to deal with the problem.

- Do local vendors offer significantly more free and inexpensive technical support than the national dealer? To find the real answer, it is a good idea to ask their references about just how easy it has been to get help.

- How important is it to establish a relationship with a local vendor? Does extra cost translate to extra service? It is comforting to have a local dealer you can call with your questions. However, small computer businesses tend to be unstable and prone to going out of business. At least the large national company will probably be around next year or the year after, even if you must endure long waits on "hold" for technical assistance.

Comparing Computer Offers

Be sure you know what you want before you begin comparing prices. Focus on the features you really need. How much money do you have to spend and what must come out of that amount? As of this writing, a well-known, national computer vendor offers a system consisting of a monitor and a desktop computer equipped with a combination CD writer and a DVD player for about $600.00. Although the exact specifications keep changing, the system offered is usually basic but acceptable. This same computer company offers high-end desktop computer systems that sell for about $4,000. For the moment, let's forget about the high-end selections, but consider the differences between the $600.00 model and, let's say, one that sells for $1,200.00.

The first thought that comes to mind is that for the same cost, two staff members could have new $600.00 computers on their desks, while only one could benefit from the $1,200.00 model. This is a very important point to consider. Computer sharing never works very well. Staff are most efficient when a computer is available when they need it. This means that your nonprofit should not purchase the $1,200 model unless there is reason to believe that either the cheaper model will not meet your needs or the more expensive one is somehow very much superior. How do you make such a decision? Begin by making a list of just what is different about the two computers and what is the same.

Points in Common

Let's begin with the ways in which the two computers are similar:

- They are sold by the same company, so the reputation of the vendor is, of course, the same, as are the vendor's quality control procedures.

- The vendor has a reputation for providing good or bad customer service, good or bad technical support. The same staff will be responding to your pleas for help, but the more expensive one probably comes with additional free technical assistance.

- The durability of the materials is probably similar. Buying a computer is not like buying a washing machine, since you generally do not get added years of use from a more expensive model.

- Many of the basic components are the same. They were manufactured to the same specifications by the same factory in China or Sri Lanka.

Differences between Computers

Now let's consider some differences between the two models:

- The more expensive computer is probably a more recent model. Not much more recent, however. Older computer models are quickly discontinued.

- Similarly, the more expensive computer represents somewhat more sophisticated technology. The processor may be faster, the RAM memory and hard drive larger.

- Features that were optional with the bare-bones computer are included with the more expensive model at no additional cost.

The computers may be produced by different divisions of a company. This means, for example, that the computer marketed for business use may be somewhat sturdier than the one marketed for use at home.

Specific Differences

Finally, evaluate the specific differences between the two computers under consideration:

- How much faster is the more expensive model? Is speed important to the applications you will be using? If you maintain a database consisting of many thousands of records, speed is important to you. If, on the other hand, it will be years before your database grows to this size, then you will probably have a new computer by then.

- How much larger is the hard drive? This is usually not an important consideration because most of the information stored on your hard drive will probably be database records and word processing documents. These require much less storage space than the music and graphics files that a home user might store. It may be worth having a large hard drive, however, so you can use data recovery programs like GoBack that, rather than deleting all your changes, store them to another part of the hard drive.

- How much additional RAM memory comes installed on the more expensive computer? Experts agree that this is an important consideration and will have a big impact on performance. A memory upgrade, however, can be as inexpensive as $60.00–$100.00. If this is all you need to run your applications efficiently, then the more expensive computer may be a waste of money.

- Can you really live with the barebones computer or would you need to "customize" it? Computer vendors sometimes offer a computer at an attractive price. However, when you look more closely, you discover that standard features like modems and CD "burners" are priced separately.

The Dell computer website (www.dell.com) has an interesting feature that allows you to start with a basic computer package and then add higher-end components. Some of the other larger online computer vendors offer similar sites. Whether or not you are considering a Dell purchase, it is helpful to use the site to experiment with different add-ons. After even a few minutes, you begin to see which features hike up the price and which are relatively inexpensive.

Of course, when you are considering computers sold by different companies, comparisons are somewhat more difficult. However, many websites like PCWorld and CNET, as well as more traditional publications like Consumer Reports, regularly review new equipment. It is very easy to find reviews of any models you may be considering. Even if you are unable to find reviews of precisely the model that interests you, you will find more than enough information about the company's reputation for quality and for customer service.

Larger Purchases Require More Research

When making any sizable investment in technology, it is essential to know exactly what you want before negotiating with a vendor. Although vendors can be very helpful in making you aware of your options, they will usually try to influence your decision, leading you toward more expensive solutions and away from smaller purchases that will naturally result in smaller commissions. Government agencies are usually required to write a Request for Proposals (RFP) whenever they plan to make a large purchase. Although nonprofits may not be required to draft such a document, it is in their best interests to do so. The RFP (see Exhibit 3.2) should be detailed enough that it is easy to compare the proposals and quoted prices of different vendors. If the RFP specifically includes an item, option, or service, it can be assumed to be included in the cost unless the vendor specifically excludes it. An RFP is important in any legal conflict, but even more important, it provides an opportunity for the organization to clearly identify its needs and state them unambiguously.

Checking References

When considering a vendor, be sure to check references, just as you would if you were hiring a staff member. Ideally, you would like to talk with people in other organizations similar to your own and ask them about their experiences with the

EXHIBIT 3.2

Writing an RFP

Imagine that your nonprofit needs to outsource some technology service or purchase a "turnkey automation system." Perhaps you want to contract with a database vendor to create a database of contributors or with a Web design firm to design and host a website. Rather than inviting vendors to tell you what they can supply, it is more effective to first tell them exactly what you want. To write an effective RFP, you will need to do the following:

- Identify your need in general terms. What problem are you trying to solve?

- Identify the type of consultant or vendor you need.

- Describe your organization, its mission, and its programs in a few sentences.

- Briefly describe your technology as it is and as you want it to be.

- Specify your needs in detail. What are the desired results? What will be different when the project is complete? Include exactly what it is you want to get out of the proposed relationship.

- If you are purchasing equipment, focus on what it must be able to do. What functions are essential and what functions are optional? Must it be compatible with your existing equipment? If you are hiring a vendor to create a database, what kind of reports should the system be able to produce?

- Clarify whether you will leave the solution to your problem open-ended to get different opinions on the best course of action.

- Describe what you want to know about vendors, including their experience with similar projects and how they have handled problems similar to yours.

- Require a timeline. When will the vendor be able to commence work on the project and when will it be completed?

- Ask vendors to include references from similar clients in their proposal package.

- Ask them to clarify exactly what their price quotation includes.

- Decide who will receive your RFP. Ask other nonprofit administrators for recommendations. Consider inviting vendors via a newspaper advertisement and email discussion lists. Find websites and publications that list vendors who specialize in this service.

vendor. Try to identify other customers not listed as official references and ask questions similar to the following:

- How would you characterize the service you have received?

- What kind of problems have you experienced working with this vendor?

- How long did you have to wait before the vendor addressed these problems? Did they ever get addressed?

- What is your impression of the vendor's business ethics and financial stability?

- Would you choose this vendor again?

Volume Discounts

It is not impossible to bargain for technology with either local or national vendors. If you are buying several computers at one time, it is well worth the effort to solicit price quotes from several vendors. Ask for the price as a package and for the individual components. Make sure that your quote indicates the discount offered for buying in volume, as well as shipping, delivery, service, and warranty charges. Consider other sources of discounted equipment (see Exhibit 3.1). Are you getting the best price available, considering support and convenience?

When you are talking on the phone with a salesperson, be sure you take extensive notes. Ask the name of the person to whom you are speaking, and clarify any ambiguous claims. Later, these notes can serve as evidence of the terms you were offered. Good companies try to keep their promises, so when a vendor fails to meet a deadline or is otherwise unable to meet all the contract requirements, ask to be compensated for your inconvenience.

Purchasing Hardware and Software at Discount Prices

Nonprofits are sometimes able to take advantage of educational discounts, and some businesses offer special pricing just for nonprofits. Before you pay full price for a computer, printer, or software program, check the following websites that offer special discounts for nonprofits:

DiscounTech (www.techsoup.org/DiscounTech) at the TechSoup website offers technology products at excellent prices just for nonprofits. Producers have donated their products, so cost is sometimes almost negligible.

501Click Marketplace (www.501Click.com) offers special prices for nonprofits, having negotiated discounts from each of its vendors. They will refund the difference if you see an item somewhere else for a lower price than you paid for it at 501Click.

Consistent Computer Bargains (www.ccbnonprofits.com) offers deep discounts to nonprofits on many name-brand software packages. It has made arrangements with Microsoft and other vendors such as Borland, Aldus, and Novell to sell certain titles to 501(c)(3) nonprofits at academic discounts.

Before Signing a Contract

If you are simply buying an off-the-shelf computer from your local discount store, you probably do not need to concern yourself with a contract. Whatever you get or do not get is in the box, possibly including a printed service agreement. However, in a sense, you participate in a contract simply by purchasing the equipment. Your invoice or sales slip is a kind of contract. When you purchase a computer online, you are usually unable to proceed until you click on a button that reads "I agree." You can see only a small portion of what you are agreeing to, but if you scroll through the whole contract, you will discover a long, complicated agreement written in legalese. Most people click the button automatically, scarcely looking at the specific terms. However, if you are planning to make a larger purchase, you will need to give quite a bit of thought to any contract you may be bound by.

Contracts are usually written by the seller and so are intended primarily to protect the company from liability. You as the buyer want to maximize the seller's responsibility so that you are fully protected. To do so, you will need to alter the terms of most prepared contracts wherever possible. If you do not understand a contract provision, ask for an explanation. Beware the salesperson who responds "Oh, that's not important."

Verbal Contracts

Remember that a contract can be verbal. When a salesperson promises you free technical support if you purchase a computer, this is a verbal contract. The trouble is that your memories of the conversation may differ. Unless you have recorded the conversation, it will be hard for you to hold the seller to such a promise. There is actually a law that covers verbal contracts called the "Statute of Frauds" that limits enforceable verbal contracts to only those that can be performed within a short period of time and that involve only relatively small amounts of money.

Contracts amounting to more than a few thousand dollars should be reviewed and edited by your lawyer. Such contracts usually include a welter of unintelligible clauses that cover everything from attorney fees to arbitration and many improbable occurrences.

Supporting Documentation

If your organization does not currently use a purchase order system, you might consider doing so—at least for larger purchases and service agreements (see Exhibit 3.3). Your purchase orders have some standing in courts of law, so consider listing a few of your important requirements. If you fail to notice a damaging clause in a contract, your purchase order may offer some protection. When there is a conflict between your forms and the seller's, the courts usually ignore the terms that are in conflict. You will be a lot better off, therefore, if you read the fine print and resolve potential problems before you sign any contract. It is usually possible to alter a contract to your advantage when a vendor really wants to make a sale. Take advantage of this opportunity while you are in a bargaining position and never sign any contract that involves a significant sum of money without reading it carefully.

TIPS & TECHNIQUES

What's Included in a Contract

Clearly, it is best not to depend on verbal contracts. Even written contracts, however, may be difficult to enforce, so care should be taken in the way they are worded. The following are some of the basic inclusions in most written contracts:

- The full names of each party, addresses, and telephone numbers. If a parent corporation owns the business with which you are dealing, their information should be included as well.

- A complete statement of the obligations of each party, including all deadlines for delivery and payment.

- A personal guarantee if you have any doubts about the stability or integrity of the business.

- A reasonable *force majeure* clause. This limits liability in case events occur that are beyond the seller's control, such as labor union strikes and natural disasters. Such a clause should be clearly stated and not open-ended.

- A statement of damages that will be incurred if either party fails to perform. For example, if a seller is unable to provide the equipment specified, the company may be required to substitute higher priced models at the buyer's discretion.

- A statement specifying which state's laws will govern the agreement and the location at which the parties must appear to resolve disputes. (If the only state in which you are permitted to bring suit against a seller is a thousand miles distant, you may want to alter the contract.)

Technology Growing Pains

As we learned in the last chapter, the Arts Council chose to install a small wireless computer network connected to the Internet through a high-speed communication line. Over the course of time, more computers were added to the network. Each

EXHIBIT 3.3

Choosing a Vendor for a Large Purchase

If your organization is considering a purchase that will cost more than a few thousand dollars, the following suggestions may help you avoid common pitfalls:

- Initially avoid talking with salespeople who make unsolicited visits or telephone calls. Although salespeople can sometimes provide excellent technical information, they can't tell you what you need.

- Do not accept product claims made either by salespeople or in promotional literature unless they are backed up by product reviews in respected magazines and journals. Some websites like *PC World* also provide reviews.

- Even when you have initiated the contact, never feel obligated to purchase from a vendor. Avoid personal relationships and do not accept favors.

- Interrupt sales pitches. Demand facts. If you do not feel comfortable about a salesperson or the information he or she is giving you, this may not be a company with which you want to do business. Trust your instincts.

- Check the references for any vendor you are seriously considering. Ask to see a list of organizations that made purchases, not a brief hand-picked list.

- Ask references about the vendor's accessibility after contracts were signed. Once the deal was "in the bag," did they notice a change in attitude?

- How will a service be performed? Make sure that the contract includes details that are important to you.

- Include penalties in the contract if equipment is not installed or services are not performed on schedule.

- Make the endpoint clear in the contract so it's easy to determine whether the vendor has met its obligations.

continued on next page

- Get the names of senior administrators in the chain of command so you can report problems to people empowered to solve them.

- Be clear about cost. Repeatedly state in writing, both in correspondence and in the contract, that costs are final and no other charges will be added without your express approval.

- Do not pay the full amount until the project is finished and you are satisfied with the result. Do not pay more than 40 percent of the total cost up front.

time a computer was added, some small modification was made to accommodate it but, essentially, the group was living with the same technology plan it created when computers were first introduced. Initially, a small group of volunteers was responsible for maintaining the network. However, only one of those original tech team members is still actively involved with the Arts Council, and responsibility for the network has been absorbed into the job description of the new director. Naturally, the Arts Council director has more pressing responsibilities than running virus scans, so she has turned over such tasks to the administrative assistant.

Increasing Dependence on Technology

As mentioned earlier, however, this is a busy time for the Arts Council, with plans for the new art museum going forward and fundraising activities occupying more time than ever. One morning a staff member logged in to the computer network but was unable to open the contributors' database. Another did the same from another computer, but the result was the same. The database just was not there! We will skip over the details of this horror story, but a dozen different people including the bookkeeper's brother-in-law tried to revive the terminally ill system. It turned out that the hard drive on the network server had died, and no amount of CPR could revive it. The hard drive was soon replaced, and the database software program reloaded, but what about all that information about the thousands of contributions and contributors that was stored on the hard drive? Yes, the administrative assistant had made a backup. When was it? Two weeks ago? A month? No, maybe it was more like two months ago.

The technician from a local computer repair business was of the opinion that a virus had gotten into the server's operating system, causing the hard drive to crash. No, that was not possible, the administrative assistant defended herself. The antivirus program was set to run automatically on the server. Unfortunately, the subscription had run out. Since the administrative assistant rarely worked with the server (there were all sorts of confusing screens and she found it easiest to just shut down and restart whenever a problem occurred), she had not noticed the warnings.

Not only was the contributor database lost but the accounting records disappeared as well. However, since bills and purchase orders were still piled on the bookkeeper's desk waiting to be filed, it was possible to reconstruct most of the data. Unfortunately, this was not possible with the recent records in the contributors database. They contained not only donation histories but also precious notes about the interests and giving habits of the contributors. Both staff and volunteers attempted to reconstruct their phone conversations over the past few weeks and some of the contributions had been mailed in accompanied by forms, but some of the information was irretrievably lost. In addition, hundreds of hours were spent rebuilding the database, hours that could have been much better spent advancing the goals of the organization.

Assigning Responsibility for Technology

It was only then that the board and administrators realized what technology really meant to them. Over the course of time, the organization had surrendered its independence to the computer system. What followed was a depressing period during which everybody blamed everybody else. At length, it was agreed to put the crisis behind them and make certain that such a tragedy never happened again. Of course, never is a very long time but from that point on, technology was given the attention it deserved.

At first, everyone had an easy answer. They would hire a technician who would take over the computer network. All technical problems would be dumped into his lap and all would be well. Unfortunately, it soon became clear that the salary they could offer attracted only the young and inexperienced. Young men (almost no women applied) who had recently graduated from video games and knew far more about computers than about the world of work. Without frequent reminders, the new technician was no more likely to remember backups than the administrative assistant. Even technically unsophisticated board members realized that some of the hardware he requested was both expensive and impractical. A crisis was finally reached when he expended his budget on one "cool" state-of-the-art computer instead of the three desktop replacements that had been planned.

Technology Is Everyone's Business

It became clear that technology was not something that could be dumped into anyone's lap. Technology required the commitment of the whole group. The last time it was necessary to get a grip on technology, a tech team was appointed and a technology plan developed. Now it was time to go back to the drawing board. A new tech team was selected and, because the nonprofit had prospered, it was now possible to hire a technology consultant to work with the reconstituted team.

Over the next few months, the tech team met weekly. At first, discussions revolved around such matters as the technician's unsatisfactory performance and the selection of new equipment. Gradually, however, it became clear that these were not the real issues. Something more fundamental was wrong. During the past few years, the Arts Council had become more professional and businesslike in its activities. It had gradually built a management structure that allowed everyone in the organization to share the same goals and work toward achieving them. It supported the arts in the community by effectively managing its budget, fundraising activities, marketing, and other essential functions. When the team took a good look at technology, however, they realized that no one felt responsible for managing this vitally important function.

Orienting Technical Staff

When the Arts Council hired its young and untested technician, members expected him to perform like an experienced manager. During an especially heated discussion, Marcia, a recently hired office assistant, brought a message to a member of the group. When she left, someone sighed "Why can't our tech be like Marcia?" Although talented and personable, Marcia was also very inexperienced. In fact, this was her first full-time job. Marcia's post-probation evaluation, however, had been glowing, while the equally young and inexperienced technician's evaluation was filled with negative comments.

When Marcia was first hired, she began as a trainee. She and her supervisor worked out a training program that would allow her to learn about the Arts Council, observe the work of other staff members, sit in on a variety of meetings, and meet regularly with her supervisor/mentor. During these first weeks, her job was to learn and every effort was made to provide written materials and personal interactions that prepared her to do her job. Even after the training period was over, her supervisor continued to meet with her frequently, helping her deal with problems and providing positive feedback. It was only when Marcia felt comfortable with her job that she was expected to work independently and meet performance goals.

Making Technical Staff Part of the Organization

When the new technician was hired, no one really knew what he was supposed to be doing. Of course, a supervisor was assigned who assured him that he could come to her with questions any time he liked. He was given a tour of the facility and a copy of the staff handbook. With this brief introduction, he was placed in charge of the Arts Council's computer system. Maybe that was why things had gone so badly. Within days, staff began to find the system down when they needed it most. Evening volunteers were unable to get to the contributors database because he had taken the server offline to run after-hours maintenance routines. When the tech team really examined the problems they had been experiencing, what became crystal clear was a "disconnect" between the technician and the Arts Council. He really knew nothing about what they did or when they did it.

When Marcia first arrived, she met with each of the department heads and she quickly assembled a clear picture of how each department fit into the "big picture." While she was making these visits, she had an opportunity to get to know a lot of people, some of whom would later become good friends. Gradually, she developed a network of contacts who connected her to the unofficial grapevine and were able to answer many of her questions. It was obvious to everyone that the technician was not connected to the grapevine. In fact, his contacts with other staff members were mostly negative ones, as when they complained about crises with the computer system. He naturally came to see them as problems, not as people.

Managers Manage Technology

As team members continued to compare the two young staff members, it became clear that the new technician had probably done the best he could, considering that he had been cut off from the support system that allowed Marcia to become a successful member of the organization. The answer to many of their problems was, therefore, obvious. Experienced managers would have to learn to manage technology. Senior supervisors who understood the goals and priorities of the Arts Council would have to become involved in important technology decisions.

Although this may sound like a simple and even obvious decision, it had enormous ramifications for the Arts Council. Technology could no longer be seen as someone else's job, and staff members could no longer pat themselves on the back for a job well done if they knew nothing more about computers than the right keys to press. At first, the prospect of managing technology seemed overwhelming and even impossible. How could mature managers master so much technical knowledge? They could not, and there was no need for them to do so. After all, they worked effectively with professionals in the arts community when they could not paint a picture or play a musical instrument. There was no reason why they could not work with their technician in the same way. Together, they could establish goals and develop strategies to meet those goals. It is true, however, that their technical vocabularies would need to be expanded for such communication to take place.

Revisiting the Technology Plan

Since effective management is absolutely essential, we will be returning to the subject in a later chapter. Now, however, let's consider the ways in which management can become a central focus of an organization's technology plan. When the Arts Council developed its first technology plan several years ago, it was a much smaller, less complex organization. In many ways, it simply is not the same organization it was, and parts of that early technology plan are now obsolete. The tech team needs to revisit the plan and take a cold, hard look at it. Does it need to be revised or does the team need to start from scratch, developing a whole new technology plan that meets the needs of the organization as it is today?

TIPS & TECHNIQUES

Keys to Effective Technology Leadership

- A technology leader is a public advocate for technology.

- A technology leader fully understands the organization's mission and how technology can support it.

- A technology leader develops relationships with many groups and individuals, both within and outside of the organization.

- A technology leader empowers others to initiate technological innovations.

- A technology leader understands how key group members feel about technology and involves them in planning and implementing technology projects.

- A technology leader inspires staff and volunteers, providing a role model of commitment and enthusiasm.

- A technology leader does his or her homework and understands technical subjects well enough to make competent decisions.

When developing a technology plan, it is necessary to make a lot of predictions about the future—both the future of the nonprofit organization and the future of technology itself. Because none of us has a crystal ball, we try to make our technology plans as flexible as possible so they will be responsive to change. However, a young organization has not had time to establish a track record and can easily fail to anticipate future developments. Occasionally, when a plan really misses the mark, it is best to start over again. However, revising an older plan offers the opportunity to compare those earlier expectations with present reality. Take a good look at the plan and the kind of guidance it provided for your organization.

Revising and Updating

The Arts Council's team decided that although a number of the sections of their old technology plan seemed downright silly, some very good work had gone into it. They

TIPS & TECHNIQUES

A Technology Plan for a Mature Organization

Just as an organization becomes more complex, a technology plan for a larger, more mature organization is similarly more complex. A good plan for such an organization should include:

- A technology vision statement for your organization

- A statement describing your organization's mission and programs

- A statement describing your organization's current use of technology

- An abbreviated inventory of your organization's current hardware and software

- A description of staff and volunteer computer skills

- A list of long- and short-term technology goals

- A strategy for meeting these goals

- A timeline for meeting these goals

- A budget that details the cost of achieving these goals

- Evaluation criteria for determining whether your goals have been met

would start with their original plan but would make some major revisions intended to create a more practical plan that emphasized management issues. In addition, the plan would encapsulate the experience they had gained over the last few years. Recent events had taught them hard lessons, and one of the main objectives of the technology plan would be to learn from past mistakes. Although it would not go into unnecessary detail, the revised plan would clearly outline the relationship of technology to the rest of the organization. It would describe the role of computer personnel and their priorities.

The Importance of a Stable Budget

Looking over the old plan, the team saw at once that it described a very different organization from the present one. Little attention was devoted to budget because there was almost no money back then. The tiny technology budget was expended almost entirely on computer security, and the materials and services needed to patch together a system was composed mainly of donations. A mature, established organization must fund technology as it does other important projects and programs. Ongoing costs had risen sharply with increasing dependency on technology. Looking back, it was clear that some really vital funding commitments had not been made, and money was released only when emergencies occurred.

As was the case in earlier years, it was not wise to expend most of the budget on new computers and software. One commonly used rule of thumb states that 30 percent of the technology budget should be used for this purpose. About 70 percent should go to technical support and training. That first technology plan made clear that people, not machines, were its focus, but somehow the group had strayed from this essential principle. Funds had not been made available to keep the system fully functional. This meant that the technical support needed for repairs, maintenance, and troubleshooting was withheld when other budget expenditures took precedence. Although training had been a big commitment at the time the original tech plan was written, the program languished as time went by. New computer users received inadequate training and even experienced users forgot skills that they did not use often. In the beginning, it was clearly realized that everyone using the computer system needed training to enhance the value of the system, not interfere with its effectiveness. No one really questioned this goal, but somehow it was never fully implemented.

Funding Technical Support

As the team has already discovered, hiring a young technician at a relatively low salary does not ensure that expertise is readily available. When fully trained and integrated into the organization, such a technician can make a substantial contribution. However, funds must also be made available to bring in professional expertise to deal with repairs that are beyond the technician's ability and to assist with planning. Hiring a carefully chosen consultant from time to time can ensure that the group routinely reassesses its priorities and moves in a productive direction.

Simply maintaining a functional computer system, however, is not enough. Many people must know how to use it. An ever-changing group of staff and

TIPS & TECHNIQUES

Allocating a Realistic Technology Budget

An annual technology budget should include:

- Repair and maintenance

- Technical support

  ○ Technician/Systems administrator

  ○ Consultants

- Replacement of older equipment

- New equipment

- Training

- Disaster preparedness

volunteers must be trained and retrained or the group's investment in technology will be worthless. Maintaining an effective, ongoing training program costs money. The technology budget should include funds to train local trainers, by bringing in consultants or "circuit riders" or by providing other opportunities for trainers to upgrade their skills. The cost of software manuals and tutorials should also be added. However, indirect costs of training must also be considered, like the time that both paid staff and volunteers devote to training.

Taking Back Control

As the team reviewed the old technology plan, it became clear that they did not use computers in the ways they anticipated. Many new programs had gradually found their way into the computer system. Individual staff members had loaded their own programs, some of which were helpful but usually illegal, since the organization had not purchased the software program or a license to use it. Sometimes, the technician spent a day or more troubleshooting a program he had never seen before, one that was loaded on only one computer. It dawned on the tech team that their original goal of having the same software available on all their computers had been forgotten.

Although compatibility is essential, not all computers should be loaded with identical software. For example, there's no need to pay for a multiuser site license if only one staff member uses a particular publishing program. However, if that one user's work is essential to the organization, there must be a way for him or her to get the newsletter or fundraising brochure out on schedule, in the event of a computer crash. This means that a vital software program should be available on at least two computers. In the next chapter, we will be discussing various types of software. Bear in mind, however, that time, whether paid or volunteered, is far more costly than either computer hardware or software. Both hardware and software expenditures must be made with the goal of making the human beings in your organization more productive.

Developing an Effective Management Structure

Possibly the most difficult aspect of the transition from a startup nonprofit to a more mature organization is the loss of informality. In that early period, volunteers usually have a lot of freedom in choosing their tasks. Although a board of directors is in charge, there is a lot of room for individuality. If volunteers are inspired to take on particular responsibilities and are willing to put in the time and energy needed, the response is usually "Go for it!" As the organization grows, maintaining this kind of flexibility becomes more difficult. Some jobs simply have to be done whether or not anyone feels inspired to do them. Conflicts arise when important tasks fall through the cracks, so written job descriptions become necessary.

Growing Need for Structure

The arrival of the first paid staff members adds new complications, and tempers flare when decision-making authority and supervisory responsibilities are unclear. Every aspect of an organization is impacted by these transition "blues," but the technology program is especially vulnerable. Once a commitment to technology is made, a certain amount of rigidity must be imposed, and that may be at odds with a nonprofit's culture. Computers can use only information that is fed to them in predefined ways.

Who will impose this structure? A new technician may lack the authority while his supervisor does not fully understand the need. Computer training is essential for everyone who uses the system, but what does one do when volunteers avoid it, insisting they are too busy to attend training sessions? Is anyone responsible for the lackadaisical volunteer whose typing is so careless that contributors are lost in the database?

Clear written procedures can solve many of these problems. Once there is a clear standard, people can be held responsible for meeting that standard. However, an organization that is heavily dependent on volunteers must make some hard decisions. Is it better to get a job done even if it is not perfect? Which computer procedures allow for some flexibility and which do not? Who makes such decisions? The experience of many nonprofits attests to the need to have technically sophisticated leaders involved at board and upper management levels. That way, technology can be a natural and automatic consideration when different courses of action are under discussion. Leadership support of technology will set an example for the membership and will usually bring naysayers into line.

Summing It Up

The transition from a young startup nonprofit to a more mature or midsized one brings many rewards. It means that the organization can do more and exert a greater impact on the community. Growing pains, however, are an almost inevitable part of the transition. It is hard for group members to accept the fact that the easy informality of the past must give way to a more structured, efficient organization. Technology can become a casualty of this unwillingness to change. As a nonprofit grows, good management practices become essential to success. High-quality technology management must become an important and ongoing commitment.

CHAPTER 4

Computer Applications for Nonprofit Organizations

After reading this chapter, you will be able to:

- Select the most useful software programs for your organization.
- Distinguish between essential software applications and frills.
- Understand how a presence on the World Wide Web can enhance the image of your organization and help it achieve its goals.
- Undertake the planning and creation of an effective website.

A Step-by-Step Guide to Choosing Software

Once a nonprofit makes some initial investments in technology and successfully implements a few basic computer applications, the question always arises: "Where do we go from here?" It may be helpful at this point to imagine a progression of computer applications beginning with some that are easy to implement and very widely used. From there, the progression leads through more specialized and sophisticated programs. Of course, the needs of every organization are different. Some of these applications may be of little use in your particular situation or they may be inappropriate, considering the skill level of your users.

Email: the Most Important Application

Let's begin with email since it is so widely used and because it can transform communication within and beyond your organization. In previous chapters, we followed the progress of two nonprofit organizations. It might be helpful at this point to peek in on yet a third group, the Taylor Teen Center. It happened that the Teen Center Board made a rather surprising decision soon after it came into being. At this point, the group was in its early, planning phase, beginning to look actively for a facility and finding communication among the group extremely difficult. For this reason, the Board decided that apart from meetings, information would be shared exclusively via email. All members and volunteers were responsible for obtaining an email account and checking it regularly.

The board reasoned that if members of the group did not own their own equipment, public computers were available at the library, the senior center, and at several other locations around town. Free email accounts could be obtained at Yahoo!, Hotmail, Google, and many other websites. The board even devoted several training sessions to demonstrating basic computer skills that included how to obtain an email account and how to take basic precautions against the dangers lurking in the online world.

Although it seemed a little drastic at the time, the "decree," as it was widely referred to, turned out to be a good idea. Computer literacy was introduced long before the Teen Center owned its own computers, and some members braved the online world for the first time in their lives. Everyone in the organization received meeting agendas, minutes, and other information at almost no cost to the group. Committees could do at least some of their work without having to get together or play endless phone tag. Volunteers were encouraged to use their email accounts to contact personal friends and relatives since they would then be more likely to check their accounts frequently. The experience was made much less painful than it might have been because the places public computers were usually available offered supportive environments with helpful staff.

Extending the Lives of Older Computers

As most of us are aware, people are always looking for homes for their old computers when they upgrade to newer ones. The Board had another inspiration. If group members had older computers to give away, they could mentor their fellow group members by giving them not only their old computers but their help in getting started. Mentors would set up their equipment at the homes of their "mentees" and help them with basic skills.

Mentees would be checking their email and saving messages on the email provider's own server. In other words, they would not have to worry about a hard drive crash or the other problems that plague older computers because their messages would still be waiting for them when they returned to the site using another computer.

Plain Vanilla Web Browsers

The other problem with older computers, however, is that they are slower and have limited memory capacity. To access their free email accounts, volunteers had to take their first plunge into the World Wide Web and web pages are usually very memory intensive. For this reason, using an older computer can be a frustrating experience. More computer-literate group members discovered that they could download free "plain vanilla" web browsers like "Opera" (www.opera.org) from the World Wide Web that needed less memory and loaded web pages much faster than Internet Explorer, a standard web browser of the Windows operating system. Although there are several other programs available, the Mozilla project (www.mozilla.org) is especially noteworthy, providing some of the best software for the Web. Mozilla's Firefox web browser and Thunderbird email client are fully functional and are somewhat less prone to virus attacks than corresponding Microsoft products. Bear in mind, however, that older computers may not be reliable. They provide a good opportunity to practice computer skills, but important information should not be entrusted to them.

Maintaining an Online Calendar

Once it becomes possible for all group members to access the Internet, it's a good idea to create an online calendar and place a computer-literate group leader in charge of maintaining it. Use the calendar to inform members about meeting dates, grant deadlines, fundraising events, committee meetings, public hearings, and all the other events of interest to your organization. You may also want to use the calendar for managing projects. For example, include the date by which articles for the newsletter must be received and the day the newsletter will be distributed. List the volunteers who will be working the phones each night of the phon-a-thon. If the group is involved in a complicated project, you can break it down into manageable pieces and note deadlines for the completion of each piece on your calendar.

Many large Web portals provide online calendars. Their chief advantage over paper calendars is that everyone in the group can view them, and if you choose, everyone can add events. Of course, you may prefer to limit the people authorized to enter information. This is sometimes a good idea because the person entering information on the calendar is also responsible for correcting the entry if the date is changed or removing it entirely in the event of a cancellation.

Creating a Yahoo! Calendar

Although there are many other choices, let's use the Yahoo! calendar as an example since practically everyone on the Web "Yahoos!" You will discover the Calendar option down near the bottom of Yahoo!'s homepage. When you click on it, you are asked for your Yahoo! ID. The first step then is to create an account for the whole group. Your goal is to choose an easily remembered ID and password. No personal information will be shared, and it's unlikely that anyone would want to hack your account, so you do not need to worry about security. Make both the ID and password as easy to remember as possible, and remind members to check the calendar frequently. There's no point in putting a lot of work into a calendar if no one checks it.

Once you have created your ID and accessed your calendar, you will see that it looks very much like a printed date book. The program allows you to view a day, a week, a month, or a year. Yahoo! automatically includes holidays, daylight savings, and other important dates. Some groups also add member birthdays. One of the nicest features of an online calendar is the ease with which you can schedule recurring activities. If your group meets the first Tuesday of the month, one calendar entry can set up your meetings for the entire year. This can be a dangerous feature in the hands of novices, however. Make sure that anyone entering recurring activities inserts an end date and checks to be sure the result is what he or she intended. It is all too easy to accidentally schedule meetings on Christmas and New Year's or change the meeting date without correcting the calendar.

In addition to alerting group members to upcoming events, an online calendar continues the process of developing computer skills and making all members of the organization comfortable in the online environment. Computer applications like email and online calendars also make it possible to share exactly the same information with every member of the organization. No one is left out; no one is forgotten.

Making the Internet Part of the Organizational Culture

This is a much more democratic way of communicating information, and places responsibility for staying informed squarely on the shoulders of group members. Small nonprofits often become unintentionally cliquish. They complain bitterly that they do not have enough members, but new arrivals to the group may feel unwanted. Procedures are in place to keep an inner core of members "in the know." Telephone trees may include only long-term members, and somehow no one has enough time to keep them up to date. After a new recruit fails to get word of a meeting cancellation and arrives for an event only to find that it has been postponed, you can be quite sure that he or she will not be returning. Of course, poorly maintained calendars can be just as frustrating. Once the commitment has been made to share information in this way, there cannot be different communication channels for the in-crowd.

Discovering Nonprofit Resources on the World Wide Web

Let's return, however, to the Teen Center group, who were learning to use the World Wide Web. As they became more skilled, volunteers learned the basics of online searching. Soon, they discovered useful information about grants (see Exhibit 4.1) and legal matters (such as how to obtain 501c3 status).

In a short time, the Teen Center obtained official tax-exempt status, a small space to use as an office, and several Windows-equipped PCs. Now that the organization owned its own computers, they needed to take on some important responsibilities. No individual or organization should own a computer if they are unwilling to take care of it properly. This means performing routine maintenance, keeping up with program updates, and protecting it against intrusion from malicious

---

EXHIBIT 4.1

Grant Seekers' Online Resources

A number of business organizations provide assistance to nonprofits seeking grants. They can be helpful if your group lacks sufficient information about available grants or is weak on grant-writing expertise. One example of such a service is:

GrantStation PRO

www.grantstation.com

Admin Fee: $599.00

GrantStation PRO provides extensive information on current sources of grant money, which includes:

- "How-to" information on securing funding

- Find-a-Funder for searching thousands of funding sources

- GrantStation Insider weekly bulletin

- Government Deadlines

- Proposal-writing tools

- News and trends

---

hackers who lurk on the Internet. No computer should ever go online unless its owners have installed a reliable antivirus software program and made sure it has been updated on a regular basis.

Software Types

This brings to mind a lot of questions about computer software. Perhaps this is a good time to discuss some general issues. Most software comes under the general heading "commercial," but "shareware" and "freeware" programs are sometimes a better choice. In addition, there are "custom" software programs that are written es–pecially to meet the needs of one customer.

Commercial Software

These programs are produced and sold by companies that strictly limit the way you may use their software and with whom you may share it. Norton and McAfee are two large companies that produce commercial antivirus programs. Both are highly regarded and both have large staffs that are constantly identifying new viruses and updating their programs.

If you use their products, you must agree to abide by the terms of a software license. When you install the program on a computer, there will usually come a point beyond which you cannot continue unless you agree to the terms of the license. Unless you have specifically purchased a multiuser version of the program, you usually have the right to use the program on only one computer. Therefore, you will need to purchase a separate copy of the software for every computer on which you want to use the program. This can be both expensive and annoying. Frustrations are endless when some of your computers can run certain programs while others cannot. You may, therefore, wish to purchase a multiuser site license that allows you to use the same program on all your computers, especially if you are maintaining a local area network.

Freeware and Shareware

In addition to commercial software, there are also "freeware" and "shareware" programs. Both types of software can be downloaded from the Internet without paying a fee. However, if you wish to continue to use shareware, you will need to pay for it. Freeware is exactly what it says it is; although you do not have to pay for freeware, you must often view numerous advertisements. In general, a lot of excellent freeware and shareware has been produced for the online environment such as Web browsers and email programs. However, you will usually need to purchase commercial word processing, spreadsheet, database, and other essential programs. Shareware and freeware vary widely in quality. Although some programs like the ones described above are excellent, you usually do not know whether a program was written by a teenager working on his bedroom computer or by professional programmers. Before entrusting your computer to a shareware or freeware program, find some reviews online. Make sure that a program is in widespread use and has been proven to be both safe and useful.

Custom Software

As organizations grow larger, they may decide they need custom programs created just for their needs. The idea of designing a program that does exactly what you want in exactly the way you want it done is very attractive. In practice, however, the result may be a far cry from what you intended. The cost of these programs is usually much higher than commercial ones since purchasers are paying for the time a computer programmer spends writing the program. By the time it has been "debugged," the number of hours tied up in one rather simple program can be astonishing, so most nonprofit administrators advise staying away from custom programming if at all possible. In addition to cost, there are added problems with reliability. Commercial software is tested and retested. Once a new program is released, customers report problems, and so errors are corrected in later versions. When you commission custom software, your organization becomes the guinea pig. You will be the ones to discover the errors, and those errors may have far-reaching implications.

Occasionally, you may learn that a nonprofit similar to yours has developed a software program and is willing to license it to your organization at what sounds like a reasonable fee. Should you accept their offer? It depends, of course, on whether the program can do something very useful that no commercial program can do. However, the best answer may be "Thanks but no thanks." When you are considering a widely used commercial program such as Microsoft Office, you can check dozens of software reviews that point out both its good and bad features. There is no way to get this kind of unbiased information about a custom-produced program since only one or two organizations are using it.

Remember that the person who wrote the program was working for the other nonprofit, not for you. Unless you have a warrantee or make other financial arrangements with the programmer, you have no right to training or technical support when the program crashes. Since programmers have highly individualistic styles, another programmer may not be able to interpret the code well enough to fix glitches. Remember, too, that because it is a custom program, it is based on the specific routines and procedures that another organization has developed. Commercial programs build in flexibility that makes it possible to adapt them to a variety of situations. This flexibility is absent in custom software.

Custom Modifications and Templates

On the other hand, many of the more sophisticated commercial programs allow users to modify them to meet their needs. This kind of custom programming is much less expensive and more reliable, since it is built on a thoroughly tested product. Sharing a custom-designed template created by another organization may also save you a lot of work. Perhaps a sister nonprofit designed a database using Microsoft Access. It took a considerable effort to design all those tables, forms, and reports. These designs are called templates. If you, too, use Microsoft Access, you may save time by copying the database structure and entering your own data.

Selecting Database Software

As long as the subject of database programs has come up, this might be a good time to talk a little about just what it is a database program does. As has been mentioned in earlier chapters, it's helpful to store information about members and contributors. A variety of programs can do this (see Exhibit 4.2), but since it allows you to create separate records for each individual, a database program is often the best choice. Since Microsoft Works comes installed in Windows computers and includes a simple word processor, spreadsheet, and database, it is a frequent choice when an organization is just getting started. The problem is that although Works is very functional and easy to use, it offers few of the more sophisticated functions. In the beginning, it's a good choice, but you will probably want to upgrade to a more powerful database soon.

Selecting an Office Suite

A "suite" is a group of programs sold by the same company that are intended to work together and be fully compatible with one another. They are often combinations of word processing, spreadsheet, and database programs with some other bells and whistles thrown in. There are both shareware and freeware suites as well as commercial ones. Many organizations make it a policy that all their computers will be equipped with the Microsoft Office Suite. One of the big advantages of MS-Office is that so many people use it. Files can be easily shared among computers and help is readily available from colleagues. In addition, all the program applications

EXHIBIT 4.2

Setting Up Your Database

Databases are almost essential to nonprofit organizations because of the vast amount of information they can place at your fingertips. Use your database to collect information on:

- Members

- Volunteers

- Staff

- Workshop participants

- Donors

- General contacts such as vendors and service suppliers

Information to be collected includes:

- Name

- Organization

- Addresses

- Day/evening/cell phones

- Fax

- Email

- Website

- Preferred contact method

In addition, you might want to include:

- The role the contacts play in your organization

- Which mailing lists they're on

- Whether they have requested information about your organization

- Whether they receive the newsletter

Use the database to track information about:

- Events

- Schedules and space availability

- Assigned tasks

- Skills

- Dates contacted, follow-ups

- Donor categories (individual, corporate, foundation, etc.)

- Donation histories

- Donation restrictions

- Donor interests and relationships

included in Microsoft Office use similar commands and keystrokes. The interface (or screen design) for each of the applications looks very similar to the others. It's a lot easier to learn to use the database or spreadsheet program when you are already familiar with the word processor.

Although it is rather expensive, Microsoft donates many copies of MS-Office to nonprofits through websites like TechSoup (more about the wonderful resources available at TechSoup later). If your organization is not eligible for a donation, you will need to decide whether it's worth the cost. Different versions are available at different prices but, unfortunately, the Microsoft Access database program comes included only in the more expensive, professional versions.

Comparing Software Suites

Because this can be an expensive purchase, you may want to consider purchasing a competing office suite. There are two main contenders: WordPerfect Office and StarOffice. The consensus seems to be that, taken on their own merits, these are well-designed program suites. StarOffice, in particular, is much less expensive than Microsoft, and if the cost is still beyond your budget, you might want to consider the free open source suite, OpenOffice. However, none of these competitors are fully compatible with the Microsoft product and so files sent from other computers or downloaded from the Web may not be usable. If file compatibility is important to you and the Microsoft price tag seems too high, you might consider purchasing an older version of Microsoft Office. Copies of older versions are often available at heavily discounted prices.

Selecting Financial Accounting Software

All of these office suites include a spreadsheet program, and so in the natural course of events, many organizations decide to use the spreadsheet to do their bookkeeping. In the Microsoft suite, the spreadsheet program is called Excel; in WordPerfect, it's QuatroPro. If someone in your organization is interested, this may be a good way to maintain your financial records. Both programs require somewhat more skill and perseverance than a Web browser or word processor. However, Microsoft Money is a personal accounting program that often comes with new Windows computers. Since it is so often free, it's another choice for organizations that are just beginning to think about maintaining computerized accounting records. Quicken by Intuit is another, somewhat more sophisticated personal finance program.

QuickBooks

Once an organization gains some confidence with computers, the financial program chosen by many is QuickBooks. Just as Microsoft Word is the word processing program of choice among most organizations, QuickBooks is the financial package used by small and midsized nonprofits, primarily because it is relatively inexpensive when compared to other business accounting programs. Some administrators suggest that you are ready for QuickBooks when you begin hiring paid staff. Few programs are as widely criticized as QuickBooks, probably because few programs are as widely used. It performs a wide array of accounting functions, and is widely recommended by accountants who are able to import QuickBooks files into their own far more complex and expensive systems. Accountants complain, however, that QuickBooks and other accounting programs almost seem to have minds of their own. Nonprofit bookkeepers may fail to notice that the program has entered the same credit twice or inadvertently deleted a large debit. In reality, of course, the program has only done what it is programmed to do, but it can be dangerous in the hands of an inexperienced bookkeeper.

Although QuickBooks has a module created specifically for nonprofits at additional cost, the basic QuickBooks package is intended for businesses. This means that if you use just the basic package (as do most smaller nonprofits), some of its features may not be appropriate. Nevertheless, many administrators call it the "only game in town" in its price range. Also compared to other accounting programs, it is fairly simple to use, providing quick access to vendors, payroll, banking, and reports.

Maintaining Your Own Website

Early in their development, most nonprofits find it useful to maintain a presence on the World Wide Web. A website is one of the best marketing tools, making it possible for millions of computer users to learn about your mission and services. A website is often at the core of many fundraising campaigns and membership drives. Because websites are so popular, group members will soon suggest that your organization maintain a site. Almost inevitably, members will volunteer the services of their sons, daughters, husbands, and nephews to create the site. Although some of these premature offers will come to nothing, there are a number of young people who would be happy to create a website for your organization. Whether or not to accept their services is often a difficult decision.

The Volunteer-Designed Website

The Teen Center planning group is currently conducting a fundraising campaign and so is focusing on adult contributors. Later, the website might aim at attracting young people to the newly opened center and so have a very different look and feel. Websites differ radically from one another depending on their purpose and intended audience.

The Teen Center Board decides to appoint Myra, an enthusiastic teen member of the planning committee, as its Webmaster. Myra will work closely with a small subcommittee and will prepare them to take over the site when she leaves for college. That means she will need to document information such as where she stores files and how she uploads pages to the hosting service. The subcommittee will choose

TIPS & TECHNIQUES

Selecting a Webmaster

The Taylor Teen Center described above has quite a number of young people actively involved in its planning committee. At least some of them can probably design a serviceable website. Here are some questions to consider before choosing your website designer:

- Has the volunteer taken a course in web design or is he or she self-taught?

- Does the volunteer appear knowledgeable about technical Web issues? Technical competence, though certainly essential, is not the main issue.

- Does the volunteer use good grammar and spell correctly? Since your website projects an image of your organization, these skills really do matter.

- Does the volunteer have any background in art or design? Although a website need not be a work of art, visitors will be repelled by cluttered, confusing pages.

- Has the volunteer designed other websites? Does he or she have a personal website that you can view?

- Do you have some assurance that the volunteer will be able to update the site on a regular basis? This tends to be one of the major problems that afflict nonprofit websites. They begin with a burst of enthusiasm but information soon gets out of date. Upcoming events are not advertised in a timely manner, and last year's news is never taken down.

- Is the volunteer a team player? Although the actual Web work may be done by one person, many others should be involved in maintaining the site, gathering news, writing articles, proofreading pages, and doing dozens of tasks that make a website effective. Will your volunteer be comfortable adjusting his or her wishes to those of the group?

- Is the volunteer mature enough to understand that content comes first and glitzy, "wow" features are not important? This is not to say that there is not a place for glitz, but it's not a priority.

one of the easier-to-use web authoring programs and commit themselves to taking a course or workshop in web design within the next six months.

The Professionally Designed Website

The Teen Center might have chosen to hire a consulting firm or local business to create their website. Although site development can be expensive when done by a professional, it might be worth the cost if the website is going to be a focus for the group's fundraising effort. If you choose this option, you will probably want to take care of routine updates yourselves, since contracting this function out is expensive, slow, and inefficient. It's important to be able to make changes quickly to share information and publicize events. An independent contractor is working on many other projects and may be unable to respond quickly. In addition, a good site needs almost constant maintenance.

If you hire professionals to create the initial design, it's a good idea to bring them to your offices and have them meet with a small number of group members like Myra's subcommittee. Ask them to designate certain pages for information that must be frequently changed like the events calendar and design them in such a way that amateurs can update them without affecting the basic page design. It's not difficult to teach the group members how to update these pages themselves. Pages that deal with the organization's goals, mission, and history need not be changed often, so the design can be more eye-catching, making use of more sophisticated programming techniques.

Checking External Links

If your site includes links to other organizations, remember that their Web addresses (URLs) may change. Few experiences are more frustrating than clicking on a link that does not work. Like updating current events, you do not want to pay a consultant just to check links, and it is not even necessary to check each of them manually. You should have no problem finding freeware or shareware link checkers at software download sites like *PC World* and Software.com on the Web. Although they are easy to use, someone must remember to run them frequently. Once you commit to maintaining a website, it must be viewed as a real part of your organization.

TIPS & TECHNIQUES

Creating an Effective Website

- Consider how you can make your Web visitor's experience as pleasant and easy as possible.

- Develop a logical organization that takes visitors quickly where they want to go.

- Do not make visitors click on half-a-dozen unwanted web pages just to get to the one that interests them.

- Avoid clutter. It should not be difficult to discover what is available and get to it.

- Create groups of clearly labeled choices. Do not sprinkle them in unexpected places.

- Choose terms that have obvious meanings to most people. Avoid "in-group" jargon.

- Think of your homepage as your front door.

- Test the site on volunteer visitors.

Publicizing Your Website

For your site to be successful, you will need to tell people about it. That means listing the URL on all your publications, including brochures, bookmarks, business cards, fliers, newsletters, and pamphlets. It's also a good idea for staff and volunteers to include the URL in their email signatures and on any promotional giveaways like pencils and magnets. Even bumper stickers can be printed with the address in large letters. Newspaper articles about the organization should emphasize that the website means your organization is open 24 hours a day, seven days a week. Emphasize that the site is a real extension of your services.

If you have done much surfing, you have discovered that there are a lot of unattractive, disorganized, and frustrating websites out there, some of which, unfortunately, are maintained by nonprofit organizations like yours. To be successful, your site must be easy to navigate, informative, and appealing. It must be designed to attract visitors and to communicate a professional image of your group. This requires careful attention to design principles. It also means that your board, staff, and volunteers will need to use the site on a regular basis. Otherwise, you will fail to notice the inaccurate information, the embarrassing misspelling, or the link that goes to the wrong page.

Getting the Most from Your Website

Be sure that the name, address, telephone number, and email address of your organization are displayed prominently on every web page. Do not assume that everyone arrives at your home page. Web visitors may reach your site by searching for a keyword in a search engine. When they arrive, they may be plunged deep into one of your site's inner pages. By the way, you too can use a search engine to help web visitors find what they are looking for. Adding a popular search engine to your site, however, may mean accepting unwanted advertisements. Site maps also make it easier for visitors to navigate to the section that most interests them.

Consider Your Users

When webmasters lack professional experience, they may forget that they are viewing the site on a particular computer using just one of many web browsers. Your online visitors are using different equipment loaded with different software. If they have older computers, they may become frustrated if your pages load slowly. Avoid large photo files that can become annoying to people who just want to read about your organization. Sound and video files are "cool," but they take up a lot of memory and may not interest some visitors. Make sure that they are optional and do not begin loading automatically.

Not everyone who comes to your site can read the text without assistance. Visitors with visual impairments should be able to use screen-reading software effectively. Color blindness is a common disability and should not make it difficult for visitors to find their

LEARN MORE ABOUT

Accessible Websites

Investigate the Telematics for Elderly and Disabled People (TIDE) Project at www.stakes.fi/tidecong.

Visit the Trace Center, which provides information on how to design accessible equipment and websites, at http://trace.wisc.edu.

Discover Usability.gov for information on how to make websites more usable, accessible, and useful at www.usability.gov.

Check out the Wave, a free Web-based tool that lets users check their sites for accessibility, at www.wave.webaim.org/index.jsp.

Investigate the Adaptive Technology Resource Center at www.utoronto.ca/atrc.

way or read the text. On many websites, you will see a small graphic of a London Bobby with the "Bobby Approved" certification (http://bobby.watchfire.com). Bobby tests web pages using officially established accessibility guidelines. You can submit your own site files for evaluation.

Choosing Reliable Equipment for Website Management

Now that the Teen Center group has appointed a webmaster and a committee to work with her, their next job is to select the hardware and software needed to design the website. Myra and the subcommittee will be putting in a lot of hours creating and maintaining the site, so they will need at least one computer devoted to their needs and others, loaded with the same programs, that will be available in case of emergency. Again, maintaining the site must be viewed as a professional commitment. The website should not be consigned to an archaic, donated computer that no one else wants.

Website Authoring Software

Web authoring software ranges from free to programs priced at several hundred dollars. Dreamweaver is preferred by many Web designers, but new programs are entering the market constantly. Sophisticated programs like Dreamweaver, however, may be beyond the skills of the group maintaining your site, or there may be no local Dreamweaver workshops or classes available. Do not worry about choosing the best or most sophisticated program. Focus on your group's own needs and abilities, and do not forget to ask around about programs in use by other nonprofits in your area. Your apprentice webmasters are going to need help, so consider purchasing a popular program.

As we have mentioned, pages look different on different computers. In addition to an authoring program, you will also need some web browsers. It is very helpful to see how your site looks on both older and newer versions of the popular browsers. Even though web browsers are either free or provided with the Windows operating system, they have heavy RAM memory requirements and so, as computers age, owners tend to stop updating their browsers.

Other Software You May Need

In addition to authoring software and web browsers, you will also need File Transfer Protocol (FTP) software if you will be sending your website files to a host. Hosting services are commercial businesses that load your site onto their large computer servers, protect it from hackers, and make sure that it's available 24 hours a day.

Photoshop is another software program you may wish to invest in if you plan to use a number of photographs on your site. It is expensive, however, and you may wish to look for a less expensive alternative. Photoshop Elements is a scaled-down version of the program and is adequate for most routine needs. A number of other functional photo programs are priced as low as $25.00.

Other Hardware Purchases

Although a website does not require a large financial outlay for hardware, there are several inexpensive equipment items that will prove very useful. In addition to a desktop computer of recent vintage, a desktop scanner is a good investment. Any image you clip, draw, or paint can be transformed into a graphics file and appear on your website. Since large files are inappropriate for the Web, expensive, high-resolution scanners are unnecessary. This means that a scanner priced at under a hundred dollars or a scanner included in an all-in-one printer will meet your needs admirably.

Another useful gadget is a digital camera and again, since web photos must be quick to load, the capabilities of the higher end, multi-mega-pixel cameras are wasted. If you will be using the camera to take photos to accompany press releases or for brochures and other marketing pieces, however, you may want to invest in a somewhat more sophisticated camera. Digital cameras provide a wonderful sense of immediacy. Your organization sponsors an event, someone snaps a few pictures, and within minutes, the experience can be shared on your website. Another nice feature to consider in a digital camera is the ability to create a brief video clip. Many digital cameras arrive packaged with image-editing software that makes it possible to correct simple problems such as photos that are too dark or need to be resized. Although these programs will perform basic tasks, they are much less sophisticated than high-end software such as Photoshop.

Finding a Host

While your site is still in the planning stage, you will need to find a hosting service. A host is actually a computer server on which your web pages are stored. It must be a computer that is linked directly to the Internet 24 hours a day, 7 days a week. It is the host computer that web surfers actually interact with and not your organization's own computers.

There are many different ways to find a host and many different pricing arrangements, as well. Internet Service Providers (ISPs) are companies that offer computer storage space and web server facilities for other organizations. They may charge a fee to host your site or make their profit by adding extensive advertising to their customers' pages. Nonprofits usually prefer to pay the fee rather than allow unrelated and possibly inappropriate advertisements to take up space on their pages. In addition, service providers usually supply a limited amount of technical support either by phone or by email.

Planning for the Future

Sometimes it is possible to obtain free website hosting from an ISP that the organization already uses for email and other Internet services. Be careful, however, that you read the fine print, because your free site may be limited in terms of storage space and bandwidth available. As long as your site is small and not terribly popular, these limitations may be acceptable, but as you grow and develop a more extensive site, your costs will rise sharply.

Most organizations should not consider becoming their own host. To do so, you would need to have a server available for this purpose round the clock. Any powerful server that is constantly available on the Web poses a huge temptation to hackers who may use your site for their own illegal purposes. Since there are many predators lurking in cyberspace, considerably more technical expertise is needed and the job of webmaster becomes much more complicated. Hardware and software capable of repelling invaders are also more complex and costly.

Integrated Software Packages for Nonprofits

By this point, your organization has grown larger and your computer applications have increased in number and complexity. Is it time to invest in a large, integrated software system designed specifically for the needs of nonprofit organizations? Such systems are similar to office suites in that they usually consist of several highly sophisticated modules.

Each module performs a different function, but all modules work together, thus saving a lot of time and training. For example, arts organizations that serve as venues for the performing arts, as well as museums, zoos, and aquariums, may purchase software that supports box office operations, fundraising, financial reporting, marketing, and customer relations management. Client information and case management software systems serve the needs of family service, counseling, mental health, and residential service organizations. Professional associations may choose software for managing membership records, publications, conferences, and continuing education.

Since there are many nonprofits, this is a relatively lucrative area for software producers. In addition to those described above, there are a variety of packages intended for the use of schools and colleges. These include modules to support the admissions, registrar's, business, and alumni affairs offices. Integrated library software systems include cataloging, acquisitions, and circulation modules. Even though fundraising is part of most packages for nonprofits, some are more sophisticated and may include modules for direct mail, gift programs, estate planning, and annual campaigns.

Calculating the Costs and Benefits of an Integrated System

When considering any of these systems, one question comes immediately to mind. Is it worth the money? In general, these integrated software systems are extremely expensive, costing many thousands of dollars. However, costs vary depending on the specific nonprofit area. For example, integrated software systems designed for the healthcare sector are generally much more expensive than systems designed for less generously funded types of organizations. Although this is sometimes justified by greater functionality, there is also a tendency to price software based on whatever the market will bear.

Software vendors would have you believe that their software will totally transform your organization. The cost will, in theory, be repaid in increased productivity. It is sometimes very difficult to determine whether such claims are well-founded. As is the case with home appliances, advertisements for software boast many features that will never be used. Even the most powerful computer system is limited in the kinds of tasks it does well. When examined closely, it may turn out that the most useful part of the system is merely a database program with some predesigned templates.

Can You Afford the Cost?

When the development of a technology plan was discussed earlier in this book, it was recommended that an organization establish a set percentage of its budget to devote to technology. That percentage should be based upon technology's value or the extent to which it contributes to the achievement of your goals. As the years pass, an organization begins to see the results of its efforts and develops a clearer picture of the amount of money needed to produce the changes and improvements it envisions. Large integrated systems often exceed an organization's established technology budget and require the transfer of funds from some other activity. When that is not possible, such a purchase may increase the nonprofit's overall administrative costs. The decision, then, must not be made lightly. In fact, it should only be made by experienced group members who understand not only the opportunities technology can bring, but its limitations as well. It is essential to get beyond the superlatives promised by salespeople and focus on what precisely the system will do for you.

What Will the New System Add?

Take, for example, a sophisticated fundraising system. Is your nonprofit currently using computers in its fundraising efforts? Maybe you have developed a contributors' database similar to the one described above. Many organizations also use one of the commercial project management software programs to plan the various steps involved in a major project or campaign. Another common application is the mail merge feature that allows your word processing program to send out personalized solicitation letters. The software programs needed for all these applications require an outlay of only a few hundred dollars. Let us say that the integrated fundraising system you are considering costs $10,000. Obviously, it can do more for you, but how much more?

Performing a Cost Benefit Analysis

To learn the answer, it is necessary to do a cost-benefit analysis similar to the one described in Chapter 2. Begin by listing all the costs involved in implementing the system. You will soon discover that there are many costs that are not described in the vendor's literature. You may need newer computers, a faster Internet connection, a more recent operating system, or a different network configuration. Do not forget staff and volunteer training, which you will probably discover is provided by the vendor at a very high price. Since this is a much more sophisticated system than your staff and volunteers are accustomed to, there's going to be a longer implementation period and there will inevitably be a "burn in" period during which everything that can go wrong will go wrong.

Now what about the benefits? Begin with a list of the functions and features provided by the system under consideration. Make sure that you have concrete information, not vague product descriptions.

- Which of these functions are you now performing using more generic software programs?

- How will these functions be performed differently when the new software system is implemented?

- Are these added features unique to the proposed system or might you be able to do some of them with the software programs you are now using?

Most computer users never fully use the features available in their software. Nonprofit administrators often find that when they send staff to software training workshops, participants are amazed at all the features they did not know about.

Focusing on Your Nonprofit's Needs

If you are maintaining a database of contributors using Microsoft Access, consider how the proposed system handles contributors. Does it have ways of organizing information that will really make a difference in your organization's ability to solicit donations? Could your Access templates be changed to do the same? On the other hand, are there some things about your Access database that you like better? You may find that the proposed system **is not** flexible enough to accommodate change. Remember that Access is the work of hundreds of professional programmers. The system you are considering was created by a much smaller group of professionals. It was also tested on a smaller group. You may, therefore, find it very rigid about what it can and cannot do.

If the sales staff waffles when you mention the small accommodation that will meet your needs, it probably has not been included in the system. In fact, there's a good possibility that the system was originally developed as custom software for one specific customer. The vendor now wants to increase profits by marketing the system to a wider audience. If this is the case, you may find that its functions are closely tied to the procedures of one unique organization.

EXHIBIT 4.3

Do You Really Need That Software Program?

Since specialized software for nonprofits can be very expensive, consider carefully whether it will significantly contribute to your success. First, ask yourself the following questions about your organization:

- What procedures most contribute to or hinder your success?

- How do other organizations similar to yours perform these procedures?

- What changes can you make to improve these procedures? Remember that a software program can simplify your procedures or make them more cumbersome.

Next, list your requirements:

- Focus on the needs that are somewhat unique to your organization or features may be left out of standard packages.

- Keep your list of requirements to a minimum so you can focus quickly on important program differences.

Get Information:

- Learn what is currently available.

- Ask about features planned for the next release but do not count on them.

- Talk to colleagues about what is working for them.

- Take the promises of software salespersons with a grain of salt.

- Focus on your real needs. Ignore features that would be nice to have.

- Divide demonstrations into separate sessions for individual modules. Invite key users of each module to use and critique the program.

- Make sure that your leaders are behind the choice and will support it.

- Try to find an online users group and ask about their experiences.

- Give careful consideration to the amount of time and training that will be needed for users to become proficient with the software program. The more time needed, the higher the cost to your organization.

Do Not Pay Twice

In the example above, we compared Microsoft Access to the proposed system. Access is a part of the Microsoft Office software suite. Other office suite modules include word processors, spreadsheet programs, and presentation software. If your organization uses such an office suite, there is no point in duplicating these same functions in an expensive, integrated software package. If the advertised features sound suspiciously familiar, you may be paying for programming that you do not need.

Unneeded Features

Basic utilities are not the only functions you probably do not need. Once you have given some careful attention to the features touted in the proposed system, you will probably discover a number of them that seem to be of little use. Just because a program is capable of doing something does not mean that anyone would ever want to do it. Computers perform certain jobs very well. They can handle large quantities of information, make rapid mathematical calculations, and accomplish a variety of tasks. When used appropriately, they can better organize your workload and save large amounts of time.

There are many things, however, that you can do just as well with a memo pad or a pocket calculator. Even better, maybe they do not need to be done at all. There's no point in inventing procedures and entering information that wastes your volunteers' time and fills up your hard drive. It is not uncommon to discover that an organization collects quantities of information just to fill in the blank spaces on forms designed for some other type of organization. If you take a good look at the database forms in use in libraries, clinics, box offices, and professional organizations, you will also discover questions that violate personal privacy while serving no useful purpose.

Consulting with Colleagues

Never forget that you are not alone. Your organization is not unlike thousands of others located throughout the nonprofit world. Whatever the specific goals of your nonprofit, there are email discussion lists that can keep you in touch with your colleagues. Whether their objective is to seek advice, learn from the mistakes of others, or just compare notes, everyone with a decision-making role in your group should sign up for at least one of these email discussion lists. Use them to ask colleagues about their experiences with the software system you are considering. There are even some online user groups devoted to a single software product. Although you will be requesting references from the vendor, the spontaneous, unsolicited comments of your colleagues can sometimes tell you a great deal about a product that you might never learn otherwise.

If the cost of the system is significant (which it usually is), you may wish to visit an organization that is using the software system. Even if this means a hefty outlay for travel expenses, it may be well worth the cost to see the system in actual operation and to hear the comments of the staff and volunteers who work with it on a daily basis.

Maintaining Computers for the Public

In addition to computers for staff and volunteer use, the Teen Center will be making several computers available to teens for personal Internet use. Increasingly, nonprofit organizations are providing computer access to their clients and customers. For example, community centers, children's programs, libraries, and senior centers often have computer labs and provide assistance to inexperienced computer users. The people who commonly use public computers may lack the financial resources to purchase their own or they may find that physical limitations make it difficult for them to use or maintain a computer without help (see Exhibit 4.4). Some of these users have disabilities that can be overcome with small modifications, usually referred to as assistive technology. Because these small adjustments can open the world of computers to people who would otherwise be left out, they are well worth the cost.

Securing Public Computers

The staff members and volunteers who use your organization's computers have similar needs, usually using the same programs and viewing the same websites. When computers are made available to the general public, it is impossible to anticipate all the uses to which they will be put. This means that securing the computers from

EXHIBIT 4.4

Adapting Computers for People with Disabilities

Approximately 10 million adults have difficulty seeing computer text. Others have trouble using the mouse or keyboard. Nonprofits can serve a broader community and accommodate staff and volunteers by making just a few simple and inexpensive adjustments to their computers:

- Install a screen magnification tool or provide instructions for enabling this feature in Windows. More sophisticated commercial programs like ZoomText are also available.

- Install a screen reading program like Window Eyes or Dolphin to convert text into voice.

- Install a voice recognition program such as Dragon NaturallySpeaking, ViaVoice, MacSpeak, or I-Listen.

- Turn on the "sticky keys" function on keyboards to eliminate the need to hold down multiple keys simultaneously.

- Consider purchasing a mouse that requires only one finger to operate or features large buttons that can be pressed by a clenched fist. Other mouse options include easy-clicking mice, foot-powered mice, even head mice that use a reflective sticker on the forehead.

- Consider purchasing a keyboard with larger keys to assist people with limited dexterity.

cyberspace predators and even flesh–and–blood predators, who "hang out" in your computer lab becomes much more important and much more difficult.

Keeping Computers Unchanged

Users should not be able to permanently save any programs or data to hard drives. Every time computers are restarted, all information from the last session should be erased. A number of hardware and software options are available for this purpose.

TIPS & TECHNIQUES

Security for Public Computers

Computers available to the public require extra security precautions, both to protect your organization and to protect users from identity theft. Here are some important precautions:

- Post signs near computers describing the dangers of identity theft.

- Discourage users from submitting confidential information such as credit card numbers from public computers.

- Set web browsers to clear "history" automatically.

- Set web browsers to reject "cookies."

- Discourage users from checking their bank accounts online. "Key logging" programs can record every key pressed, and the information can be retrieved later by criminals.

- Users should not be able to permanently save any programs or data on hard drives. Every time computers are restarted, all information from the last session should be erased.

They include:

Deep Freeze. Allows the administrator to maintain several workstations that look and behave exactly alike. Deep Freeze resets the entire desktop each time the computer is rebooted. (Note: "Assimilator" is the Mac equivalent of Deep Freeze). Price: About $300 for 25 licenses.

Drive Shield. Software-based hard drive protection from Centurion Technologies. Allows anyone to reset a system back to its original configuration with a simple reboot. Write-protects the hard drive (similar to the way you write protect your floppy disk by setting the write-protect tab). Price: About $59.00 per computer.

Centurion Guard. Offers similar benefits as DriveShield but is hardware-based. Reboot causes all changes to disappear and the computer returns to its default configuration. Protection is enabled and disabled with a lock and key.

PC Guardian. A hardware solution that protects your hard drive from viruses, errors, and program malfunctions. Price: About $40.00 per computer.

FSLogic Protect. A software solution that separates the core of the operating system from the changes and preferences of the user. Price: About $80.00 per computer.

Fortres Clean Slate. Allows administrator to disable some features like the control panel, controls which applications users can run, and where files will be saved. Price: About $325 for a 15 user license. Additional software called Central Station (costs $300) is needed if you want to administer workstations centrally.

Educating Users about Security

Neither hardware nor software solutions will secure your public computers, however, without the cooperation of your users. It is essential to provide written guidelines about what may and may not be done with the computers. Especially when users are children and teens, it is important to take precautions against online stalkers who may be lurking in chat rooms or using instant messaging to entrap their prey. It's always difficult to balance safety with the interests of young computer users. Since banning messaging, email, and chat rooms is a good way to assure that the computers will gather dust, it's important to find a compromise that works for everyone.

Guarding against Theft

Theft is an important concern with public computers. Depending on your situation, you may want to secure larger pieces of equipment like computers and monitors with cables attached to the work surface. There are several configurations made for this purpose. Laptop computers are especially vulnerable to theft and should not be used in a public-lab-type environment without securing them. The Teen Center should also be careful of projection equipment connected to laptop computers. The program presenter or the teen volunteer who is showing the feature film on DVD may walk off and temporarily lose track of equipment. Smaller items such as keyboards and mice usually cost less to replace than to secure.

TIPS & TECHNIQUES

Internet Use Policy

If you are making computers available to the public, you may want to consider writing an "Internet Use Policy." Depending on the people who will be using the computers, you may want to include some of the following restrictions:

- Parental approval for users under 18

- Limits on chat rooms or email use

- Provisions for purchasing floppy disks and/or CDs

- Limits on food and drink at computer workstations

- Ban on installing personal software or software downloaded from the Internet

- Sign-in procedures

- Supervision of children by accompanying parents

- Statements on plagiarism and copyright restrictions

Summing It Up

As a nonprofit grows, its activities become more varied. Similarly, the software applications that can make it more productive are also more varied. No matter what the size of the organization, however, it is essential that software be wisely and carefully limited. It is far more desirable to have one application that staff and volunteers know how to use effectively than a dozen applications that are incompatible with one another and do little more than confuse their users. Having a program available on all computers will ultimately be more important than the luxury of having a program for every task you might think up. In addition, it takes time for computer support staff to master the quirks and problems associated with any given program. If they are spread too thin, they will be juggling too many crises with too many programs to do their work efficiently. Once again, effective management practices are far more important than the specific hardware and software chosen by a nonprofit.

CHAPTER 5

Obtaining Technical Support

After reading this chapter, you will be able to:

- Take control of your computer system.

- Anticipate technology-related crises and prepare for them.

- Decide when it is preferable to outsource technical support and when in-house support is needed.

- Develop a set of written procedures and documentation to assure the safety and functionality of your computer applications.

Determining Your Technical Support Needs

No matter what the size of your organization, more than one individual, whether paid staff member or volunteer, must take responsibility for your computer system. As a nonprofit grows and changes, confusion about responsibilities and failure to anticipate crises can wreak havoc with its goals and priorities. The key to maintaining a safe and functional computer system is a clear understanding of both your technical needs and your technical support options.

People, not machines, must always be the focus of a good technology program, and knowing the strengths and limitations of your fellow group members is essential. For example, how much technical expertise is available within your group?

Which tasks can be performed by staff members or volunteers, and which should be left to paid professionals? Some aspects of your technology program will always require professional support, but where will you find it? When is it more cost-effective to outsource technical support and when should you hire an in-house technician or systems administrator?

Caring for Your Computer System

Soon after most small organizations computerize some functions, they discover that computers do not take care of themselves. This may come as a shock to people who have had little computer experience or whose home computers hold little information of value. They might view a computer much like a refrigerator or dishwasher that can function for years on end with only occasional attention.

The kinds of tasks that a nonprofit organization entrusts to computers, however, are very different. Like maintaining a contributor database, they soon become essential. In the event of a computer failure, you may not know how much money you have, which bills are past-due, or who has made contributions to your organization. Such information is in another league entirely from your son's Dungeons and Dragons game. If the data is really lost and cannot be retrieved, months of work may be lost and a permanent setback may result.

Assigning Responsibility for Technical Support

This means that maintaining and protecting the computer system is an essential job, one that is much more important and time-consuming than most nonprofits anticipate. That is why before any computers are placed in operation, a technology plan should first be developed. As discussed in Chapter 2, one of the most important elements of the plan is assigning responsibility for both routine maintenance of the computer system and for dealing with major problems. Appointing a tech team is the best way to begin, especially in smaller organizations in which the responsibilities of individuals tend to be too fluid to ensure continuity. The tech team is usually a group of the organization's more sophisticated computer users who will oversee the nonprofit's technical development. The tech team may be strictly a planning group or may be responsible for day-to-day computer support. It is best that the tech team be given its charge by the board of directors and play a formal role in the organization.

Putting It in Writing

After the creation of a technology plan, one of the first responsibilities of the tech team should be the development of a set of written procedures or a manual that serves as the foundation for all computer-related activities. Such a manual should include the rights and responsibilities of the systems administrator, assignment of responsibility for backups, storage of backups, antivirus protection, and possibly even data input requirements. It is important to anticipate the inertia that always seems to set in after the installation of a computer system. At first, backups and virus scans are performed regularly. Training programs inspire enthusiasm, and staff and volunteers take extra care. Gradually, however, early enthusiasm is replaced by a more relaxed attitude and a certain amount of confusion about who is responsible for what.

Written procedures alone cannot reinvigorate the project, but they can clarify responsibilities. They can make clear what should be happening and who is responsible for making it happen. When an administrator or board member begins to notice that a problem exists, he or she can consult the manual and determine just how far the group has drifted from its goals.

The Experience of a Small Nonprofit

Let's revisit the Pleasantville Family Advocacy group during those early days when it was just getting started. As you may remember, it used a small office lent by another local social service agency. Volunteer counselors used the office in the mornings so it was available to the rest of the group only during afternoon and evening hours. With no paid staff and a technology budget of $500.00, the Pleasantville Association represented the very small nonprofit. Their membership base was similarly limited and included few people with computer skills. As you may also remember, they chose not to network their donated computers and made do with a dial-up phone line providing only limited access to the Internet. Pleasantville is a good example of a small nonprofit that knew its limits. In the beginning, it used the computers almost entirely for communicating with one another and for developing a contributor database.

Reviewing the Technology Plan

Pleasantville's tech team consisted of four retirees who had used computers over the course of their business careers plus a somewhat more technically sophisticated spouse who played the role of technology advocate. None were what you might call "techies," but all had seen first hand how computers made certain tasks easier. Each had experienced some sort of crisis that alerted him or her to the dangers that await the unwary. Thus, they were off to a good start. The technology plan they created consisted of just a few pages, but it was long enough to serve their immediate needs. In those early days, when they sat down to write their technology plan, it quickly became clear that the plan would have to address two basic issues:

Reliability. The donated computers would be used by volunteers who were very inexperienced. Precautions would need to be taken to assure the safety and functionality of the computers, in particular the integrity of the membership and contributor databases. When someone accidentally deleted records, imported a virus, or otherwise compromised the safety of the system, recovery procedures were essential. Instructions for backing up data, removing viruses, and reinstalling software were the first contributions to the new computer manual.

Privacy. Counselor-Client confidentiality was central to the Pleasantville mission but what about donor confidentiality? The records in the database would contain a variety of information. Contribution history, biographical information, and even hearsay about donors' financial resources would find their way into the database. This was highly confidential information that should not be passed around among group members or outsiders. Who would have access to the database? Who would simply be given the information needed to initiate a contact? The tech team decided that for these and other reasons, they would restrict the number of members who had access to the database, and a special password would be needed to see highly confidential information.

Evolving Needs

Technical support first arrived at the Pleasantville Association in the form of the son of one of the volunteers who set up the first computers and loaded the software. He promised to come back whenever they had a problem, Of course, by the time a problem actually did occur, he had gone off to college in a distant state. Since they could not wait until Christmas vacation, the tech team decided to enlist the services of a local computer repair business. There followed a confusing period when no one really knew what was happening with the computers. A technician might arrive when a counseling session was in progress or a bill might be received for a service call that no one remembered.

After much initial confusion, it was decided that, except in emergencies, the same technician would check the computers about once every six weeks. Of course, the computer business had a high turnover rate, but the owner was kind enough to send the same technician whenever possible. One of the members of the tech team was chosen to be his contact. She would be present whenever he was working on the computers and would maintain a log of his visits, repairs, and recommendations. This arrangement worked very well; both the technician and the tech team member got to know the little peculiarities of the system and were able to deal with the few emergencies that occurred.

Online Technical Assistance

It was about this time that the tech team discovered online technical support. Team members were understandably skeptical because their experience with telephone technical support had been stressful enough to raise their collective blood pressure several notches. Each team member had his or her own story of waiting on hold for an hour or more, only to discover that the staff member on the other end of the line spoke little English, failed to understand the problem, or charged for the service by the minute. Team members imagined that online support would have similar drawbacks, plus the confusion of an Internet chat room.

TechSoup

Their first and most exciting discovery was the TechSoup website. Team members could hardly believe their eyes. Here was a website just for nonprofits, and here were the answers to many of their technical questions. If they did not see what they were looking for, they needed to only email a question. Although the group continued their surfing adventures and discovered many other great sites, they returned to this favorite again and again. TechSoup (www.techsoup.org) should probably be your first stop on the information superhighway as well. A project of CompuMentor, a large nonprofit assistance agency, TechSoup provides almost every kind of technology resource that you might need. In addition to making available online information and resources, it also serves as a headquarters where nonprofits can obtain donated and discounted technology products, provided by corporate partners.

Other Useful Websites

The TechSoup site was so user-friendly that the tech team decided to take a closer look at the resources they already knew about. The Microsoft site came as a happy surprise. Although the layout of the huge site is somewhat confusing, a number of web pages are devoted specifically to the needs of nonprofits. However, the tech team was especially impressed with a section aimed at small businesses called The Learning Center (www.microsoft.com/smallbusiness/learn/hub.mspx). Among the large collection of articles are probably the best materials on computer security to be found anywhere on the Web. In fact, team members realized they could profitably spend several hours at the Microsoft site. However, in the event of a real crisis, this was not the place to be. Online technical support works best when you are calm and unruffled. If you have a real honest-to-goodness crisis on your hands, you need a human being.

Searching for Online Help

Unfortunately, most of us tend to put off our technical reading until we have a problem. For example, the times when the Pleasantville group were likely to go online seeking assistance might follow the appearance of ominous-looking screens with messages like "root.exe status code 200 yields 579." All too often, they discovered, such messages preceded computer crashes. Both Norton Anti-Virus (www.symantec.com) and McAfee (www.mcafee.com) maintain excellent websites that allow you to search for a particular virus symptom that might be worrying you. Simply typing the mysterious message into Google (surrounded by quotation marks) will sometimes yield good results as well.

LEARN MORE ABOUT

Online Technical Support

Visit TechSoup's Community Message Boards at www.techsoup.org

Consider joining the Nonprofit Techie Listserv at
www.supportcenter.org/resources/techie_listserv.html

Discover Tech24.com at www.tech24.com

Look into Topica at www.topica.com

Visit TechKnow-How.com at www.techknow-how.com

Try Microsoft TechNet at www.microsoft.com/technet/default.mspx

Go to ExpertCity.com at www.expertcity.com

Seeking Professional Tech Support

As we know, however, the Pleasantville Association grew rapidly. Donated space gave way to a new building and the two donated computers were eventually replaced by a local area network consisting of a number of desktop computers and a network server. New members were drafted into the tech team. Responsibilities were assigned and reassigned and re-reassigned. It became inconvenient for a small group of volunteers to have exclusive access to the system, so more and more people were given passwords. Two of the most computer-literate volunteers shared the title of network administrator but they found the ever-growing system overwhelming (see Exhibit 5.1).

Coping with Change

Suddenly, without warning, Pleasantville's local computer service went out of business. No longer would their young technician make regular "house calls." Some new arrangement would need to be made and made quickly. Frequent crashes signaled serious problems, and the novice systems administrators desperately needed help. Although another computer repair business was called in, the tech team was

EXHIBIT 5.1

Technical Support Assessment Questionnaire

To better assess their technical support needs, the Pleasantville tech team members might have asked themselves the following questions. They may help you better understand your own needs.

1. Is your present technical support level sufficient? Are enough people with good technical skills available to meet your needs?

2. Is your technical support budget adequate? Bear in mind that approximately 70 percent of your technology spending should go to support and training.

3. Roughly how many staff or volunteer hours are spent on computer maintenance each month?

4. How many hours are spent on software installation and troubleshooting?

5. How many hours are spent on network administration?

6. Are these tasks clearly assigned or are they done when a staff member or volunteer has time available?

7. Whether a systems administrator or capable volunteer, is there someone able to answer technical questions clearly in plain English?

8. Is someone assigned to train staff individually, as well as organize group training sessions?

9. Has someone been appointed to keep a network log or other written record about the computer system?

10. Has a backup technical support person been identified and trained? In other words, if the person in charge of the computer system is ill, is there someone else who can capably take his or her place?

11. Have you identified an independent contractor such as a computer store or consultant that can meet unexpected technical support needs or help you deal with emergencies?

12. Have you appointed a system administrator?

13. If so, how many hours does he or she work (on a paid or volunteer basis) per week?

14. Is the system administrator able to get work done on time or is there always a large backlog?

not really satisfied. The technology plan really did not seem relevant. Technology needs had grown just as rapidly as the organization while technology planning lagged behind. Although some of the newer volunteers had good computer skills, there was a general feeling among the group that the computer system was out of control. It was clearly time to revise the technology plan, but the tech team needed help. What was needed, members believed, was a consultant to advise them.

Hiring a Consultant

As you have probably noticed, consulting for nonprofit organizations is a field that has exploded in recent years. You may be most familiar with fundraising consultants who guide nonprofits through capital campaigns and other important fundraising activities. Technology consultants, however, need not specialize in nonprofit organizations. Computer systems are much the same whether they are found in for-profit businesses or nonprofits.

However, the human side of the organization is quite different in nonprofits. In a business, a local area network the size of the Pleasantville system is used by a small number of paid staff. The Pleasantville system, on the other hand is used both by its small paid staff and by its large corps of volunteers. As we learned, attempts were periodically made to limit the number of volunteers given computer passwords. However, the more dependent an organization becomes on computers, the more people need to use the system to do their work effectively. Although any good technology consultant can help you plan your technology future, a consultant who specializes in business customers may find it difficult to comprehend these human considerations.

Although it had grown rapidly, the Pleasantville Association still did not have money to throw around. On one hand, they wondered how much they would have to pay for a good consultant and hoped they could find a bargain. On the other hand, some members of the group remembered the consultants who were routinely hired by their former employers. These consultants seemed to live on another planet and offered impractical suggestions that were rarely acted upon. No matter how high or how low the consultant's fee, the money was wasted.

TIPS & TECHNIQUES

You May Need a Consultant When

The following are some situations when hiring a consultant might be your best course of action:

- Your organization has no expertise in the area of need.

- Your need will end, either on a specific date or when a task is accomplished.

- Your organization has not been successful when it attempted to do this task internally.

- There is disagreement among organization members about how to meet this need. They need an objective, unbiased perspective.

- No one else in your organization is willing or able to take on this task.

- Grant funds are available to hire a consultant; a grant may even require that you hire a consultant.

Seeking Recommendations

Consultants are usually paid a flat daily fee plus expenses. These expenses include air travel, hotels, meals, and other related costs. The Pleasantville group wondered if a local person might meet their needs, since the savings would be considerable. The tech team began by choosing a number of nonprofits in their area and asking each about its experience with consultants. Naturally, they chose somewhat larger organizations, rightly assuming that they were more likely to have encountered similar problems along the way. Fortunately, the Pleasantville board and staff members had made it a point to get to know their colleagues in other nonprofits. During the last few years, they had sought them out frequently and gotten a lot of good advice. Whether asking about technology matters, job descriptions, or tax issues, they were able to avoid "reinventing the wheel."

Collecting Information about Consultants

Some organized system was needed for collecting information about possible consultants, so team members devised a form. Each team member would make several visits or phone calls to colleagues, ask relevant questions, and complete the forms. In a few weeks, they would get together to discuss the results. Once they had gotten past the first big question and determined that a nonprofit had at least hired a technology consultant, what else would they ask? The first few questions like the name, address, and phone number were obvious. What then? Initially, they decided simply to ask what a consultant had been hired to do and how successfully he or she accomplished the task.

After only a very few organizations had been queried, the tech team discovered that most of the people they talked with had been faintly dissatisfied with their consultants. Some seemed unable to pin down the source of their dissatisfaction, but it was obviously present. Whether the team spoke with an administrator or board member, the consensus seemed to be that the consultant had not done what was expected. A little further delving made it clear that no one was quite sure what the consultant was supposed to do, but whatever it was, he or she had not done it.

Establishing Realistic Expectations

This is such a frequently encountered response that we would do well to spend some time discussing what it is we want the consultant to do. Too often a group underestimates its own ability and overestimates the consultant's expertise. They imagine that a consultant will walk in their door and immediately understand their problems. They imagine that in the one, two, or three days for which they have contracted, their consultant will solve all those problems or write their technology plan or perform some other task that really requires hundreds of hours to complete.

You will probably be happiest with your consultant if you decide in advance exactly what it is you want accomplished in the agreed upon time. Consultants are at their best when they are sharing information. In the few days available, most of the consultant's time should be spent listening and talking. When he or she leaves, the group should be better able to tackle its challenges. They should have more information at their fingertips to allow them to make better decisions. The consultant does not (and probably should not) write your technology plan. Your group should be better prepared to write it because of the knowledge the consultant has shared. The consultant does not solve your problems but rather makes it possible for you to solve them yourself.

Maximizing the Consultant's Time

Tech team members also discovered in their conversations with colleagues that much of the consultant's time was spent simply learning about their activities. This is inevitable because you do not want recommendations that are really better suited to other organizations. However, some of this time might have been better used. These groups might have made better use of preliminary interviews and phone conversations with the consultants they were considering, giving them as much relevant information about their organization as possible. Once they had selected a consultant, they might have sent out a packet of materials about their organization. Rather than simply gathering up all their reports and brochures, they might have condensed important information so it could be read and understood quickly.

It is also probable that those dissatisfied groups did not organize their consultant's time effectively. They could have scheduled an informational meeting at the start of the first day and planned carefully what they would discuss. Although members should feel free to share their thoughts, they must be made aware of that clock ticking away. Almost any group can easily get off-topic and spend precious time reminiscing or arguing. Similarly, most groups have members who are known for their loquaciousness. A prepared agenda with topics to be discussed and the amount of time to be devoted to each would have kept such groups on-task. Effective group facilitators can gently discourage "talkers" from monopolizing the discussion and make sure essential information is presented as succinctly as possible and different factions are represented.

Creating a Consultant's Job Description

Thus, the Pleasantville tech team got more from their discussions with their colleagues than they had bargained for. Contacts with other nonprofit organizations provided not only the names of some possible consultants but a lot of "food for thought." It became clear that a lot of preliminary work would need to be done to prepare for a consultant. The Pleasantville tech team had also imagined that a consultant would solve all their problems. Now, they saw that they would need to be more specific in their expectations. Why not create a job description for the consultant before they proceeded further? Clearly the consultant would advise them, but what about? What were the specific decisions that lay ahead? Together, team members made a list of the questions they had been asking one another:

1. What kind of technical support was needed to maintain their local area network?

2. Was the present budget adequate to maintain the network?

3. Could their network continue to expand or should they be thinking about major changes (with corresponding higher costs) in the near future?

This list was only decided upon after many other questions had been discarded. In fact, team members had questions concerning training, funding, equipment purchases, and a host of other troubling matters, but they were not hiring superman or superwoman and they had a tight budget. These three questions would be more than enough.

Once these questions had been identified, it was easy to create a section labeled "Objectives" in the consultant's job description. Clearly, the consultant would be successful if he or she empowered the team to respond to these questions with sound decisions. Members of the tech team felt justifiably pleased with themselves for it occurred to them that their unhappy colleagues in other organizations had never gotten this far.

Deciding on Basic Qualifications

Now that they had hammered out specific objectives, they could begin to address the question of qualifications. What experience and documented expertise did a consultant need to achieve these objectives? During the course of their phone calls and meetings, they had met repeatedly with negative comments about consultant qualifications. It seemed almost anyone could set him- or herself up in business as a consultant. Of course, there are professional organizations that weed out the real opportunists, but the qualifications of even professionally recognized consultants seemed to vary widely. It was decided that the most important qualification for any consultant was experience. The team was looking for someone who had encountered these same problems before in a variety of different environments. There is no substitute for experience, they reasoned, although academic credentials were important.

Occasionally, you will encounter consultants who think they can do anything. If you look on their website or read their marketing pieces, you will find just about every area of nonprofit specialization listed. They will happily consult on fundraising, legal issues, grant writing, management, membership building, or technology planning. If this is really one individual claiming to possess all this expertise, you would do well to go elsewhere. Very likely such individuals worked for nonprofits in one capacity and found it profitable to consult in that area. Soon, however, they began receiving inquiries about other specialties. Rather than admit that they knew nothing about them, they quickly gathered up enough information to put on a credible performance. A performance is not what you are looking for, but rather in-depth knowledge. Each consultant comes to the profession with a different background, but the combination of past experience, educational qualifications, and recent consulting experiences must add up to the specific expertise you are seeking.

By now, Tech Team members made almost daily visits to the wonderful TechSoup website and they found a lot of excellent articles about choosing a consultant. In addition, they found lists of professional associations in the field and learned of the experiences of many more nonprofit organizations in other parts of the country. Eventually, with the help of their colleagues, TechSoup, and various professional associations, they assembled a long list of possible technology consultants.

Selecting the Search Committee

Next, it was time to choose a small number from the list who appeared to best meet their needs. Interviews can be conducted by phone or in person. Interviewing a consultant is a lot like interviewing a job applicant and should be approached in much the same way. However, you will probably want to include more people on your consultant search committee than on a staff search committee. The Pleasantville Tech

Team decided to ask another board member and an administrator to join them on the search committee, as well as the chairperson of the fundraising committee. The organization will be richer in knowledge and more likely to implement the resulting recommendations if such leaders can work closely with the consultant. Be careful, however, that the group does not become unwieldy. The committee must remain small enough to work together as a cohesive unit.

Preparing for the Interviews

As is the case with employment interviews, all consultant prospects should be asked the same questions, which have been prepared in advance. The specific questions you ask will differ depending on your organization's own unique needs.

An applicant's responses to the questions, however, should not be the only basis for your decision. Personal fit and communication styles are at least as important as technical expertise. As we have discussed, in most cases, a consultant does not perform a task but rather empowers others to perform it better. Therefore, success must be judged, at least in part, on the ability of the consultant to communicate effectively. Communication is influenced by a variety of factors including personal style. Good consultants are good listeners, so it is important to note how much applicants hear. Is it clear that they are really trying to understand your organization or are they focused on selling themselves? If you sent out materials about your organization prior to the interview, does it appear that they have read them? Do they ask thoughtful questions and really listen to the answers?

One of the reasons for hiring a consultant is to get an outsider's view. You are seeking someone who has no ties with your organization and no axes to grind. This objectivity can be lost, however, if a consultant is tied too closely to some other organization. Word some of your questions to bring such prejudices or preconceived ideas to the surface. If applicants respond to several questions by telling you how they handled the same situation in their former place of employment, then you might rightly infer that they are not noticing the ways in which your situation is different. This may be an indication that an applicant's experience is too limited and he or she has not had time to learn that one size does not fit all.

Getting the Interviews Off to a Good Start

Begin the consultant interviews as you would employment interviews. By this I mean introducing participants and providing some preliminary information about both your organization and the specific reason why you are seeking a consultant. Try not to depend on speakerphones when conducting telephone interviews. Although conference calls are more expensive, they ensure that everyone can both hear and be heard. After a few minutes getting to know one another, it is time to begin asking questions from your prepared list.

Learning from the Interviews

Your search committee will undoubtedly learn a great deal, both about the consultants and about your own situation as viewed by an outsider. If you have done a good job of structuring the interviews, you should receive quite a bit of free advice.

When the Pleasantville committee got together for the first time after the interviews, they never got around to talking about the consultants' qualifications. What really interested them were the other organizations that had been discussed. It was fascinating to hear about their problems and see how a professional went about analyzing them, separating out nonessentials and concentrating on core issues. With such good examples set before them, the committee naturally viewed their own situation differently and even wondered if they still needed a professional consultant.

Although it was true that the interviews had provided what almost amounted to a course in technology planning, the committee concluded that they still needed a professional. However, the interviews made it possible for them to narrow their focus, separating the questions they could probably answer themselves from the ones that still confounded them. Of course, this meant revising the consultant's job description, but the group now felt they knew what they were doing and were happy to make the needed changes.

Choosing Substance over Charm

It was not until their next meeting that they finally got down to the real business at hand-selecting finalists for further consideration. Some candidates could be eliminated almost immediately because they lacked relevant experience with similar

TIPS & TECHNIQUES

Questions for Consultant Applicants

Although any list of questions should be modified to reflect the needs of your organization, here are some general ones you might consider including:

- Would you tell us how you became a consultant?

- Would you tell us about your experience with technology? With non-profit organizations?

- Would you tell us about some of the organizations you have worked with that had needs similar to ours?

- Could you choose one of them and tell us about the problems you encountered and the recommendations you made?

- Did you remain in contact with that organization? How did they implement your recommendations? What were the results?

- Although we understand that you still know very little about us apart from the information we sent you, how would you compare our situation with the one you just described?

- What particular strengths do you have that would be especially useful in working with our organization?

- As an organization, we have had very little experience with consultants. Could you tell us briefly about the way that you usually work? How might you divide your time? How would you work with our tech team, our board, our administrators and group members?

- Would you be working alone or would anyone from your organization be working with you? (Note: if other people will be involved, the search committee should interview them as well.)

- What would you expect of us? How might we make a consulting experience more successful?

- How much time would you need to deal with the issues we have outlined?

- What could we reasonably expect to have accomplished at the end of that time?

continued on next page

TIPS & TECHNIQUES CONTINUED

- When would you be available to work with us?

- Would you tell us about your fee structure?

- What else should we know about you that would help us make a decision?

organizations or because they seemed more comfortable with computers than with people. One of the people interviewed sounded perfect, in fact too perfect. Making a living as a consultant is difficult. Some of the more successful ones learn to "sell" themselves, and they become skilled at knowing what to say and how to impress.

A Pleasantville search committee member remembered the complaints of a colleague who had worked with an unsatisfactory consultant. That group had hired a real charmer who "wowed" the board and submitted a report that was obviously meant for some other client. This is not uncommon. When a large number of group members are involved in the selection decision or when the search committee does not really know what it is looking for, personality often wins over ability. Sometimes ability and personality go hand-in-hand, but you may want to be somewhat more skeptical about the candidate who was so charismatic but never quite answered your harder questions.

Comparing Consulting Fees

Up to this point, the committee had paid little attention to cost. To be quite truthful, they had begun their search with almost no idea what it might cost to hire a consultant. It appeared that most of the fees they had been quoted were roughly comparable to one another, with one much higher and one much lower than the rest. In general, cost may be less a reflection of quality than an indication of the kind of client a consultant seeks to attract. The consultant at the high end marketed his wares to larger businesses and so had little to offer the Pleasantville Association.

At the low end of the fee scale was a local man who was getting started in the consulting business. On the negative side, he lacked the extensive experience of many of the other applicants. However, he was personable, easy to talk with, and as a local resident, he already knew quite a lot about the Pleasantville Association. Also on the positive side, he was available for telephone calls and even an occasional personal visit that would not go on his bill. Of course, his references were few. In fact, he admitted that he was offering to take the job for a smaller fee because he would like to use Pleasantville as a reference in the future. The committee was undecided about just how much experience they really needed. "After all," said one member who could not resist the shopworn cliché, "it's not rocket science." They agreed to put him on their list of finalists for the time being.

Checking References

Now it was time to learn whether the image the consultants presented in the interviews tallied with the way they were viewed by their clients. Although resumes and interviews are essential, nothing counts more than a consultants' track record, and by far the best information comes from their former clients. As we all know, job applicants tend to pad their list of job references with personal friends who can be counted on to sing their praises. The same is true of consultants. When you make a reference check, be sure you understand exactly what the consultant was hired to do. In fact, was he or she really hired at all? Although many people do pro bono work to help nonprofit organizations, it is not really the same thing as getting hired to do a job. You will want to talk with clients who paid the going rate for services and expected results. Ask consultants to provide complete lists of their recent clients. That way, you can pick and choose among them. If you are not satisfied, you can continue to make calls until you have a clear picture of the consultant's work.

Consider carefully who will make the reference calls. In general, people tend to be more candid with a caller who they perceive as being like themselves. In other words, an executive director might speak more openly with another director than with a board chair or tech team member. Most people are reluctant to make negative comments and will be especially reticent if they do not really trust the caller to maintain confidentiality. Although consultants may list specific names or titles, there's no reason to contact only those people. You can easily obtain the names of administrators, board members, and others involved in an organization, especially now that most nonprofits have websites. It may be worthwhile to contact two or even three members of the same organization for references.

Dealing with Reluctant References

As you have noticed, some of the best questions ask the respondent to make judgments. If you encounter a reference who is reluctant to respond to such questions for legal reasons, you might substitute the following questions that merely substantiate factual information:

- What was the problem the consultant addressed?

- What were his or her specific duties?

- How long did the project last?

If you encounter no difficulties with these questions, you may wish to be somewhat braver and ask whether the reference would recommend the consultant to a colleague, given a similar situation.

Interpreting responses is always difficult. None of us likes to be critical of a nice person, so we try to think up positive comments. We mention what a pleasing personality the consultant had, how punctual he was, and similar comments that really do not answer the questions. When you suspect that a reference has to reach to think of something positive to say, it is important to pay attention to what is not being said. Sometimes it helps if you say out loud what you think the reference may be thinking. For example, you might say "I had the impression that Ms. Jones does not feel comfortable working with a large group. Was that your experience?"

In the end, the Pleasantville search committee identified two consultants who seemed best able to meet their needs. Since travel costs for one would be substantially lower than for the other, budget was the final deciding factor. It is important to note that the group did not allow cost to influence its decision until near the end. Occasionally, when the budget is inflexible, as when the consultant's fees are being paid from grant funds, it is not worth spending time interviewing consultants you know you cannot afford. However, even then, applicants will sometimes lower their fee if they understand your situation.

TIPS & TECHNIQUES

Questions for References

As we all know, some people will talk on and on while others volunteer as little information as possible. Prepare for both extremes. Avoid questions that can be answered with a "yes" or a "no." Try to keep your questions open-ended whenever possible. Once callers have introduced themselves, clarified the reason for their call, and verified that the reference can indeed speak about a paid consultation, here are some other questions you may wish to ask:

- Could you tell me about your organization and why you decided to hire a consultant? Ideally, you are looking for reasons that might be similar to your own.

- Why did you choose this consultant?

- How would you rate the consultant's ability to communicate effectively with your group?

- How would you rate the consultant's technical knowledge?

- Would you say that the consultant was a listener? Did he or she come prepared with a basic understanding of your organization? Was he or she responsive to your unique needs?

- Can you describe the consultant's greatest strengths?

- What do you consider to be his or her weaknesses?

- What were some of the recommendations, and did you implement those recommendations?

- Was the cost what you expected it to be?

- Would you hire this consultant again if you needed the same kind of expertise?

The Consultant's Visit

No matter how carefully your consultant is chosen, you must expect to get out of the experience only what you put into it. The tech team has a lot of work to do before they greet their new consultant at the airport. One secret to a successful consultation is to plan the visit as early as possible. Most consultants have developed a format for meeting with clients, gathering information, and then presenting their recommendations. You, on the other hand, want to be sure that the consultant meets with the members of your organization who can present the problem most clearly and who can get the most out of the visit. You are going to have to strike a balance between the democratic goal of providing broad access to the consultant and the more practical need to use the limited time available in the most efficient manner possible.

Putting Together an Itinerary

Big meetings are usually not very productive. Many of those attending have not been involved in technology planning and may send the meeting off on unproductive tangents. What large group meetings do accomplish, however, is to make people feel they are part of the process. It is essential that the tech team not be seen as a small, exclusive clique who make decisions without consulting others. As your group sets up the schedule, allow time for the consultant to meet the larger group, but focus on small group meetings and meetings with individuals who are most responsible for technology planning.

Work with your consultant to plan the schedule. You may want to appoint one person from the tech team who stays with the consultant throughout the day, making sure that meetings begin and end on time. Make it clear to everyone, including the consultant, that staying on schedule is the only way to be fair to everyone. When there is no advance planning, group members may arrive at meetings unprepared. Important issues may be forgotten. In trying to find something to say or keep the discussion going, members may ramble about the organization, its history, and even their pet peeves. The consultant, who does not yet fully understand the problems confronting the group, may also ramble or ask irrelevant questions if members are not forthcoming about their situation.

Preparing the Consultant

A month before the scheduled visit, the Pleasantville Tech Team talked with their consultant by phone. She described a typical consultation and volunteered to fax the schedules of some of her recent visits. In exchange, the team sent her some introductory materials about their organization and asked what else she would like to know about before the visit. Notice that they did not send a huge packet filled with brochures, flyers, press releases and annual reports. They assumed that such materials would not be read.

Avoid Overwhelming Your Consultant

It became clear that the consultant liked to begin with a broad overview of the organization so she would be better able to understand their specific questions. One team member suggested covering this information in a breakfast meeting, but the others objected. Breakfast meetings are for eating and getting acquainted, they argued. It is nearly impossible to spread out papers or take notes. The overview was, therefore, made the responsibility of the executive director and scheduled for the first meeting after breakfast. Since time was limited, the director would briefly describe the work of the organization, its priorities, and its plans for the future. Technology issues would be saved for later.

When an individual or group was asked to meet with the consultant, it was not an open-ended invitation. Each meeting was intended to serve a specific purpose, and each individual was responsible for gathering, condensing, and presenting certain information. Most of this information, however, should be presented in response to questions, not imparted in the form of endless monologues. The consultant can quickly become bored if she is overwhelmed with a barrage of facts and figures. Remember that the consulting relationship is a collaboration. The consultant cannot do his or her job without your help, but that does not mean that you can take over the proceedings. Some nonprofits discover when looking back that they gave their consultant no time to make suggestions or express opinions. All they really got for their money was a written report.

Willingness to Change

Many organizations hire consultants, pay their fees, read their reports, and then continue to do exactly what they planned to do in the first place. In other words, they gave only lip service to the possibility of change. There is simply no point in wasting your organization's money unless you are willing to give serious consideration to the consultant's recommendations and implement at least some of them. Occasionally, it seems as if a consultant has not fully understood your situation and makes impractical recommendations that really cannot be implemented. If, however, you have done your job and made available all the relevant information needed, a consultation should result in change.

Well, the Pleasantville consultant has come and gone. In general, members were very pleased with her visit and avoided most of the pitfalls described by their colleagues in other nonprofits (see Exhibit 5.2). They also feel much better able to tackle their own technology problems. With the consultant's help, they developed a three-year plan for upgrading the existing computer network. Thanks to her, they have a much better understanding of new directions in technology and are more savvy about touted high-tech innovations that are headed for oblivion. Their three-year plan will mean spending a little more money than they anticipated, but it will be money well spent since they know what they need. At the end of three years, they will have a stable, reliable network specifically tailored to their needs.

Focusing on Technical Support

As a result of the consultant's recommendations and the group's own discussions, it became clear that their most serious problem was the absence of adequate technical support. In the early days when they had only three computers and few of their records were computerized, occasional service calls by a local technician met most of their needs. Since hardware and software additions had come so gradually, no one had stopped to consider how many functions the computer system had taken over. Now that they were so deeply dependent on their expanded network, they could no longer afford to take chances. One person with advanced technical skills must be put in charge of the network.

We all know the jokes about committees. They are great for ideas but not so great when it comes to practical accomplishments. Essentially, the Pleasantville computer network had been installed and maintained by a committee. Over the course of time, different people took on different responsibilities, only occasionally guided by a computer professional. That meant that hundreds of small system changes and adjustments were made that only one or possibly two people knew about. This was one of the reasons that computer crises were becoming so common.

EXHIBIT 5.2

Bad Ways to Hire a Consultant

- Hiring a relative, friend, or acquaintance of a group member.

- Hiring a consultant who doesn't understand your kind of organization or is not comfortable in your kind of work environment.

- Hiring a consultant without defining the problem he or she must address.

- Hiring a consultant without buy-in from key members of your organization.

- Hiring a consultant who has preconceived ideas about what your organization should be doing.

- Hiring a consultant without documenting expectations, responsibilities, and remuneration in a clearly stated contract or letter of understanding.

- Hiring a consultant without clarifying the roles of board members, staff, and volunteers in the consultation.

- Hiring a consultant and later unofficially broadening the scope of the assignment and/or the time required.

- Hiring a consultant without believing fully in the process.

- Hiring a consultant and then taking a back seat, allowing the process to get off course without making every effort to get it back on-track.

Outsourcing Technical Support

Since hiring, training, and supervising technical support staff are among the most difficult aspects of technology management, we will be devoting much of the remainder of the book to this discussion. However, before we proceed further, let's give some thought to whether your organization really requires a technical staff member or if an independent contractor might meet your needs just as well.

In recent years, the practice of outsourcing work once performed by full- and part-time staff members has become common. The consultant the Pleasantville Association hired was actually an independent contractor. She was under contract to perform certain agreed upon tasks. An independent contractor, however, may

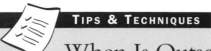

TIPS & TECHNIQUES

When Is Outsourcing a Good Choice?

Outsourcing, whether bringing someone in or contracting work out, is sometimes a good solution when:

- You have a sudden temporary increase in your organization's workload and do not wish to hire additional staff.

- You need ongoing help but a few hours a week would probably be sufficient.

- You do not want to take on the responsibility of supervising a technical staff member.

- You have a project planned that has a beginning and end. After completion, you will no longer need the staff member who performed the work.

- Your organization does not have anyone on-staff who possesses the needed skill.

- The cost of outsourcing a task or project is lower than doing it in-house.

- The job must be done quickly. There is insufficient time to retrain existing staff or hire new staff.

- By outsourcing a project, your organization has access to more sophisticated equipment or expertise than if you depend upon your own resources.

have a continuing relationship with an organization or may even do his or her work at another location.

Smaller organizations may find outsourcing useful because they require just as wide a variety of skills and services as a larger organization, but they may need them only occasionally. Although independent contractors are generally paid 20 to 40 percent more an hour than employees might be paid for the same work, it may be possible to obtain exactly the skill you need when you need it, with no downtime for training. A small organization may also have an unstable budget. Hiring a staff member is a long-term responsibility that you may not want to take on. Few experiences are as stressful as having to let a staff member go because of budget constraints.

Understanding What an Independent Contractor Does

Independent contractors generally own their own businesses. They are not your employees. Instead, they contract to perform work using their own skills and methods. You specify the end result, but you may not control their working conditions. In general, independent contractors determine their own working hours but not always. For example, Pleasantville's consultant had to be available at specific hours to work with members of the organization. Consultants are, nevertheless, classed as independent contractors because their responsibilities are spelled out in the contract, their work is performed in a manner of their choosing, and they have no further obligations when the job is done.

Similarly, you may want to contract with a local technician to work on your computer system for a specified number of hours each month. The contract might be for six months or a year, but it always has an end. The contract should also specify exactly what work is to be performed. You will remember that the Pleasantville Association hired a local computer repair business to maintain their computers. That business was functioning as an independent contractor. The arrangement worked pretty well, but the business had other customers and other priorities. It was not always able to make service calls when it was convenient for the tech team and was sometimes unable to respond promptly to emergencies.

On the positive side, however, Pleasantville was burdened with few responsibilities except to pay their bills on time. Since the technician was not on their payroll, they did not have to pay Social Security or Medicare taxes, unemployment insurance, workers' compensation, retirement contributions, or health insurance premiums. Almost all the recordkeeping was the responsibility of the business owner who deducted tax contributions and filled out required government forms. In addition, he was responsible for hiring, training, supervising, and even firing technicians on his staff.

Meeting Government Regulations

Care must be taken, however, to meet the federal definition of an independent contractor or you may incur legal penalties. The designation has been abused by some employers, who were trying to avoid paying Social Security and other fringe benefits for their staffs. Here are some tests you can use to determine whether your relationship meets federal and state requirements (see also Exhibit 5.3):

- Does the contractor have a separate place of business?

- Do you have the right to control how the contractor accomplishes the job?

- Where is the work performed?

- Does the contractor provide his or her own tools and supplies?

- Does the contractor have other clients or is he or she entirely dependent on your organization?

- How long will the relationship last?

EXHIBIT 5.3

Employee or Independent Contractor?

Sometimes it's difficult to tell the difference between an employee and an independent contractor. Which of these descriptions comes closer to your situation?

Independent Contractor	Employee
Operates under a business name	Has no separate business
Has own employees	Has no employees
Has a separate business checking account	Has no business checking account
Advertises business's services	Never advertises services
Invoices client for work performed	Paid a regular salary
Has more than one client	Works only for your organization
Has own tools	Uses the organization's tools
Sets own hours	Works hours as assigned
Keeps business records	Keeps only records that remain in your organization's files
Decides how duties will be performed	Performs duties as assigned
Provides own training	Trained by your organization

It is not necessary to pass all the tests. For example, a technician may do work on your premises but it is not his primary place of business. Since there are so many kinds of business relationships, it is very difficult to come up with exact definitions.

Creating a Paid Technical Support Position

It was the Pleasantville consultant's opinion, however, that the organization needed to hire a part-time or full-time technician. Many nonprofit administrators will tell you that no personnel matter is more difficult than creating and supervising this new staff position. The reason is that most of the other staff members have similar backgrounds and do similar work. Most Pleasantville staff members have worked in other nonprofit organizations and/or have a background in psychology or social work. Of course, such groups do have some entry-level positions, but new arrivals have plenty of help learning the ropes and are quickly integrated into the staff. In this case, however, neither the tech team nor the director had the slightest idea what a technician does, knows, or is paid.

As a nonprofit grows, it almost inevitably finds itself in the position of needing a staff member who is responsible for technical support. Since this is both so common and so necessary, the next three chapters will be devoted to hiring, training, and supervising technical support staff.

Summing It Up

Deciding how much and what kind of technical support your nonprofit requires is always difficult. Smaller organizations usually progress from volunteer technical support to some combination that includes both volunteers and independent contractors to handle more complicated tasks. When outsourcing technical assistance to an independent contractor, organizations need to be aware of the legal issues involved, since the federal government has strict guidelines regulating such agreements. A consultant is another example of an independent contractor who can provide expertise that may not be available within your organization. When a nonprofit's needs can no longer be met by outsourcing technical help, it is usually time to consider adding a technician to the paid staff.

CHAPTER 6

Hiring Technical Staff

After reading this chapter, you will be able to:

- Decide when it is time to hire a staff member to maintain your computer system
- Design a job description for a systems administrator
- Evaluate the qualifications of technical job applicants
- Select the most qualified applicant for a technical position

When Technical Staff Become Necessary

By way of setting the stage, let's imagine that the Taylor Teen Center group has become heavily dependent on computers. Fundraising, bookkeeping, budgeting, marketing, and most routine clerical activities require staff and volunteer access to computers, while teenagers beg for ever more computers to surf the Internet. It has grown both in membership and in financial resources.

However, the workload of the group has grown as well. Although a director was hired, and later an administrative assistant, much of the work of the group is still performed by volunteers. Two years ago, a board member's husband set up a small local area network in the building the center occupies. Gradually, the network has expanded as one function after another is computerized. Unfortunately, the couple has moved away and the group has been depending on a local computer repair service when problems arise.

Disaster struck when a malicious computer virus attacked the bookkeeper's computer. Computer security had been treated as an afterthought even though the surfing teens made the system especially vulnerable to attack. Of course, it was not really the bookkeeper's computer. At least half a dozen volunteers had used it to write "thank you" letters and assemble grant applications. No one was really responsible for updating the antivirus software and in hindsight, several members remembered the screen warning that their subscription was expiring. However, they assumed that someone else would take care of it.

What's Everybody's Business . . .

Although the computer repair service removed the virus from the system and did its best to rescue the files on the terminally ill hard disk, some essential records were lost. Recriminations were rampant, and some staff members stopped speaking to other staff members. At length, the board and the director decided that something must be done. Someone must be made responsible for the health of the computer system. What is everyone's responsibility, they reasoned, is no one's responsibility.

Looking around, however, they realized that there was no one on staff or among their volunteers who possessed much more than basic computer skills. Sure they could check that virus updates were downloaded, but wasn't that just putting a band-aid on the problem? The time had come to hire their own in-house technician, someone who would be on the spot, dealing with each crisis as it arose and figuratively holding the hands of computer-challenged staff. Such an idea has tremendous appeal. Nothing sounds more soothing than the presence of an expert, a computer professional who doesn't panic at the words "fatal error." It is in part this desperate urge for someone who will "solve all our problems" that can doom the organization to a future of endless technology-related problems.

Creating a Technical Position

Once the decision has been made to hire a technician, where does one begin? In some ways, it is like hiring any other staff member; there are procedures to be followed, and laws and regulations to be considered. However, before becoming involved in such routine matters, it's important to come to grips with this white knight image that is mesmerizing the board or administrative staff. What is this person really being hired to do? Is there really enough work to make it worth hiring a full-time technician, or would it be better to start on a smaller scale with a part-time arrangement?

Budget considerations play a big role in this decision. Hiring a technician will probably mean that some other plans will have to wait on the back burner. Where does a technician on staff really rank as a priority? What sacrifices will be required to pay his salary? Before making a commitment, take a good look at all your needs. Right now, it may seem that getting the computer system under control is the only thing that matters, but that may not be the way you feel tomorrow.

Deciding on a Salary

Next, consider the matter of salary. How much will you pay the technician? This is a surprisingly complicated question that can cause a lot of unhappiness later. On the one hand, you must be prepared to offer a competitive salary. In most places, there aren't enough technicians to go around and they are able to demand relatively high salaries. On the other hand, nonprofit organizations typically have low pay scales. Staff members tend to be paid lower salaries for more advanced qualifications than they would receive in the business world. They choose to accept this situation because they are being paid to "do good." They believe in the work of the center or agency. They understand that funds are scarce and are willing to make personal sacrifices.

In most cases, a technician does not fit this description. Rarely does a technician start out as a volunteer and evolve into a staff member. In most cases, he arrives with no knowledge of or interest in the organization. It is just another job. He knows what his services are worth and expects a nonprofit to pay what any other employer might pay.

Dealing with Gender Issues

Notice that I used the masculine pronoun "he." Although it is customary to be inclusive, assuming that a new employee might be masculine or feminine, I am going to make a deliberate departure from this practice. Of course, there are many female technicians, but nearly all smaller organizations with limited budgets will discover that their applicant pools are composed mostly of males, and most of these males will be in their late teens and twenties. Because of this homogeneity, it is possible to make some inferences about them that would not otherwise be possible. Such an applicant pool is neither better nor worse than others, but it poses special challenges and opportunities for organizations that traditionally attract middle-aged women to their ranks.

Considering Staff Morale

Let us get back to the technician's salary, however. It may be difficult to stretch the budget to meet a technician's salary requirements, but there is another problem with paying a technician the going rate. Other staff members have willingly accepted their inadequate wages because they understand that the budget is tight, and because everyone is in the same boat (or more literally, on the same pay grid). The small salary variations are a reflection of educational qualifications and longevity. The moment that one staff member gets preferential treatment, the others may no longer be willing to accept their lot. They may come to feel that they are unappreciated or believe that they are the victims of discrimination.

Salary Information Is Not Really Confidential

This places the administrator in a nearly impossible situation. If the salary is too low, then no qualified technician will accept the job. If it is too high, staff morale will plummet. Occasionally, you will hear it said that what one staff member earns is no one else's business. Taking this attitude is akin to fiddling while Rome burns. Maybe other staff members should not care, but you can be absolutely certain that they do care. Whether or not it is their business, they view their relationship with the organization as a mutual commitment. They will make sacrifices for their employer, and they expect their employer to come through for them. When the employer fails to meet its obligation, employees may feel they are no longer bound by their part of the agreement.

To be quite truthful, there is no really good solution to the problem. The only satisfactory strategy is usually to affect a compromise. The technician's salary is set as low as is reasonable but high enough to attract at least a few qualified applicants. It's a good idea to take a look at ads for technicians in local newspapers and magazines. Choose a figure a little above the lowest salary you see advertised. Ask other people who regularly work with technical staff whether it looks right to them. Ask local business owners or bank managers whether they think you can attract qualified applicants for that salary.

After this decision has been made, explain your actions to the staff. Everyone on the Teen Center staff was aware of the computer meltdown, so the proposed salary didn't really come as a shock. Nevertheless, it hurt and will probably hurt even more if a very young man with little experience in the work world is hired. Some administrators prefer to say nothing about salary, believing that there's no sense in inviting trouble. It will be time enough to deal with a problem if and when the word gets out. You know your own staff; you have first hand experience with the grapevine.

Creating the Job Description

Before announcing the decision, however, you will want to prepare a job description for the new position. This is one of the more difficult tasks in the hiring process. Your organization has probably developed some boilerplate language, but the duties and requirements for this job are going to be very different from those listed in other job descriptions. Because your own experience with technology is probably limited, you may have little idea how the technician will be spending his time or what qualifications he will need to get the job done. This means that you will need some help.

What Will You Ask For?

The director of the Teen Center might look to a state agency for help or seek out the director of a larger nonprofit that includes technicians on its staff. Spend some time with other experienced administrators going over their job descriptions for technical staff, but merely copying someone else's job description is not enough. It is important to know what really lies behind the impressive sounding phrases. What does the technician really do? Which are the more time consuming tasks? Which ones require the most skill?

TIPS & TECHNIQUES

Beware of Jargon and Buzzwords

It sometimes happens when we don't quite know what we're looking for in an applicant, and we must somehow produce a job description, that we resort to keywords or buzzwords. When the opening involves technical support, the buzzwords are likely to consist of what's often called technobabble. We're not really sure what any of these impressive phrases mean but we've seen them in other job descriptions and announcements. Although our applicants may also be in the dark, you can be quite sure that they will study your advertisement and your job description carefully, then replicate all those buzzwords on their applications. In such circumstances, the best bluffer usually gets the job.

Next, focus specifically on your own position. What qualifications can reasonably be expected for the salary being offered? It comes as a revelation to supervisors that technicians often have few formal qualifications. Much of their experience comes from experimenting with their own personal computers. Many have learned programming languages to tweak their video games or achieve some cool effects. This does not necessarily mean that they are not qualified to become your technician. However, it makes it much, much harder to evaluate their credentials. Experienced technical recruiters tell us that it's probably better to word qualifications as required skills rather than as formal educational experiences. However, that brings up another hard question. What skills will you require?

What Will the Technician Be Doing?

It's not possible to know what skills will be required without knowing what the technician will be doing with his time. Smaller organizations, whether in the business or nonprofit world, depend on personal desktop computers that use the Microsoft Windows operating system. Macintosh computers are popular in the arts community, but the skills needed to maintain them are not unlike Windows skills. Windows-based computers are usually networked to a server so that they can share information and access the Internet. Managing this network will be your technician's main job.

There are many other skills that are nice to have (like the ability to make minor equipment repairs), but most of the time, your technician will be maintaining and troubleshooting this network. The job title that usually goes with such responsibilities is Systems Administrator (see Exhibit 6.1). Including this title in your job description and help wanted ads will clarify the job you have available. The term "technician" can mean almost anything, including laboratory technician, accounting technician, or any of a wide variety of other specializations that have little relationship to your organization.

Systems Administrator Requirements

Although the definition of systems administrator varies with the size of the organization, here are some basic responsibilities included in most job descriptions:

- Staff training and support

- Software installation, maintenance, and upgrading

- Hardware installation, maintenance, and upgrading

- Research and troubleshooting

- Routine network administration and maintenance

- Network documentation

- Database development and supervision

Essential Qualifications

If these are the principal tasks your systems administrator will be performing, the following skills will be needed to do them successfully:

- Knowledge of and experience with your type of network

- Knowledge of and experience with your software applications

- Knowledge of and experience with hardware installation and upgrades

- Knowledge of recent technology trends

- Ability to train staff and volunteers to use the network and the software loaded on it

EXHIBIT 6.1

Microsoft's Definition of a Systems Administrator

Many employers, if they had their "druthers" would hire a Microsoft Certified Systems Administrator. If you can afford one, great! However, you can also analyze Microsoft's certification requirements to better focus your job description. Assuming that your computers are Windows-based, your new technician will ideally possess as many of the skills included in the program as possible. Microsoft says that its program prepares technicians to "implement, manage, and maintain a typically complex computing environment." The following are some of the skills they need to do this:

- Perform and troubleshoot an installation of Windows XP Professional.

- Troubleshoot failed installations.

- Monitor, manage, and troubleshoot access to files and folders.

- Connect to local and network print devices.

- Implement, manage, and troubleshoot disk devices.

- Implement, manage, and troubleshoot display devices.

- Implement, manage, and troubleshoot input and output (I/O) devices.

- Manage, monitor, and optimize system performance.

- Restore and back up the operating system, system state data, and user data.

- Configure and manage user profiles and desktop settings.

- Configure and troubleshoot the TCP/IP protocol.

- Configure, manage, and implement Internet Information Services (IIS).

- Configure, manage, and troubleshoot an Internet Connection Firewall (ICF).

- Configure, manage, and troubleshoot a security configuration and local security policy.

That should give you a start. The list can be condensed, of course, and other tasks added that are specific to your own situation. Don't forget that your technician is probably not going to sit at a computer eight hours a day. In fact, it's not a good idea to isolate him. The more your technician participates in the normal day-to-day work of the organization and becomes part of the group, the more successful he will be. Again, it's a good idea to get some help from a larger organization that has experience with technical staff before deciding how much time should be available for nontechnical activities.

Describing Your Needs

That should take care of the technical side of your job description, but are you really satisfied with the other sections, especially the boilerplate material that was probably copied from another nonprofit or an HR manual long ago? For example, what does your job description have to say about your work environment? A few sentences describing the goals of your organization can tell an applicant a lot about the position he's applying for. Emphasize functions that the technician supports. Make it clear that what's important in your computer system is not technical sophistication but reliability. Your technician will not be encouraged to do a lot of experimenting, so it's only fair to make that clear from the beginning.

How Much Previous Experience?

What will you require in the way of previous work experience? This, of course, depends on how much you're willing to pay. Most supervisors say they'd rather not hire a technician right out of high school, even if his technical skills are acceptable. They scan resumes for what might be called a "real job," in other words, one that involves more than a few hours after school and on weekends. It's exhausting to be the first boss who ever explained the importance of deadlines, and no one wants the onerous job of being a punctuality monitor. Keep in mind that other staff members will be watching. If the new technician, whom they view as earning an inflated salary, can't manage to get to work on time, resentment is bound to boil over.

Unless an applicant has a real work history, no references will be available to attest to his skill, reliability, or work habits.

Comparing Older and Younger Applicants

Although most of your applicants will probably be young and somewhat inexperienced, you may find yourself evaluating resumes that seem to boast too much experience. Why are these people applying for your entry-level job when they have years of relevant experience? Why would such highly qualified applicants be willing to accept such a low salary? The computer industry has long been the preserve of the young, and it is not uncommon for older staff to be "put out to pasture" long before traditional retirement age. Sometimes, this is clearly discriminatory, but in other situations the older employee may simply have been coasting on the job, failing to update his skills to keep up with changes in the industry.

Most nonprofits do not have "state-of-the-art" needs. They just want a good reliable workhorse of a network and someone to manage it efficiently. If they choose an older applicant, they can expect a mature staff member who should have learned acceptable work habits decades ago. An older technician may also have more in common with other staff members and his higher salary can be more easily justified by his extensive experience. The only question is just how out-of-date are his skills?

Evaluating Skills

There is probably no way to discover the answer to this question without an interview. If possible, invite someone with good technical skills to sit in with you. If you must conduct it alone, stay focused on "Windows" skills. You don't want to hear about his experiences with Cobol, Fortran, or mainframe computers, so don't allow the discussion to dwell on the past. Sooner or later it will be clear that the applicant can or cannot perform the tasks on the list. Occasionally, an applicant will argue that with his superior experience, it will be easy to brush up on newer developments. The question you must then ask is why he didn't do it long ago. Nevertheless, the better fit with your organization, as well as the lower turnover rate typical of older workers, may tip the scales in his favor. If so, consider an agreement that obligates him to take some refresher courses at the local community college.

Will the technician be working at more than one location? Does the organization have satellite centers? It's common to base a technician at the main location and expect him to make "house calls" at satellites. The Teen Center may reduce costs by sharing a technician with a sister organization. In either case, the technician will need a vehicle and a valid driver's license. This should be included in the job description.

Advertising a Technical Position

Once your job description is in good shape, you will need to advertise the position. Some organizations are reluctant to advertise a salary, fearing that it will scare off better applicants. However, it's best to be open and above board. There's no point in wasting your time interviewing individuals who will only consider your job as a last resort. Even if they accept a position, they will soon be moving on.

It is at this point that staff usually learn about the salary being offered, if they haven't already been told. Remind them of the crises of the past and emphasize the danger of continuing to operate in this manner. Read off the list of tasks the technician must be able to perform.

Hiring from Within

It often happens that someone on the staff thinks himself or herself qualified to do the job. Maybe this is the staff member who has been maintaining the network and who may be feeling unappreciated. Explain that there is nothing you'd like better than to see an in-house person get the job, but the skills listed in the job description are essential. Since the list was based on Microsoft Systems Administrator Certification, you might want to work out an arrangement whereby the staff member accepts a trainee position while working toward certification. This might involve an interim salary, possibly some tuition assistance, and some scheduling flexibility to accommodate coursework.

You are not, however, obligated to accept an unsatisfactory arrangement just to keep the peace. You have learned from painful experience that the present staff does not possess the technical skill needed to maintain the computer system. Now is not the time to back down and accept a compromise that will not solve the problem.

Creating the Help Wanted Ad

Let's consider the advertisement that will appear in your local newspaper. In addition to the job title, salary range, benefits, brief description of duties, and a sentence describing the organization, what else is needed? Interested readers will need to know what they must do to start the application process. Some administrators place a high value on that first glimpse of an applicant, specifying that applications be picked up in person. There's something to be said for this approach, but other options should be available for out-of-towners.

Your willingness to list a phone number probably depends on the number of applicants you're expecting. Some administrators lean toward accepting telephone inquiries if it's not too inconvenient. Just be sure that staff know to whom the calls should be directed. Consider whether you want to appear technically savvy by listing your fax number or email address. Faxed applications usually pose no problems (unless you routinely allow your ink cartridge to run low) but the small, slightly blurry type font used in help wanted ads makes it easy to misdirect an email inquiry.

Fine-Tuning the Application Process

What will constitute a complete application? Will you insist that applicants complete an in-house application form? Many supervisors believe that a resume alone does not provide enough information and require such a form. Resumes need not be written by the applicants themselves and information can be fudged or omitted. When hiring a technician, you must be able to confirm work history, skills, and

TIPS & TECHNIQUES

Advertising Nonprofit Staff Openings

Look into the Chronicle of Philanthropy Careers, which has a large online nonprofit jobs database at http://philanthropy.com/jobs.

Consider advertising in Nonprofit Times Jobs at http://nptjobs.nptimes.com.

educational qualifications. Although an applicant has a right to conceal certain personal information, recent employment dates must be clear, as well as reasons for leaving previous jobs.

Employment counselors sometimes encourage their clients to prepare functional rather than chronological resumes to minimize the impact of "job-hopping" or conceal periods of unemployment. An application form makes this kind of unsatisfactory work history more obvious. In addition, most forms include a statement and space for a signature certifying that the information included is true and the applicant understands that any falsification or willful omission will be sufficient cause for dismissal or refusal of employment.

If you don't currently use an application form, it may be time to develop one. Adapt one that was created by a human resource professional, since there are a number of questions that you may not legally ask. Smaller nonprofits (and even larger ones) too often run afoul of the law when they ask personal questions regarding age, health, and family, that are really none of their business. Be sure your form meets legal requirements.

Getting the Announcement to the Right People

Where are you going to advertise the position? The first and probably best answer is the local newspaper. When people are looking for jobs, they routinely check the newspaper. However, you may want to post announcements in other places, as well. For example, businesses that sell computer parts and manuals might be willing to pin up an announcement on their bulletin boards. Think about other places where technically sophisticated young people "hang out." Are there local newsletters that would be appropriate? Don't forget to post an announcement on your own organization's bulletin board and include it in your publications. Your colleagues who work for other local nonprofits might also post your announcement, and don't forget the placement office of the local community college. Ask around about local websites where technicians congregate. Many national websites like Monster.com have sprung up to connect employers with job seekers. Some of these maintain a database of resumes.

You may be in the habit of advertising positions in your own professional publications. This could be helpful, but remember that most of the people who will apply for your position don't read these publications. Discover the information sources they do check. Finally, don't forget employment agencies and government programs that place job seekers.

Reviewing the Applications

Once applications begin arriving, they will need to be reviewed. Who will do this? It's a good idea to have more than one person involved, so search committees are common. Since smaller nonprofits have little experience filling staff positions, there may be some groundwork that needs to be done before the search committee begins its work. What procedures will ensure that all committee members have input into the decision? In case of disagreement, who will have the last word?

Consider what each potential committee member will bring to the task. At least one should be able to interpret the technical component of the application. If there is no one in the organization who is able to do this, identify an experienced supervisor of technical staff in your community and enlist his or her help in evaluating technical credentials. This could be done on a volunteer basis or you might offer a fee for the service. It would be a good idea to develop a short form for the purpose. List the technical qualifications you are seeking and leave room for a comment on each. In other words, the form is a little like a report card and will allow you to more easily compare applicants with one another.

Should You Readvertise?

Since you may never have advertised for a technician before, you will probably be surprised at the applications you receive. If your efforts don't generate enough applications that meet your minimum requirements, consider readvertising or expanding your scope to include additional newspapers and other publications. If most of the applicants are underqualified, maybe you need to reword the advertisement emphasizing requirements or reconsider the salary you are offering.

Evaluating Technical Skills

Some organizations insist that no consideration be given to applications until they are complete; in other words, until the application form, resume, references, or other required materials have all arrived. This can waste valuable time, since many of these applications will be quickly rejected. Instead, many experienced administrators recommend that a preliminary evaluation of technical skills be made as quickly as possible.

It's a good idea to ask your search committee's technical advisor to do this initial written evaluation of technical qualifications soon after applications arrive. Then the evaluation form can be included when photocopying or circulating application materials. Be sure that your advisor really understands your needs. Get together before applications begin arriving to decide which technical skills are essential and which merely desirable. Once again, let me stress that this evaluation be in writing and available to all committee members when they are considering applications because misinterpreting qualifications is such a common problem.

Based on these evaluations, divide the applications into three groups: candidates who appear to have all or most of the qualifications being sought, those who possess some technical skills but not precisely the ones being sought, and those who simply are not qualified for the job. Put these unacceptable applications aside so you don't keep coming across them again and again and don't waste time collecting further information.

Evaluating Nontechnical Qualifications

Once it has been determined that applicants possess the technical skills listed in the job description, take a careful look at their work histories. Is it clear which positions are volunteer, part-time, or college work-study? Is it clear when each work experience began and ended? Since many of your applicants will be young men who have only recently entered the job market, you can expect to find some short-term service jobs like flipping hamburgers at fast-food restaurants or repairing computers on an informal basis. Such jobs in themselves don't raise red flags. However, some evidence of a successful, responsible work record is essential.

One supervisor in my acquaintance says she looks for evidence of commitment and indications that an applicant works to support himself or pay his college expenses, rather than to purchase a new car or stereo system. College work-study jobs should be closely examined. Some student workers actually administer networks and perform other high-level technical tasks, but many student supervisors may ask for little more than warm bodies. Although Burger King and other traditional student employers experience high staff turnover, too many jobs in too short a time span is still a bad sign.

Overblown descriptions of work experiences that seem to be borrowed directly from "how to write a resume" manuals should also raise alarms. When clerking at a local discount store is described as if it were a desirable management opportunity, you have reason to wonder whether the description of technical qualifications isn't similarly exaggerated.

Cover letters can be a good indicator of an applicant's verbal skills. Although a resume may be written by a placement service or professional writer, cover letters are more likely to be an applicant's own work. You've probably discovered that nonprofits tend to draw staff from the humanities and the social sciences. It is probable that applicants for technical jobs do not possess the same verbal skills, and that's perfectly understandable. However, the new technician must be able to communicate effectively. It doesn't matter if his spelling is a little weak in the cover letter, but if he can't express his thoughts clearly, you can be sure that he will not be inclined to document the settings and changes he makes to the computer network.

The Interview Process

It is customary in many organizations to winnow the pile of applications down to three finalists and invite only this select group for interviews. In general, this practice does not work well when interviewing applicants for technical positions. Nonprofits, accustomed to hiring professional staff, limit the number because such marathon interviews constitute a substantial outlay of time and money. In the case of entry-level technical positions, it's a good idea to limit reliance placed on written materials and schedule a lot of brief interviews. Since it is more difficult to evaluate the credentials of candidates who lack formal educational preparation or lengthy work records, the only way to determine their suitability for the job may be to meet them in person.

Another way search committees often narrow the field is to conduct telephone interviews with semifinalists. From the group interviewed by phone, finalists are selected who will be invited to face-to-face interviews. This technique is also less useful when hiring technical staff than it is for other staff positions. The telephone interview tends to prejudice committees in favor of the more verbal candidates, and verbal skills, though desirable, are not the real priority. Making a good impression, while enduring the stress and confusion of a conference call, is one of those skills that is acquired with experience and may not offer a young applicant the opportunity to display his competence or suitability for the job. This is another reason why it is really more effective to schedule a larger number of half-hour, on-site interviews. Since most applicants live nearby, top candidates can be invited back for a second interview with little inconvenience.

Conducting the Interview

Of course, there are other young people who work for nonprofits, but to be quite honest, applicants for most positions tend to be middle-aged and accustomed to the interview environment. To a young person, confronted by three or more search committee members with a long list of questions, an interview may feel like an inquisition. This means that it's important to find ways to make the interviews less formal. For example, you might sit in lounge chairs, rather than around a conference table. Try to chat comfortably; don't start right in on your list of questions. Take a few minutes at the beginning to distribute coffee cups and get to know one another.

When interviewing for other positions, you probably expect applicants to possess some knowledge of your kind of organization. In other words, applicants make a sort of "sales pitch," telling you how they would fit in and how they would make your organization more effective. Since technical applicants may be only vaguely awareness of your organization's existence, committee members must make those connections themselves. This means that they will need to place questions in context, providing an overview of the sort of environment applicants would be working in. Don't be reluctant to share information that might help applicants formulate better answers. Help them along when they seem to be at a loss for words. This does not mean, however, that committee members should do all the talking. Most of us have attended disastrous interviews at which the applicant could hardly get a word in edgewise.

Preparing a List of Questions

It's a good idea to have a list of questions prepared in advance. Search committee members are frequently given photocopies of the questions with space to write their comments. Your technical consultant, who initially interpreted technical qualifications listed on resumes, should be asked to formulate several questions that will further clarify the applicants' technical knowledge and experience. Ideally, he or she should be present at the interviews, but if this is not possible, the search committee will need some coaching on what constitutes a good or a bad response.

Once you've greeted applicants and tried to put them at ease, explain that you'll be asking a series of prepared questions. Encourage them to interrupt to ask questions of their own or to bring out experiences and qualifications that they want the committee to know about. It is inevitable that reading "canned" questions will take some of the spontaneity out of the interview. Do some ad-libbing and follow up on applicants' responses, probing significant comments more deeply.

Recognizing Good Applicants

When you interview applicants for other positions, you come to the interview with a clear mental picture of what the job entails. Over the course of time, you have gotten to know the qualifications and personal characteristics that translate into the right person for the job. Many of those same qualities are still important, so don't lose sight of them. For example, you look for evidence of good work habits. When applicants arrive late, inquire into the reasons. If they forgot to set their alarm clock, failed to estimate the length of the drive, or got lost because they forgot to bring a street map, they didn't plan ahead. Their failure to arrive on time may simply be an isolated incident, but it may also be evidence of disorganized work habits.

Although you may feel unsure about precisely what you're looking for in a technician, you have probably developed some excellent tools over the course of interviewing many applicants for a variety of jobs. You have grown a set of virtual antennae that help you distinguish between applicants who really know what they're talking about and those who don't. Those same antennae can usually gauge intelligence, and when you combine these signals with more objective information, it's not difficult to determine whether an applicant has the intelligence needed for the

TIPS & TECHNIQUES

Coaching the Search Committee

Many inexperienced search committee members are not aware that their decisions are based on subconscious preconceptions and prejudices. It is helpful to tactfully remind committee members of these potential pitfalls when setting up interviews. Ask committee members:

- To avoid making quick or snap decisions about applicants.

- To avoid stereotyping applicants based on sex, weight, ethnic background, minority status, physical attractiveness, or physical disability.

- To avoid asking questions unrelated to the job.

- To look at the whole individual and avoid placing too much weight on a few characteristics.

- To avoid asking "loaded" questions, which one must be an insider to understand.

- To be consistently positive and supportive of all applicants. It's not fair to make one applicant uncomfortable while encouraging another.

- To focus on the job description and objective evidence of an applicant's fit.

job. Computers are such complex machines that intelligence and imagination are essential to troubleshoot them. The technician who possesses limited intelligence may do well working under close supervision and performing routine tasks. However, when there's a crisis, he will have difficulty sorting out the many possible causes and focusing on the root of the problem.

Another essential qualification is the ability to work independently and manage one's own time. Imagine the new technician on the job. Although the supervisor will establish priorities and assign projects, the technician must determine how his time can best be spent. Young, inexperienced workers often fail to anticipate the amount of time needed to complete a job. They may become engrossed in something that interests them, losing track of the larger goal. When a deadline approaches, work must be hurried to completion and quality may be sacrificed.

It is a good idea to ask a question that calls upon applicants to describe some complex project they were responsible for and how they approached it. The project need not be a technical one. Organizational skills are needed in many situations, whether one is directing the high school play, coping with a power outage at Mac-Donald's, or building a backyard shed. Be sure that you include a question on this topic when you make your reference checks. A former supervisor may be able to make a more accurate assessment of an applicant's organizational and time management skills than the applicant himself.

Guiding the Interview

Because the search committee is on shaky ground when it comes to interpreting technical information, it's a good idea to maintain somewhat tighter control over the interview than usual (see Exhibit 6.2). Make sure that your questions are specific, to minimize evasive answers. Because younger workers will have only brief work histories, devote a little more time to clarifying resume information. You're looking for evidence that applicants take their work seriously. All of us have had an unhappy work experience, but a pattern of negative comments about unfair supervisors or excessively hard work is an indication that an applicant hasn't completely made the transition into the adult work world. Be sure to ask applicants to distinguish between part-time and full-time jobs, as well as those that were connected to academic programs (college work-study or high school vocational education). What exactly did they do on a day-to-day basis? Why did they quit?

Drawing Out More Information

You might even want to create some hypothetical scenarios. Describe imaginary situations. Ask what applicants would do if faced with angry customers or conflicting demands from staff members? How would they prioritize their workload when there was too much to do and too little time? How would they approach a particularly troublesome problem? Yet another scenario might be devised to show whether they see their control over the computer system as a source of personal power or an opportunity to support others in the organization.

Ask what parts of their jobs applicants liked best and what parts they liked least. This can give you an idea whether an individual likes to go off by himself or work with the group. Be wary of the technician who does not really enjoy being with people, because a "loner" is likely to make computer decisions in isolation. This question also provides an opportunity for applicants to display enthusiasm. It's quite likely that if they felt no enthusiasm for their previous jobs, they're not going to be very enthusiastic about your position. Be wary if they wax poetic about hardware and software but tend to forget the people experiences.

EXHIBIT 6.2

Interview Tips from the Pros

Many experienced managers believe that the best predictor of future job performance is past performance. Since you cannot be a fly on the wall observing an applicant at work, it's important to find other ways to gain such insights.

- Do not count on a resume to clarify experience. It may have been written by a friend or a commercial service. The same job title can involve many different levels of performance, and applicants often make up or enhance job titles.

- Job hunting books and employment services also coach applicants on handling trick questions, so this strategy is less than reliable.

- When you are setting up appointments for interviews, why not give the applicants an assignment? Ask them to visit your organization's facilities and learn about your program and services. At the interview, ask for their impressions, observations, and even recommendations. Of course, a young technician may understand little of what he sees, but you will discover that some applicants are much more perceptive than others. In addition, the requirement will serve to weed out some who are not really interested in your job.

- When applicants already know something about your organization, you are much better able to set up hypothetical situations or scenarios and ask how they would handle them. Again, young applicants have little experience but it's often possible to tell whether they are natural problem solvers or individuals who allow problems to continue without addressing them.

- Remember that interviews really test how well someone interviews. Do not respond to acting ability rather than competence.

- Of course, you want the people you are interviewing to like you and your organization, but do not waste the interview selling yourself. Let the applicants do most of the talking.

- Help your applicants along when they seem shy or hesitant but do not put words in their mouths.

- Ask questions that focus on past experience like "What would your former employer say about you?"

- Treat applicants fairly. Give them roughly the same time and opportunity to express themselves. Bring closure to interviews by saying something like "we have about five minutes left. What else would you like to tell us about yourself?" It often happens that applicants say something quite important when they know that this is their last opportunity.

- Be sure you ask questions that you understand. That way, you can tell the difference between a knowledgeable applicant and one who is just very articulate.

- Consider conducting second interviews if applicants are tied or the search committee is not in agreement. First impressions are often at odds with later observations. If your technical advisor was unable to be present at the interview, he or she might be able to talk with applicants by phone.

- No matter how strong your personal reactions to applicants, do not rely completely on your instincts. Back them up with reference checks and do not simply lead the reference to confirm your beliefs.

TIPS & TECHNIQUES

What Interviews Can and Cannot Do

It is important to understand the limitations of the interview process. Interviews provide opportunities for evaluating applicants that make them essential to the hiring process. However, they have certain inherent and sometimes unavoidable disadvantages.

Interviews are useful:

- To evaluate communication skills, including grammar and fluency

- To assess social skills

- To obtain additional information

- To evaluate job knowledge

- To get some indication of compatibility between the applicant and organization

Interviews interfere with the search process when they:

- Lead to subjective evaluations

- Encourage snap judgments

- Encourage interviewers to make decisions based on stereotypes

- Place members of minorities at a disadvantage

- Put greater weight on negative than positive information

- Allow highly verbal applicants to mislead interviewers

Interviewing Younger Applicants

Most interviews include a question about why an applicant wants to work for this organization. Administrators caution that young people may move in a totally different orbit and be scarcely aware of your organization's existence. They may be unaware that libraries provide public access to computers or that arts councils do anything but hang paintings. Don't take their ignorance too seriously. Such responses are not necessarily an indication of a bad fit. If most of the people who work for

TIPS & TECHNIQUES

Holistic Hiring

When you hire a new employee, try not to focus on one or two characteristics. Consider the applicant's:

Behavior

Interests

Energy level

Personal interaction

Enthusiasm

Intelligence

Sense of humor

Grooming

Verbal skills

Directness

your organization are in their forties or fifties, you may be unaccustomed to interviewing representatives of Generation X or Generation Y. These young people are more likely to focus on salary and benefits than older staff. Such a focus need not detract from their suitability for the job. However, if they show no real interest in your organization, its hard to imagine them becoming part of the team once hired.

Customize Each Interview

Don't worry if you don't get around to every question on the list. Other questions may come up in the course of the interview, and they may provide more insight into applicants' abilities than the prepared questions. There is no need for each interview to be exactly like all the others. However, although it is inevitable that you will keep some candidates longer than others, it's rude and humiliating when a search committee loses interest in an applicant after the first 10 minutes. You may cut some questions when it becomes obvious that an applicant is not qualified for the job, but never give the impression that you're just going through the motions of an interview. Applicants should leave the interview feeling good about themselves and about the people with whom they have been meeting.

Never offer the job at the interview and never tell an applicant that he has been removed from consideration. Let applicants know when you will be making your decision and how you will contact them. It's helpful to ask whether they will be out of town during the next few weeks and if you might have a contact phone number. Some administrators say that email is a more reliable way of getting in touch with technical applicants than telephone calls.

After the Interview

After goodbyes have been exchanged, hands have been shaken, and applicants have left the room, it's a good idea for the committee to briefly review responses to questions. Although it's far too early to evaluate candidates or compare them with one another, this is a good opportunity to be sure everyone heard the same responses. When someone says "I thought he said" and someone else disagrees, it's still possible to reconstruct the exchange from memory. When the committee later gets together to reach a decision, sometimes a week or more after the interviews, memories have faded and it's no longer possible to accurately reconstruct the interview.

Narrowing the Applicant Pool

Once interviews have been concluded, it's time to select a small number of well-qualified applicants for further consideration. If the committee still has questions about the suitability of some of the applicants, they may wish to invite one or more back for a second interview. However, if it is the consensus of the committee that there really were no satisfactory applicants, they'll need to decide whether to re-advertise the position or lower their standards.

This is always a hard decision. Consider the amount of public exposure you gave the opening, including advertisements, announcements, and word-of-mouth recruiting. Is it probable that most of the people who would be interested in applying for the position have already done so? Possibly, an advertisement failed to make the newspaper's deadline or some other problem kept the word from getting out. However, if it seems clear that the position has been advertised widely, you can probably assume that a second round of advertisements will not produce more qualified applicants. Unless you are prepared to raise the salary or add some other attractive perk, you will probably have to make your selection from the applications you have in hand.

Considering Each Interview in Its Entirety

Most search committee members have probably been involved in a number of interviews. Sometimes they played the role of interviewer; sometimes they were the one being interviewed. This creates what you might call an interview community in which the same questions are asked repeatedly and the good and bad answers become community knowledge. Certain responses come to be known as "the kiss of death" to applicants' chances. They become easy ways for a search committee to eliminate applicants and narrow the pool of serious contenders.

We ourselves might have stumbled into some of those responses if we were not interview savvy. Remember that many of your young applicants have not yet joined this community and may say whatever pops into their heads. Don't allow yourself to focus on one or two questions. Consider the interview as a whole. You may be getting more honest responses than you would with a seasoned veteran, and that's not a bad thing. There are no magic words that will reveal the right or wrong applicant, so don't look for shortcuts.

Checking References

In recent years, the checking of references has become possibly the most difficult part of the hiring process. Once a small number of finalists have been identified, the committee will need to contact former supervisors, mentors, and colleagues. Many supervisors, who have hired an applicant after making only cursory reference checks, live to regret their hasty decision.

Contrary to the popular saying, what you see is not necessarily what you get. Interviews tend to bring out qualities like charm and verbal agility that may not translate into a competent, reliable employee. The only way to learn how someone will perform in your job is to discover how he has performed in other situations.

Ideally, those situations should be as much like your work environment as possible. However, young applicants may never have worked at comparable jobs, so academic and personal references may also be contacted.

The reason that the process is so difficult is that many businesses and government agencies do not allow their supervisors to give out references. It may be possible to confirm the dates of employment but little else. Nevertheless, you must garner evidence of integrity, reliability, competence, and good work habits before making your decision. Otherwise, all you have are the committee's "gut feelings," and there's ample evidence that such strong, personal reactions are unreliable.

We all find ourselves responding positively to certain people and negatively to others. If you look closely at the political arena, you'll see that again and again charismatic and physically attractive candidates are chosen over others with stronger credentials. Neither of these characteristics is an indicator of competence or character. There is simply no way to know what lies beneath the veneer except to look closely at the track record.

Expanding the List of References

How can you do this if no one will answer your questions? You will simply have to make a great many telephone calls. First, make sure that you have the applicants' written permission to do so. The best way to get candid references is to protect the rights of the persons providing the information. The statement signed by the applicant should make it clear that you have the right to call anyone you think may have relevant knowledge. Applicants may exclude their current employer, but otherwise you should have a free hand.

Begin with a list of prepared questions concerning the applicant's job responsibilities, special projects completed, overall performance, ability to get along with coworkers, and reasons for leaving. Include some character questions toward the end, but you will usually find that people are more willing to answer objective questions than subjective ones. Divide calling responsibilities among members of the search committee and be sure that applicants have provided the names and phone numbers of all their former supervisors. If more complete information or additional names are needed, don't hesitate to contact them again.

Dealing with Reluctant References

Begin calling only former employers. These are, by far, the most relevant references. When you reach a supervisor who is not allowed to answer your questions, confirm the dates of employment. Then ask if the employee is eligible for rehire. This is a little different from the more personal question "Would you rehire?" This is not the opinion of a supervisor but information stored in a field of the same computer record that includes the dates of employment. Since sharing such official information carries with it less legal liability than expressing personal opinions, supervisors may be willing to respond. They might also refer you to someone in the HR department authorized to do so.

Despite the cautions of attorneys, there are still many people willing to give an informative reference. In general, you will probably find some who will speak freely, some who are allowed to say nothing, and a third group who will share positive information but retreat behind company policy when an employee's work has been unsatisfactory. This situation makes it extremely difficult for search committee members to evaluate what they are hearing.

Once again, the only way to interpret such confusing responses is to make more phone calls. Do committee members know of others who might be acquainted with an applicant's work record? If you live in a small town, the answer will probably be "yes." Reputations are widely known. Half the town may be able to speak to the strengths of a young person who has grown up in the community. In a more metropolitan environment, the job of gathering information is much more difficult. If you've run out of references, get back to your applicants and ask for the names of others who could reasonably be expected to know of their work and work habits. Ask about customers, colleagues, Boy Scout Leaders, teachers, ministers, or rabbis.

Interpreting Reference Responses

Once you have a substantial list of names, the big question is how to interpret their responses? Begin with the assumption that a personal reference will be glowing. These are personal friends, family friends, and older adults who want the applicant to succeed. If you ask a general question, you can usually predict the answers. Instead, ask references to describe situations in which applicants exhibited the qualities you're

TIPS & TECHNIQUES

Choosing between Skills and Fit

Experienced human resource managers frequently recommend hiring the applicant who is the best personal fit for the organization. He or she can learn the job later. It's true that character, a common outlook, and good work habits will go a long way toward a successful work relationship, but a technical position is different from the others in your organization. Who will teach the new staff member his job when no one else possesses the needed skills? Who can suggest books to read, courses to take? A young, inexperienced technician needs guidance. The difficulties of supervising technical staff are compounded when the blind must lead the blind.

asking about. Encourage them to talk freely, letting memories surface and forgotten stories come to mind. It is in these stories that you will get a picture of your applicants in "real life." How do they compare with the impressions they made in the job interviews? Are these clearly the same people or do you detect some dissonance?

It is not uncommon for a frustrated search committee to make the minimum number of reference checks, collect enough superficial information to complete their questionnaires, and stop. This is certainly understandable. There's almost no task more unpleasant than trying to pull scraps of information from people who don't want to talk with you. I say "almost" because there is one task that is even more painful, and that is firing an unsatisfactory employee. When a mistake has been made and the wrong person has been hired, it is not just the search committee who will experience the anguish, but the whole organization. Time spent on the unpleasant task of collecting reliable references now may well mean that you needn't endure such misery later.

Verifying Credentials

Once the committee has completed its reference checks, it is almost ready to offer the job to the person they consider the best fit for the organization. However, there may still be parts of the application that have not arrived, primarily verifications of academic work (usually diplomas and transcripts), as well as proof of other training and work experience that were factors in the committee's decision. Let the successful applicant know that he is the committee's choice and let him know, too, what it is that you're waiting for. Perhaps he can speed the process along. There have been so many revelations of invented credentials in recent years that you can accept little on faith. Make sure any commitment is provisional until all required verifications have been received.

Summing It Up

Selecting the right employee for the job is one of those decisions that will have enormous impact on your organization's future success. Even though technicians may be very different from the people who are usually attracted to your organization, you will find that your past experience will serve you well. Supervisors with limited technical skills can do an excellent job if they set about the task in an organized way and don't "cut corners." The secret is really knowing what characteristics and qualifications you're looking for and the ways to recognize them. If each step of the process is carried out in a thorough, professional manner, the result should be a new staff member who will become an asset to your organization, not a liability.

CHAPTER 7

Training Volunteers and Staff

After reading this chapter, you will be able to:

- Train volunteers and staff members to use computers effectively.
- Assimilate technical staff fully into your organization and its mission.
- Master the skills needed to prepare young and inexperienced employees for technical positions.
- Facilitate communication between technical and nontechnical staff.

Training: A Key to Success

It is no exaggeration to say that everyone in a nonprofit organization needs a formal training program to perform effectively. Too often, staff and volunteers are given some basic instructions and then "turned loose" without guidance or support. Although this holds true for every job, it poses special problems in the case of technology responsibilities. Most staff members and volunteers use computers on a daily basis, often with little or no preparation. Computer technicians usually know far more about computers than their colleagues do, but they may know almost nothing about your organization or how it seeks to achieve its goals. Both kinds of ignorance will significantly interfere with a nonprofit's success. In addition, the absence of effective training can result in a "great divide" or gulf between technical and nontechnical personnel. Each group disdains the other because it does not speak its language or understand its needs. Each blames the other when things go wrong, as they inevitably will. Only when an organization initiates a formal training program is it really possible to identify problem areas and remedy deficiencies.

Although formal training programs are essential, every new employee also needs a personal initiation into the organization provided by a coach or mentor. When administrators or board members assign responsibility for the computer system to a technician, whether to paid staff or volunteer, they often feel that they have little further involvement. Similarly, they may believe that staff and volunteers will "pick up" both computer skills and a sense of commitment to the nonprofit's mission. Neither of these assumptions is true. Without a close association with at least one other staff member or experienced volunteer, new arrivals are likely to remain outsiders, lacking the knowledge base and personal involvement to make informed decisions.

Revisiting the Taylor Teen Center

When the Taylor Teen Center group was just getting started, it depended entirely on volunteers. Do you remember that daring decision made by the board to use email for most routine communication? Only one or two volunteers openly admitted to being unable to use a computer. However, it soon became apparent that others just avoided the issue. They arrived at meetings unprepared or failed to show up at all when they had not heard about a postponement. It became all too clear that many volunteers lacked the skills needed to use email effectively. Unless the board was prepared to rescind the email "decree," a formal computer-training program would be necessary.

At first, the board approached the problem rather casually, asking a member of their teen advisory group to attend the next volunteer meeting and explain how to get online. Although this sounded like a good idea, the impromptu training session turned out to be a complete flop. The teen zipped through screens, quickly confusing most of the group. After half an hour, many of the volunteers were staring at the ceiling or looking at their watches.

Later, the board got together to critique the training session. Although their teen volunteer was an accomplished computer user, she was not a teacher. Many of the volunteers were retirees whose last years in the workplace had been characterized by low self-esteem, precisely because of younger colleagues who seemed to be born with microchips embedded in their brains. This teen volunteer reminded them of those past humiliations. She was unable to step into the shoes of older, inexperienced volunteers who felt overwhelmed and even frightened by computers.

Getting Serious about Training

Fortunately, one of the board members was a high school teacher and made an excellent suggestion. A colleague taught the computer classes at her school and she felt sure he would be happy to help them. Jim was his name, and the teacher promised to give him a call. Well, Jim turned out to be a treasure. Being a high school teacher himself, he fully understood the need for a new teen center and promised to do anything he could to help. A few days later, he invited the board members to visit him in his high school computer lab and tell him exactly what it was they wanted him to do.

Well, it was simple really. They just needed him to teach their group to use email. Jim was not sure it was all that simple. What did group members already know about using computers? Some had their own home computers, but the majority were starting from scratch. That meant that there was no point in discussing email until they learned basic Windows skills. Then volunteers would need to use a Web browser like Internet Explorer. Finally, it would be necessary to navigate to a free email website, sign up for an account, and learn to send and receive mail. No, this was not going to be so simple. Even though their teen volunteer had sailed through all this information in under an hour, several training sessions would be needed.

Hands-On Experience Is Important

Where would these sessions be conducted? At that first disastrous computer introduction, everyone had clustered around one desktop computer. How could anyone even see the screen, let alone learn new skills? Jim would check with his principal and see if he could use the high school lab. School labs usually provide the best opportunity for computer training, and nearly every school has at least one computer lab that goes largely unused during evenings and weekends. Although libraries and senior centers also have computer labs, school labs are designed to accommodate whole classes. They usually have enough workstations to allow each member of the group to use a different computer.

Making Training Enjoyable

The next big hurdle would be convincing volunteers that they should attend the training sessions. It was not going to be easy after that first unsuccessful attempt. The board had started out on the wrong foot, and now group members had even more negative feelings about computers than before. "Why not turn the first training session into a party?" the board chair asked.

Another board member had heard about small training grants available to nonprofits in their area. An application was quickly put together that included funding for lunch, tasty coffee breaks, printed "handouts," payment of a cleaning charge for the use of school facilities, and a small honorarium for Jim. The board decided a little subterfuge was also in order. They called each of the volunteers personally to invite them to what they were calling a "workshop and fun get-together." Computers were mentioned casually in the course of the conversations.

Providing a Good Learning Environment

The workshops were held on Saturdays when the group had most of the school to themselves. There were enough desktop computers to permit all the volunteers to have their own. Because the room had been designed for just this purpose, lighting conditions were ideal. Window shades controlled natural light while overhead fluorescents provided even, glare-free illumination. Environmental conditions like lighting and temperature are very important to the success of training sessions. When people are uncomfortable and cannot see what's going on, their thoughts naturally stray.

Most trainers prefer a one-to-one ratio of computers to users. Certainly, no more than two trainees should sit at one computer. However, when trainees must share a computer, do not place an experienced computer user with an inexperienced one. Naturally, the experienced one will end up controlling the keyboard, and the inexperienced one will merely look on, learning little.

Other Environmental Factors

Older volunteers may have difficulty seeing their computer screens. It is a good idea to allow some time before the training session begins to adjust text size and screen brightness to meet the specific requirements of each user. At this point, trainees do not have the skill to do this themselves but it is important that they understand that computers can adapt to their changing needs. In many cases, older people can continue to use computers, even when they are unable to read most printed text.

The high school computer lab is equipped with a projector that is connected to the instructor's laptop computer. Its purpose is to let the class see what the instructor is doing so they can repeat the keystrokes and mouse clicks. It often happens, however, that less experienced users become confused. A software program is often available on the instructor's workstation to take control of all the computers in the lab and bring them to the correct screen.

 TIPS & TECHNIQUES

Discovering Other Training Opportunities

The Taylor Teen Board was certainly fortunate to find an experienced trainer who was willing to give them both his time and access to a well-equipped computer lab. Although every nonprofit does not have its own Jim waiting to be of assistance, there are many places you can turn for help. Of course, a class specifically tailored to your computer needs is ideal, but there are probably many computer classes and workshops in your area that are free or available at little cost. Here are some questions to get you started:

- Does your group belong to a local or regional association of nonprofits? Since all members have similar needs, the association may sponsor computer workshops.

- Does your organization belong to the local chamber of commerce? Even if you are not a member, you may be able to take advantage of their programs and classes.

continued on next page

- Is there a sizable business located in your area? Larger employers often provide basic computer skills classes for their employees. Including your volunteers in their program would solve your problem and provide a sizable tax deduction for the business.

- Can you negotiate for a discounted fee from a large corporate trainer? Through Gifts In Kind International, three companies (CompUSA, New Horizons, and Executrain) offer a 50 percent discount to nonprofits. To qualify, a nonprofit must pay to become a member of Gifts in Kind. Visit their website for more information.

- Is there a community college, four-year college, or university within easy commuting distance? Your volunteers may be entitled to take classes free or at a significant discount. Check the EduPoint.com website for its database of continuing education opportunities nationwide.

- If there is no college nearby, would a distance learning program serve your needs? These are courses usually taught via a video link from a university campus. Obviously, it is much more desirable to have instructor and students in the same room, but this may be the only way to get training on more advanced topics. The Management Assistance Program for Nonprofits offers resources on distance learning, including many useful links.

- Would you consider hiring a consultant to do the training? Consulting fees are usually high, but training is an area where grants are a little easier to obtain than for most of your other needs. A consultant might also work with your group to design the training sessions, but your own computer-savvy volunteers would do the actual teaching.

- Are you fortunate enough to have a Community Technology Center nearby? These are local organizations that maintain computer labs and sometimes offer training classes to the community. The Community Technology Centers Network maintains an online national database of more than 350 community technology centers.

- Investigate the Management Assistance Program for Nonprofits' links to programs like LearnKey.com, DigitalThink, SmartPlanet.com, and Learn2.com.

Nurturing In-House Trainers

Jim has gotten the group off to a good start, but Jim will not always be available when new group members need training and more experienced members need to brush up their skills. Therefore, the Teen Center leadership is going to have to find a way to do at least some of its training internally. A good solution is to have some of the more experienced volunteers pass on their knowledge to others. Otherwise, the gradually shrinking core of experienced computer users will create a bottleneck, limiting both data input and access to information.

Most people, however, are not natural teachers and sharing skills with others is different from simply knowing how to do a task. However, within most organizations there are some natural teachers. Ideally, these would be volunteers with professional teaching or training experience, but you can probably identify others who possess the gift. With proper preparation, this group can take over a significant part of the training responsibility. However, you will need to find ways to "train the trainers."

Training the Trainers

Maybe the Taylor Teen leadership can work with Jim to plan some training sessions just for the group's budding trainers. Another possibility is to hire a consultant to develop a computer training program for the whole organization. If funds are not available for this purpose, consider writing a grant proposal that will include not only the consultant's fee, but the cost of duplicating training materials. Once your in-house trainers are provided with lesson plans and training materials, training ceases to be such a "hit or miss" affair. Training schedules can be planned well in advance and computer training can become a normal part of the volunteer experience.

Training Content

Once these very general questions are answered, take a good look at the group of staff members and volunteers who will participate in the training program. By this point, we will assume that your computers have been acquired and one or more software programs installed. If, for example, you will be using a database program to keep track of information about contributors, one of your training objectives is to enable trainees to use the database program effectively. That will mean creating, updating, and deleting records, as well as designing forms, tables, and reports.

TIPS & TECHNIQUES

Taking Time to Plan

If you are unable to obtain the services of a professional consultant, you can still create a successful training program. The secret is planning. Planning is essential to the success of a training program. Before any training sessions take place, get the trainers together and consider the following questions:

- Who will be trained? Will you begin with a small number of trainees? Just the people who will be using the computers on a daily basis? Even if you start small, be prepared to expand the training program as quickly as possible. Almost everyone in the organization may need to use the computer system occasionally.

- What should trainees be able to do after they complete the program?

- How might you break down these expectations into specific skills that can be taught?

- How can these skills be grouped together into one- or two-hour training sessions?

- How will training sessions be scheduled? How long will each last? How many sessions will be conducted?

- What do you know about your trainees' skill and motivation level?

- Will you have one or more remedial sessions for the least skilled trainees? Will advanced trainees be able to skip early sessions that are very elementary?

- Has any training been done with this group before? What were the results? What worked well? What problems were encountered?

- Do you have a training budget? How will you pay for printed training materials, coffee break goodies, and so on?

- What teaching/learning techniques will be used? Consult an experienced teacher or trainer for ideas.

- If there will be more than one trainer, how will you make certain that every trainee is presented with the same information? One solution to this problem is to develop a written outline of each training session. Ask all trainers to follow the outline.

- Where will training sessions take place? Can you borrow a computer lab in a school or library just for the training sessions? If training occurs off-site, there will be less likelihood of interruption and training sessions can take on a more formal character.

- How will you measure the success of the training program? How will you know whether training sessions have achieved their objectives? Will trainees be evaluated when they complete the training sessions?

Can you reasonably expect the trainees to perform all these functions? If your group is like most others, some members of the group will be capable of little more than routine data input. Others can be relied on to perform more sophisticated tasks. If trainers underestimate the abilities of their students, they will teach at too elementary a level, graduates of the training program will be able to do only simple tasks, and the organization will suffer because no one is able to perform more complicated ones. If trainers overestimate the abilities of their students, inexperienced computer users will be trusted with too much responsibility. The database will be unprotected and serious errors will result.

Getting Started

Begin the first training session with basic computer skills. Unless you are working with a more advanced group, it is a good idea to review basic skills to refresh the memories of volunteers who do not use computers frequently. If the questions above revealed that many of the trainees were unable to perform basic Windows tasks, you might begin with copy and paste, file locations, mouse skills, startup and shutdown. If it appears that some of the trainees already possess good Windows skills, they might be scheduled to arrive later or skip the first training session entirely.

Ideally, it is a good idea to separate trainees who have very different skill levels. If this is not possible, try to keep training classes small. Occasionally, a trainee who possesses very poor skills or has a learning disability can disrupt a training session

TIPS & TECHNIQUES

Performing a Participant Training Assessment

Take a closer look at the group who will be trained. Called a training assessment, this is an excellent opportunity to look around you at the people who are active in your organization. To be effective, training must be custom-designed to meet their needs.

1. Decide exactly what each person who uses the computer system should know. Called competencies, these should be worded as very practical, easily learned skills. You may want to establish a minimal set of competencies that everyone must master before they are given a password for the computer system. To perform more complicated tasks, some volunteers might be asked to master a second set of more advanced competencies.

2. Determine a method for evaluating trainees' skill levels in a non-threatening, nonjudgmental way. Most people find it difficult to accurately describe their computer skills. Inexperienced computer users may know so little that they overestimate their skill level, imagining that there is little more to be learned. Experienced users, on the other hand, may underestimate their skills because, unlike "newbees," they know what they do not know. The following questions might elicit more useful answers:

   - Do you own a computer? How would you describe it?

   - What software programs do you use regularly?

   - Have you ever had a computer virus? How did you deal with it?

   - If you wanted to send the same email message to a group of people, how would you go about it?

   - When and how do you back up your computer files?

There are many other questions you might ask, but the point is to focus on specific computer skills rather than asking a vague, open-ended question.

and hold the rest of the group back. If you know ahead of time that one of your volunteers will not be able to keep up with the rest of the group, a "one-on-one" session timed to precede formal training might be appropriate. That way, you can begin the group session at a level that is neither boring nor confusing.

It is always a good idea to provide written instruction sheets and use them as a basis for the training session. Encourage trainees to make notes on their copies and keep them nearby when working at a computer. Do not try to cover too much information in a short period of time. Schedule more training sessions, each covering less information. The amount of information that can be covered depends on the skill levels of your unique group, but in general trainees are more likely to retain information that is presented to them in small doses.

 TIPS & TECHNIQUES

Adult Learning Principles

Most people enjoy learning something new but there are ways to help adults learn more easily and retain what they learn for a longer period of time. Here are a few basic principles of adult learning:

- Focus on problems in the real world, or more specifically the nonprofit's world.

- Find ways to address those problems.

- Choose problems that really matter to trainees. Make it clear why they matter.

- Encourage trainees to think "outside the box," applying new information to what they already know.

- Encourage them to exchange ideas with one another and get feedback from others. This expands the pool of experience from which trainees can draw.

- Limit note taking and memorization. Adults learn better by doing than by listening.

People get tired of listening. They are much more likely to remember what is taught if they have something to do. Therefore, focus on hands-on activities and reduce lecture to the bare minimum. Most adults have a relatively short attention span. Although, unlike children, they will appear to listen, their attention soon drifts to other thoughts. If you are working with a group of very inexperienced computer users, consider the high level of stress they may be experiencing. Find ways to make training sessions more enjoyable. Create activities that are fun and take frequent breaks.

Circuit Riders

Computer trainers who travel from place to place are often called "circuit riders." These are professionals who are skillful teachers and who have taught hundreds of people to use computers. Somewhere near you, there's probably a circuit rider unpacking a dozen or so laptops and setting up a portable computer lab. Maybe a local insurance company has arranged for a trainer to come out to its main office. Maybe a local bank or chamber of commerce has made the arrangements. It is even possible that you already belong to an organization that can provide a circuit rider for your group.

 LEARN MORE ABOUT

Circuit Riders

- Read Sean O'Brien's "A Week in the Life of a WAJF Circuit Rider" at: www.gristmagazine.com/grist/week/obrien100499.stm.

- Look into "The Management Assistance Program for Nonprofits Technology Circuit Riders" at: www.mapfornonprofits.org/.

- Read about "Technology Intermediaries: Pros & Cons" at www.nponet/powerpoint.

- Sign up for Riders Listserv, a community of nonprofit (NPO) and nongovernmental (NGO) technology assistance providers and Circuit Riders at: http://npogroups.org/lists/info/riders.

- Look into NinthBridge, which has an especially good resource section on training at www.ninthbridge.org.

Remember that the business and nonprofit organizations in your area have many of the same technology needs that you do. They purchase the same kinds of computers and similar software. In the past, technology might mean all sorts of proprietary machines, each of which worked differently from the others. One photocopier was totally unlike another manufactured by a different vendor. Early computers had different operating systems, and peripheral equipment was also unique. It is now safe to say that most businesses and nonprofits in your area need training on Windows computers and Microsoft software. Even if you have chosen Macintosh computers, you can probably find other organizations that have done the same.

Why not get together? Consider forming a local computer training partnership. Make it a somewhat official organization held together with memos of understanding or other legal documents. The purpose of the partnership is to hire a trainer who will be shared by all the members of the group. Of course, each of the participants will have somewhat different needs and budget limitations that should be thoroughly discussed before a trainer is hired. Members might consider purchasing some of the same software programs so that they can help one another and share some of the training sessions.

Training Is a Top Priority

Some people might question why the fledgling Teen Center organization decided to put so much effort into computer training, even when it did not own its own computers. The answer is that a successful technology program depends much less on hardware and software than on people. In general, nonprofits should plan to spend no more than about 30 percent of their technology budgets for equipment and software. The rest should be devoted to the human side of the equation—training and technical support. No board should consider computer purchases until they know that their group has the skills to use them. Most of us have friends who went out and purchased the most powerful, high-tech computer they could find. Those computers are still sitting in their dens gathering dust because their owners never had the time or interest to learn to use them. Our nonprofits have been the recipients of some of those same never-used computers, often donated to our organizations when they were too old to be useful. We must not make the same mistake.

EXHIBIT 7.1

One-on-One Training

Sometimes group training is not the best option. Funds may be unavailable or an individual just doesn't seem to be making progress in a group-training situation. As we all know, different people learn in different ways and one size does not fit all. Sometimes one-on-one training is the most effective way to create a community of technically skilled volunteers. Here are some suggestions for developing a successful program:

- Some people are visual learners. If they can see a picture of a screen or watch another person perform a task, they will be more successful. Opportunities for visual learning may be limited in the group-training environment.

- Aural learners do better by mentally processing what they hear. They are typically the individuals who do well in workshops, but if environmental conditions or physical disabilities interfere with their ability to hear the trainer, they may need special accommodation.

- One-on-one training can be very effective when one peer trains another. What peer trainers lack in skill may be more than made up for by increased empathy. Having learned the same task recently, they remember what was difficult or confusing.

- When trainer and trainee can sit down together at the same computer, there is a greater sense of camaraderie and the trainee's comfort level rises.

- One-on-one training can progress more rapidly because it focuses on exactly the knowledge and skills that a trainee needs.

- When peer trainers are used, training can usually take place in the work environment and even on the computer the trainee will be using every day.

- Peer trainers and trainees should begin with well-established goals that both understand. Since peer trainers are inexperienced, they can get off-track themselves or be led away from the topic by the trainee.

- Peer training is especially effective when some group members need different skills from others. If only a few volunteers will be performing a task, it is wasteful to train the entire group.

- A big advantage of one-on-one training is that it can take place at exactly the right time. A trainee can learn to perform a skill and almost immediately use the skill in a work assignment.

- Peer training is especially effective when the trainee's schedule does not permit attendance at a workshop.

- Not everyone can be a peer trainer. There is a big difference between being able to do a task oneself and being able to show someone else how to do it. A training coordinator or someone in a similar position should monitor training sessions and identify the natural teachers.

- One-on-one training can work even in a group situation if a professional trainer pairs experienced and inexperienced trainees. However, the more experienced trainees must understand and accept their roles as mentors.

- When everyone in the group needs to learn the same skills, one-on-one training is usually too time-consuming and should be used only as a follow-up to group training. One-on-one training might then be available for volunteers who need more help.

- "On the job" training may be less effective because of distractions like ringing phones and noisy coworkers. In such cases, group training away from the workplace may be more effective.

Who Should Be Trained?

Another question you might ask is why the Teen Center board wanted to train its whole corps of volunteers. Would it be better to train only the small group who will really be using computers on a daily basis? The obvious answer, of course, is that they want everyone to send and receive email. There's another and possibly more important reason, however. If computers are to be an integral part of their organization, they have to part of the planning process, a consideration in decision-making, and a shared responsibility.

LEARN MORE ABOUT

Training Yourself

It sometimes happens that only one or two people need to learn a particular software program. Although it is always better to take a class or participate in a training session, it is not always possible or worth the expense. Sometimes, individuals will simply need to train themselves. There are a number of websites, CDs, books and DVDs, and videos on the market that can make the task easier. These include:

- **PeachPit Press:** How-to computer books

- **MacAcademy:** Videos and CDs for both Macintosh and Windows software

- **LearnKey:** Self-paced training, including CDs and videos on office and systems applications

- **Datacal:** Datacal offers CDs and videos on common software programs

- **CDI Communications, Inc.:** Videos on network, office applications, and web design

Nonprofit boards and administrators are all too experienced with the "gung-ho" volunteer who enthusiastically takes on a sophisticated computer project and then finds himself or herself unable to finish it. Again and again it has been proven that the best computerization programs are those approached as shared responsibilities. The value of a group of reasonably computer-literate volunteers will always outweigh that of one guru, even though such a person can be very useful to an organization. He or she needs the solid backup of others who can carry out a project when the guru's attention turns to other interests.

People Investment First, Then Nuts and Bolts

A few months ago, I visited a small nonprofit that maintained a database of grant information on a ten-year-old computer. Over the years, the database had become priceless. It contained the cumulative experience of all the volunteers and staff members who had sought grants. It listed the names and phone numbers of key individuals, the gist of conversations with foundation representatives, and all sorts of vital information about the requirements and preferences of each funder. Even though the technology used to create the database was archaic, the database itself was one of the group's most precious resources.

Although the database had been carefully backed up over the years, there would soon be no working computers of that vintage on which it could be loaded. A vendor was being hired to migrate the database to a modern database program so that it could be used with new equipment. I use this example to illustrate that the value of technology is not in the computer equipment or the computer software, but in the opportunities they provide for human innovation. Again and again, the expertise that had been captured in the database became the basis for successful grant proposals. It is impossible to know which of those proposals would have been rejected without the database, but it is safe to say that the database was responsible for several hundred thousand dollars in revenue over that ten-year period. Once it is available on new equipment, the database will be easier to search and sort. Again, however, its value is the information that has been amassed and saved by dozens, even hundreds of individuals over the years. The really valuable resource is people, not computers.

Training Technical Support Staff

You may remember that in Chapter 3, the Anytown Arts Council hired Tom, a young technician, to take charge of its computer system. He was a personable, computer-literate young man who had recently graduated from high school and was attending classes at the local community college. It was not long before the Arts Council director and her board realized that paying a technician's salary did not ensure that their multiple computer problems were solved. Tom really did not understand how staff and volunteers used the computer system, primarily because no one told him. He treated the system as if it were his own personal equipment, since most of his experience consisted of working on his own personal computers.

Technicians Need Training, Too

Although Tom could cope well with the types of crises the Arts Council had formerly experienced, he created new ones. For example, the organization had grown rapidly and the number of staff and volunteers had multiplied several-fold. Since more and more information was being stored in the computer, nearly all these people needed some level of access to the data. When one poorly trained volunteer accidentally lost some records, Tom reacted by restricting everyone's computer privileges. When they logged in, they found that they could not get at the information that was vital to their work.

Since so many people needed to use the computers, it was essential that a large number of lower-end workstations be available for their use. Tom, however, spent most of his budget on powerful, high-end computers with no thought to the many older computers that were scheduled for replacement. Then it was discovered that the latest version of the database program would not run on the older computers. Funds had to be borrowed from other projects to meet the emergency and Tom's reputation, already shaky, descended still further.

Integrating Technical Support Staff

As you may remember, the Arts Council tech team wondered why Tom could not be more like Marcia, the young office assistant who merited an outstanding evaluation. Both were about the same age, and both had had little work experience. Yet Marcia caught on quickly and soon became a highly respected member of the group.

When the tech team gave the matter some thought, they realized that Marcia had spent several weeks in training. She was sent to every department to learn about their work. She attended many meetings that enabled her to understand the important issues that the nonprofit was grappling with. Marcia's supervisor knew exactly what she wanted Marcia to accomplish and presented her with clear objectives.

Why had not Tom received similar training? There were several reasons, but most boiled down to confusion on the part of his superiors about the nature of his job. Tom was the first technician who had ever been hired, and no one had really thought out his role. Yes, of course, he had a job description but what did it mean? Because the senior staff members who would supervise or interact with Tom felt insecure about their knowledge of technology, they expected that Tom would somehow know what to do when he arrived. They imagined a computer wiz who would magically know all the answers. Instead, the reality was a bright, inexperienced young man who needed just as much supervision and guidance as any other young, apprentice staff member.

Management Is the Key

The Pleasantville Association also grew rapidly, and like the Arts Council, experienced a number of growing pains with its computer applications. It, too, decided that it was time to hire someone to manage its computer system, but it was fortunate to have an experienced manager among its board members. Having been through the "technology wars," she knew that technicians were not mysterious beings from the planet ROM, but flesh-and-blood young people whose skills and work habits could be honed to meet the needs of the organization. It was this same board member who made many of the suggestions that were incorporated into the job description.

While interviews were still being conducted, senior staff members gathered to discuss the technician's job. What did they need from him and what would he need from them? Naturally, discussions began on an unrealistic plane. They needed Superman, and they had no idea what he might need from them. As they began to focus on the young people who came to interviews, they reluctantly conceded that these were not technology super heroes. Gradually, they began developing a training program similar to the one designed for Marcia. In the beginning, the new technician would make recommendations rather than decisions. Each recommendation would be discussed thoroughly with his supervisor.

Focusing on Communication

Both supervisor and technician need to learn to speak the other's language. At the Arts Council, Tom had found it useful to spout impressive jargon when he wanted something. Here at Pleasantville, the technician would need to learn to explain his needs in simple English. At the Arts Council, the supervisor had been chosen with little attention paid to her computer skills. The Pleasantville board member made it clear that it was not fair to ask a technician to report to someone who really had no idea what he was doing. Sophisticated computer skills are not necessary in a supervisor, but communication skills are. Communication will not take place if the supervisor is completely ignorant of technical terminology and recent innovations.

One reason that the supervisor needs to understand the basic technology needs of the organization is that he or she should be the one to control the technology budget. Decide in advance how much the technician can spend without supervisory approval. Make the sum large enough that a faulty CD drive or network card can be replaced when the need arises but new computers or other expensive items cannot be purchased without authorization. As the technician becomes more knowledgeable about the organization, this amount can be increased.

At the Arts Council, staff accused Tom of becoming the computer czar, imperiously deciding who might have what rights on the system. The new technician should not be the one to make such decisions. Of course, access decisions should be made in consultation with the technician, but all staff members and volunteers have a right to the computer support needed to do their jobs effectively. Only someone who understands the nature of the work and the goals of the organization should decide who has access to the system and who does not, or who gets a new computer and who must make do with an old one.

Technicians Are Staff Members, Too

Tom at the Arts Council felt isolated, rarely interacting with other staff members during the course of his day. During the training period, the new Pleasantville technician will spend at least half of every day talking with staff, attending meetings, serving on committees, and generally becoming an integral part of the organization. There is no way that a technician can be expected to understand the needs of other members of the group if they do not tell him. He will need to know that whenever possible, maintenance routines should be run at night. Only in an emergency should the system be taken down during the workday. If volunteers make fundraising phone calls in the evening, then the computer system should be available to them. Tom's own schedule may need to be adjusted for special projects such as a fundraising campaign or a teleconference.

Becoming Accustomed to the Work Environment

Inexperienced young people generally need help establishing good work habits. When the new technician arrives 15 minutes late his first week on the job, it needs to be explained that staff members are expected to be at work on time. Since he is supporting the work of so many other people, his lateness or absence will negatively impact their work. This can be explained in a conversational tone without coming on as a hard-nosed boss.

There will be times when schedule adjustments must be made, both for personal reasons and for the sake of the organization. These should be planned ahead and approved by the supervisor whenever possible. Do not allow a problem to go on for weeks before the technician is called on the carpet. By then, other staff members are complaining that the technician is getting special privileges and hostile work relationships are already developing.

Establishing Consistent Expectations

Once a nonprofit becomes established and hires several staff members, you will quickly discover that they all have somewhat different views of their rights and responsibilities. A supervisor may make a "command decision" in one situation and then reverse it in another. One staff member may be given permission to take time off when another is refused. Still another staff member is chastised for breaking a rule he did not know existed. The result can be both poor morale and poor productivity. As human beings, we are quick to react when we think we are being treated unfairly, and we find it harder to accept our lot when someone else gets an undeserved perk. The only way to send out the same message to everyone and to create consistent expectations is to put it in writing. It is, therefore, essential to develop a staff handbook or manual as soon as possible (see Exhibit 7.2). In fact, if you have a volunteer handbook, the staff manual can evolve from it. However, employees have many more legal rights than volunteers and so a staff handbook becomes a legal document, a kind of contract between employee and employer. It is, therefore, a good idea to ask an attorney or human resource professional to read over your handbook and alert you to any potential legal problems.

Working As a Team

As is becoming clear, a new technician should not be given more independence than other staff members. In the interviews discussed in the last chapter, the search committee asked questions intended to reveal the applicant's working style. Was he a loner or someone who sought out other opinions? Once on the job, this personality trait

EXHIBIT 7.2

Creating a Staff Handbook

Although the specific information included in a staff manual or handbook will vary with the unique characteristics of an organization, there are a number of sections that should be included in all of them. Here is a partial list of the most important points to be covered:

- Introduction (including history, mission, long-term goals, and values of the nonprofit)
- Performance expectations (both general and specific)
- Equal opportunity statement
- Pay and performance issues (when paychecks will arrive, and so forth)
- Promotions and wage increases
- Classification of employees (part-time, full-time, on-call)
- Salary advances, leaves without pay, overtime
- Rights of internal job applicants
- All types of leave, including sick, parental/maternity, military, funeral, personal, family, medical, and jury duty
- List of paid holidays
- Pension or profit-sharing plans
- Standards of conduct
- Sexual harassment
- Use of alcohol, drugs, and tobacco
- Preemployment screening
- Performance review
- Causes for which employees will be terminated, including criminal activity, insubordination, poor performance, dishonesty, absenteeism, security breaches, policy violations, health, and safety threats
- Grievance procedure

- General information like parking, organization chart, personal telephone calls
- Confidentiality statement
- Appropriate dress
- Work hours
- Workplace safety
- Copies of forms (sick leave, vacation, grievance filing, travel reimbursement, accident reporting)

Attorneys advise employers to include a disclaimer to the effect that employment can be terminated at any time for any reason. They suggest a statement like the following: "Our organization recognizes our employee's right to resign at any time for any reason; similarly, we may terminate any employee at any time, with or without cause." Attorneys also caution against using the term "probation" or "probationary period," since they may imply that employees are entitled to continued employment after the probationary period is over. It is a good idea to ask employees to sign a form acknowledging that they have been given a copy of the handbook and understand that they will be held responsible for its contents. The form should be placed in their personnel files.

becomes vitally important. If a technician has difficulty functioning as part of a team, he is going to be unhappy with the nonprofit environment. He is going to want to proceed on his own, making his own decisions, and implementing them with minimal input from his supervisor or other group members. This is not the kind of person you want working in this position.

In many cases, however, it is not the technician's fault but the fault of the supervisor who does not make these expectations clear. If the computer system has been particularly troublesome, the supervisor may believe that the technician's time is better spent remedying these problems. The real purpose of a training period, however, is to give the trainee a clear picture of what the job ought to be. Even if technical problems are urgent, it is essential that team spirit and team goals be instilled during this period.

Clarifying Reporting Lines

Nonprofits, in general, tend to be somewhat more informal than business organizations. They evolve from a group of committed volunteers, and both staff and volunteers continue to be motivated by that mission. Gradually, of course, structure is imposed on the organization. Committees are formed, chairpersons appointed, and reporting lines are clarified. Gradually, staff are hired and supervision responsibilities assigned. Nevertheless, the organization continues to have the feeling of a group of friends getting together to help their community.

This kind of informality may be difficult for a new technician to understand, and it may also be difficult for the group to understand the technician's role in the organization. For example, he will need a clearly identified supervisor. Because of his youth, inexperience, and lack of familiarity with the organization, he will need somewhat close supervision, at least in the beginning. However, if several group members feel compelled to take on this task, he will naturally become confused and dissatisfied. From time to time, every computer user will eventually need his help. How is he to understand just what his responsibilities are to each of them?

Learning Time Management Skills

It will be necessary for the technician to learn to balance solitary periods when he can really focus on computer problems with time for personal interaction. This balance is not learned instinctively, and it is important that the supervisor explain how it is done. Some organizations set up a schedule that limits the times when their technician is available to offer assistance. In a nonprofit where volunteers come and go, however, this may not work. Some set aside a time when the technician is not to be bothered except in a "life and death" emergency. Whatever solution is chosen, the technician should understand that helping staff and volunteers really is part of his job. It is not simply a distraction from his real work. His supervisor should make it clear in advance that group members will be asking questions and may not be able to continue their work until he provides answers.

Prioritizing our time is another skill that most of us learn only with experience. Since so many people and so many projects will be competing for the technician's time, it is a good idea to familiarize him with basic time management concepts. It is also important for your technician to understand your organizational priorities. In meetings and coaching sessions, keep reminding him of the "big picture" and help him understand that he has an important role in helping to achieve your mission.

Confidentiality

Young people sometimes have difficulty understanding why personal information should not be shared. At this point in his life, he has probably not experienced medical problems and may not understand why such records must be kept strictly confidential. He has been supported by his parents most of his life and may not understand the sense of humiliation people feel when their poverty or credit problems are revealed. He may receive requests for mailing lists or other information that seem perfectly legitimate and may respond without giving the matter a thought. Make it clear that all personal information stored in the computer system should be considered confidential unless he has been given specific permission to share it.

Summing It Up

Successful nonprofits have learned that training for their group members is one of their most important priorities. To use technology effectively, an organization must develop a corps of staff and volunteers who can be trusted to use computers effectively, understand the ethical issues they pose, and recognize the security risks they present to the organization. Even though technicians may arrive with all the requisite technical skills, they lack an in-depth knowledge of your organization, its mission, and its goals. This knowledge is even more important than knowing about USB ports or Bluetooth standards. Well-planned, comprehensive training brings everyone in the organization together, working toward common goals. Training provides a common framework into which the efforts of both staff and volunteers fit together to create a successful team effort.

CHAPTER 8

Supervising Technical Volunteers and Staff

After reading this chapter, you will be able to:

- Know the characteristics of a good supervisor.
- Supervise technical staff effectively.
- Identify performance problems and effectively coach technical staff members.
- Prepare for staffing emergencies.
- Reduce turnover among technical staff members.

Whether your technical support is provided by volunteers or paid employees, they will need thoughtful supervision and coaching if they are to be successful. Although recruiting a talented volunteer or hiring a skilled technician will point your organization in the right direction, do not assume that your work is done.

Supervising Volunteers

Many people are under the mistaken impression that volunteers **do not** need supervision. Because they donate their time to the organization, they may be viewed as free spirits. Of course, they are free to come and go as they like, but to be effective they must be fully integrated into the organization and its mission. This means that they must be assigned tasks that are well suited to their skills and interests. When volunteers are not guided toward productive endeavors, they may feel lost and ineffective. If they are allowed to create their own jobs, they may be working in directions that are counterproductive and which may ultimately interfere with the ability of the organization to accomplish its mission. Technical volunteers are different from others only in that they have certain unique and valuable skills.

When an organization is just getting started, it is almost entirely dependent on volunteers. Gradually, as it grows larger, a small staff of paid employees is hired. This transition can be a somewhat painful one and many organizations lose valuable supporters in the process. In the beginning, volunteers may do everything, performing every task required of them and some of their own making. A colleague of mine is fond of saying that volunteers are "self-propelled. Unless there is strong leadership, volunteers move in directions of their own choosing. However, what they may lack in organization and efficiency, they make up in enthusiasm and dedication. When paid staff arrive, they may view volunteers as annoying amateurs. Volunteers, on their part, may view the paid staff as lacking dedication or as servants to be ordered around.

Recognizing the Time Constraints of Volunteers

Whether laboring in a small nonprofit or a large one, volunteers are the backbone of the organization. They provide time, money, and dedication. When their work is effectively coordinated and supervised, they can make the difference between success and failure. Technical volunteers are among the most sought-after members of an organization because most other volunteers have skills that are nearly interchangeable with one another. Replacing their enthusiasm and commitment may be hard to do, but replacing their skills is not usually very difficult. On the other hand, replacing technical volunteers, who possess sophisticated and very marketable computer skills, can be a real challenge.

All volunteers, however, must put their personal and professional responsibilities first. Most of their time is devoted to making a living and being with their families. The organization usually plays only a small role in their daily lives. Well-meaning volunteers may begin a task and then find that they have no time to finish it. They may leave for an extended vacation with a computer program only partially installed. Managing volunteers is, therefore, quite different from managing paid staff, since the work of the organization cannot come to a halt while Marian winters in Florida. Time constraints and competing obligations must be taken into consideration whenever duties are assigned.

Remember that although they may be well meaning, some volunteers are actually harmful to your organization. You may depend on a volunteer to perform an important function only to find that promises are not kept and opportunities are missed. Volunteers may enthusiastically sign up for responsibilities without really understanding that they are taking on a real commitment. People with technology skills are among the most sought-after volunteers, and so they may be pulled in several directions at once.

Some volunteers may also lack the interpersonal skills to be successful. Occasionally, the work of a nonprofit is disrupted by a volunteer who repeatedly sows seeds of conflict among the group. Like the other unfortunate situations described above, the failure to effectively supervise volunteers is often at the root of the problem. Like paid staff, volunteers need to know their limits. They need to understand their role in the organization and their responsibilities to others. It is usually when volunteers find themselves in confusing, unstructured environments that they are tempted to take on authority that is not legitimately theirs.

Meeting Your Goals and Their Needs

Retaining talented technical volunteers who actively embrace your nonprofit's mission and work to achieve its goals is not easy. Their skills are in high demand, and without careful nurturing, volunteer relationships often atrophy. Some of the best may move on to other interests, while domineering and disruptive ones are given a free hand (see Exhibit 8.1). Here are some suggestions for making sure your volunteers enhance, rather than impede your organization:

- Consider your technical volunteers' needs and interests. Listen to what they have to say and show them respect. In too many organizations, highly trained volunteers are treated like incompetents who cannot be trusted with responsibility.

- Meet regularly with technical volunteers. Even if they do much of their work at home, do not let them work in isolation. It is very difficult to understand the needs of the organization without frequent contact with its members and leaders.

- Tactfully limit the projects your volunteers take on. Although it is important to take advantage of their talents and expertise, do not let their enthusiasm cloud your vision. If a project is not directly related to the mission of your organization and its goals, then it is best to steer your volunteer toward higher priority activities.

- Make sure that your volunteers really know how to perform their assigned jobs. Volunteers sometimes fail to understand how much skill is needed to perform a task, especially where computers are involved. They may offer to design a brochure with only a nodding acquaintance with desktop publishing or create a website after an hour-long website design workshop.

- Consider using volunteer contracts. Even though volunteers are not paid, it is a good idea to clearly spell out expectations, time commitments, and special responsibilities. A volunteer who offers to create a database may later remember only a commitment to help or advise. A contract can avoid such misunderstandings.

- Ask technical volunteers to research their proposed computer solutions and present their recommendations to supervisors or board members before plunging ahead. Make it clear that no individual "owns" the organization's computers. Without adequate supervision, technical volunteers may approach your organization's computer system just as they do their own home computers, for example, installing a program or reconfiguring an operating system without getting input from others.

- Be wary of any project that a volunteer begins without an ongoing commitment. Every technical responsibility involves some element of continuing oversight and maintenance. The hours that any volunteer can spend are limited. Be sure that those hours include not only innovating but also supporting new applications with written documentation, testing, and training.

- Understand what obligations your volunteer is burdening the organization with. If a volunteer moves away, how will his or her work be continued? Will you have to hire a computer professional to continue the project? If the project does not have a high priority, this could be a waste of scarce funds.

- When talking with technical volunteers, be specific about your needs. Make sure that any project is designed around your organization and its mission. Too often a volunteer writes a program, designs a website, or plans a database that can do everything but serve the need for which it was intended. If you were outsourcing the project to an independent contractor, you might write a Request for Proposals that describes in detail the results you are expecting. A similar but less formal written document may be a good way to clarify your needs to your technical volunteer.

- Create a project schedule and arrange regular meetings with volunteers to review the schedule. Establish interim deadlines and completion dates. It is inevitable that interruptions will occur, and your volunteer may not progress as speedily as anticipated. However, if several deadlines are missed, it is probably best to reassign or rethink the project.

- Try to find that special niche where each of your volunteers is comfortable and productive. This means matching the interests and skills of each volunteer with the tasks assigned. If you make a mistake, try again. Do not wait until a volunteer fails or loses interest in your organization. No nonprofit is so rich in human resources that it can treat volunteer burnout lightly.

EXHIBIT 8.1

When Your Volunteer Is a Pro

If you are fortunate enough to have a computer professional among your volunteers, count yourself blessed. However, volunteers naturally must put personal and professional responsibilities above their commitment to your organization. In addition, they may lose interest if they are not given satisfying assignments. Here are some ideas for keeping technical volunteers happy and productive:

- Do not throw everything at your technical volunteers at once. Although computer professionals may have plenty of enthusiasm, their time is limited.

- Define your basic needs before you enlist help from professionals. Remain open to new ideas but do not get sidetracked.

- Work together with your computer professional to create a plan of action. Develop a manageable set of tasks.

- Use computer professionals to help with training whenever possible. Leverage their time by sharing their knowledge and solicit their help as one-on-one trainers. Do not assume, however, that simply knowing about computers means that they will be effective teachers.

- Ask your web professional to create a simple website that does not require frequent updating. It's not usually a good idea to entrust a website to one person unless it functions like a brochure and doesn't become an embarrassment if it's left unchanged.

- Even better, ask him or her to coordinate the planning of the website and train a small group of members to design and maintain it.

- Ask your computer professional to set up a small local area network and train other volunteers to manage it.

- Make your computer professional a hardware and/or software troubleshooter. Be specific about what needs fixing. Volunteer professionals should refrain from making changes in the system without being requested to do so. Ask them to document their work in writing.

- Ask your volunteer professional to evaluate donated equipment and make recommendations about upgrading your existing equipment.

Senior Volunteers

Seniors make up the core of many volunteer groups. They naturally have more time available than younger volunteers who must fit in their volunteer hours between pressing work responsibilities and the needs of their young families. Many seniors, however, have not had the opportunity to learn computer skills on the job. They may have found themselves at a disadvantage in the workplace where younger colleagues had access to computers and computer training even in elementary school. Such experiences may result in some seniors developing a negative attitude toward technology or hiding their ignorance behind assertions that they can do a job better without the aid of a computer. If your nonprofit wants to attract seniors and fully integrate them into the work of the organization, computer training should play a large role in your planning.

It is far better to assume that everyone will need extensive training and support than to humiliate senior volunteers who may find themselves taking a back seat to younger group members. Seniors may ultimately become some of your most productive volunteers. Most of the uses to which nonprofits put their computers involve repetitive tasks. In the long run, the ability to input numbers and other information accurately can be far more important than more sophisticated computer skills. As long as very basic computer literacy is mastered, the volunteer who is good with details may be more valuable than the computer whiz who bores easily and makes mistakes. Part of the traditional conflict between paid staff and volunteers may have to do with their attitudes towards computer use. Younger staff may complain bitterly about volunteer ineptitude without ever accepting responsibility for mentoring or training.

Short-Term Memory Limitations

Easy-to-understand written materials are essential when training senior volunteers and later when they are becoming familiar with their computer responsibilities. Even when they perform the same duties every day, short-term memory problems may destroy their self-confidence and make them reluctant to use computers. Keeping an easy-to-understand, written manual of computer procedures nearby will reduce their anxiety. Occasionally, a senior volunteer simply cannot perform computer tasks

Senior Volunteers

Senior volunteers can be one of your best sources of technical help. For more information about using senior volunteers effectively, contact:

CyberSeniors
www.cyberseniors.org
One Monument Way, Portland, Maine 04101
info@cyberseniors.org

Environmental Alliance for Senior Involvement
www.easi.org/index2.html
8733 Old Dumfries Rd., Catlett, VA 22019
easi@easi.org

Green Thumb
www.greenthumb.org
2000 N 14th Street, Suite 800, Arlington, VA 22201

National Council on the Aging
www.ncoa.org
409 Third Street SW, Washington, DC 20024
info@ncoa.org

National Retiree Volunteer Coalition
www.nrvc.org
1660 Duke Street, Alexandria, VA 22314
voa@voa.org

SeniorNet
www.seniornet.org
121 Second Street, 7th Floor, San Francisco, CA 94105
Phone: (415) 495-4990, Fax: (415) 495-3999

Seniors Community on MSN
http://communities.msn.com/seniors

Senior Corps - RSVP Program
www.cns.gov/senior

Service Corps Of Retired Executives (SCORE)
www.score.org

reliably even after extensive training. Such a volunteer may continue to interrupt staff and other volunteers with questions and crises long after others have become competent computer users. There comes a point when a supervisor must admit that it is unlikely that the volunteer will ever master basic computer skills and must tactfully redirect the volunteer's efforts. It is important, however, that such a decision be based on observable behavior and not preconceived prejudices about older people.

Virtual Volunteers

Technology makes it possible to make use of the expertise of volunteers who may never be able to attend meetings or work on your premises. A virtual volunteer might be a local mother with young children who has plenty of time to work at home but rarely gets out of the house. Conversely, a virtual volunteer might live a thousand miles away, but believe passionately in the work of your organization. There are many things they can do from their home base, even linking their computers into your computer network as part of a wide area network (WAN). In fact, a distant volunteer is often sought out to expand the work of your organization. Distant volunteers might even start a new branch or chapter. Supervising virtual volunteers, however, is more difficult than supervising traditional on-site volunteers. There are many more opportunities for misunderstandings to arise and it is more difficult to both supervise and evaluate their work.

Who Becomes a Virtual Volunteer?

A virtual volunteer may be a member of your organization whose responsibilities, like the care of an older parent or young child, make it difficult to leave home. Another volunteer may live thousands of miles away, participating in the organization entirely via technology. When virtual volunteers can occasionally meet with their supervisors face to face and interact with other members, they can gather a much clearer idea of your mission and goals. However, this is not always possible. Although volunteers who live in other parts of the country may become involved because of a shared commitment, they can easily acquire an unrealistic picture of how your organization functions. It is only with considerable personal support and encouragement that such volunteers can be effective.

Are You Ready for Virtual Volunteers?

Before you decide to recruit virtual volunteers, however, take a good look at your organization and decide whether you are ready to take the step. Here are some questions to ask:

- Have you been successful in recruiting traditional, face-to-face volunteers?

- Are volunteers screened to identify their interests, talents, and challenges?

- Is there a system in place for making assignments, managing work-flow, evaluating performance, and getting feedback?

- Are volunteers valued and respected in your organizational culture?

- Do staff and volunteers fully understand your organization's mission and work together as a team?

- Is there a system in place to communicate easily and effectively with volunteers without the need for face-to-face contact? Are schedules, news, and other information regularly sent out to everyone via email? Do volunteers regularly share information with one another? If virtual volunteers are dependent on email, then they will be cut out of the communication loop by anyone who is unwilling or unable to communicate in this way.

- Is one person responsible for managing volunteers? If so, is this person knowledgeable about human resource issues? Does he or she inspire enthusiasm? Does he or she have access to a computer and an email account during work hours?

- Is the volunteer supervisor prepared to manage virtual volunteers? Remember that virtual volunteers should be supervised and support-ed like any other volunteer. They should feel as if they are part of the group, receive training and encouragement, communicate with their supervisors and other volunteers regularly, and identify enthusiasti-cally with the organization.

TIPS & TECHNIQUES CONTINUED

- Do you include a box for email address on your volunteer application? Are you ready to recruit virtual volunteers via email?

- Are your volunteer coordinator and others who work regularly with volunteers committed to reading and responding to email within 48 hours? Virtual volunteers need to have their questions answered quickly if they are to be effective.

 TIPS & TECHNIQUES

Job Descriptions for Virtual Volunteers

Considering that virtual volunteers do most of their work offsite (home base may be in another state or even another country), here are some jobs that can be designed to minimize face-to-face interaction:

- Providing technical assistance. This may require special software to allow them to interact fully with your computer system.

- Conducting grant-seeking research, using their own personal computers.

- Editing your organization's newsletter. This requires the same software used by staff and traditional volunteers for exchanging articles and images.

- Providing legislation alerts based on information gathered online.

- Providing professional consulting expertise on human resource, accounting, or legal issues.

- Writing speeches and/or creating PowerPoint presentations.

- Setting up a video conferencing event.

- Using a CAD program to draw a floor plan or preliminary architectural design.

continued on next page

TIPS & TECHNIQUES CONTINUED

- Posting information on appropriate Internet discussion lists and newsgroups.

- Translating documents written in another language or being accessible by telephone when a client does not speak English.

- Proofreading or copyediting text for a website and printed publications.

- Designing a logo for the organization or illustrating a brochure.

- Planning a marketing campaign.

- Registering your website home page and other pages with online search engines.

- Designing a database system.

- Managing other virtual volunteers.

Supervising Technical Volunteers

It is not uncommon for supervisors, after their first few discussions with new technical volunteers, during which they understood little, to feel they are out of their depth. The amateur or professional technician sounds as if he knows what he's talking about, and so supervisors are reluctant to interfere and possibly make fools of themselves. Such an attitude is usually the beginning of an unsuccessful relationship. A new volunteer technician must come to understand the goals and expectations of the organization. To be productive, he or she must become an integral part of the staff and of its work. This is not a technical problem but a "people" problem similar to others that supervisors routinely face. We must not lose sight of the fact that technical volunteers are there to support others and give them the tools that will help them achieve their goals.

Taking Supervision Seriously

Technical support, however, is provided by a wide variety of individuals, especially in smaller nonprofits, and so supervision can be a complex task. As we have discussed, most organizations begin with volunteers taking responsibility for technology. The organization may progress through a stage when the job description of someone on the small staff includes computer maintenance responsibilities. It is only when the organization grows a little larger and somewhat more stable that it is usually in a position to hire a technical staff member. Finally, activities may expand to the point that a small department is needed to manage technology. Let us begin our discussion of supervision at the lowest support level and progress gradually to larger organizations.

Supervising volunteers can be a challenge. After all, they are contributing their time because they believe in the work of the organization. They are, in a sense, making a gift of their time, and a supervisor naturally feels unwilling to look a gift horse in the mouth. When volunteers have strong feelings about what should and should not be done, it can become difficult to alter their direction or convince them to work as part of a team.

Technology Is a Team Responsibility

Some volunteers may claim ownership of a particular function like technology and erect a figurative fence around their territory. When a group is just starting out and volunteers can easily be fitted into a living room, you may feel fortunate if you can find just one person who can be placed in charge of technology. If that person is reasonably diligent and knowledgeable, the larger group may forget about technology altogether until a crisis arises. Sometimes, of course, this scenario is all but inevitable but it is one that will almost always get the organization off to a poor start.

We have already discussed the need for a tech team and a technology plan. This small group should be appointed as early as possible since the concept of team responsibility is critical to future success. Even if your tech team consists of only two or three members it is a start. In addition to a focus on teamwork, it is important for the individuals involved in technology to establish a reporting relationship, probably with the board of directors. Most of us who have spent much of our lives working or volunteering in nonprofits are aware that personalities play an extraordinary role in determining success or failure. People become volunteers to meet a variety of personal needs. When one has a strong need for power, the result can be highly destructive. It must be clear from the beginning that there will be no empires. No individual will be permitted to seize turf as his or her own. A responsibility like technology must be shared and decisions must be subject to review by others.

Appropriate Computer Use

When a number of volunteers use computers on a regular basis, many issues arise that require discussion and ultimately decisions. Volunteers who have little experience with computers may fail to understand the harm that can be done when they are misused. Once computers become part of the everyday work experience of volunteers, it is essential to develop a policy that covers such issues as privacy, piracy, and other matters that may have major legal implications for the organization (see Exhibit 8.2).

Conscripted Technical Volunteers

Since one of the goals of this book is to describe nonprofits and their needs as realistically as possible, it may be time to talk about "conscripted husbands." It is not unusual in nonprofits that attract largely women to their ranks for group members to draft their husbands to perform tasks that they are unable to do themselves. Sometimes this means performing manual labor like moving furniture, but it can also mean assuming computer responsibilities. Of course, husbands may draft their wives as well. Draftees should never be underestimated, since they help keep so many nonprofits afloat. Nevertheless, a draftee does not share the same allegiance to the organization as the other volunteers, and this must be recognized when assigning responsibilities. Draftees are at their best when sharing information with others. As consulting members of the tech team, they excel. As advisors to search committees hiring technical staff, they can also perform an invaluable service. However, draftees should not be made solely responsible for a computer system, and they should not take on computer responsibilities that are not fully understood by other group members. Some draftees eventually get so interested in their volunteer assignments that they become permanent members of the group, but it is unfair to count on them. They are doing a favor for both their spouse and the organization, and they cannot be expected to continue doing favors indefinitely.

EXHIBIT 8.2

Developing a Computer Use Policy for Staff and Volunteers

Every nonprofit that uses computers on a regular basis should develop a Computer Use Policy covering the basic legal and ethical issues that staff and volunteers may encounter. Although policies will differ from one organization to another, the following are some basic components of a good policy:

- Rules concerning acceptable use of computer equipment

- Client and donor privacy violations

- Definition of and prohibition against software piracy

- Limitations on personal email (email, voice mail, and other electronic communications may be monitored)

- Inappropriate or prohibited email, including inflammatory, defamatory, impolite, discriminatory, or pornographic messages

- Use of the organization's equipment for personal activities

- Prohibited activities like using the nonprofit's systems to look for another job, knowingly opening a virus, or sending or forwarding chain letters

- Unacceptable behavior including representing personal views as those of the nonprofit (for example, in Letters to the Editor)

- Consequences of violating the computer use policy

- Consequences of disseminating harassing or offensive materials, knowingly accessing pornographic or other blatantly offensive content, or soliciting or advertising unrelated to the nonprofit

- Statement prohibiting the copying of licensed software

- Clarification concerning staff and volunteers authorized to install software programs, whether they are purchased programs or downloaded files

Evolving Technical Responsibilities

Sometimes, technology responsibilities evolve without conscious planning. A volunteer uses his or her own computer to maintain financial records or publish a newsletter. As quickly as possible, these computer applications should be transferred to group-owned computers and housed in the group's facility. Otherwise, these volunteers can inadvertently hold their organizations hostage. If they decide they are unappreciated or if they choose to depart for some other reason, they can leave the organization incapable of carrying on with these projects. Essential information like financial records can also disappear.

 TIPS & TECHNIQUES

Distributing Technical Responsibilities

If technology responsibilities have not yet been assigned in your organization, you have the opportunity to do it right. Job descriptions can clarify responsibilities and reporting lines. However, if you have acquired a technical "lone ranger" who does not readily share information or authority, you may have a problem. You will need to decide whether the situation is a tolerable one or a tinderbox that may soon ignite and do a lot of damage. Give some thought to whether this situation can really be allowed to continue. It may help to answer the following questions:

- Is one person in your organization making all major technology decisions?

- Does your technology "guru" make regular reports to the board and/or the membership about what he or she is doing?

- Does this person readily accept suggestions from the board and from other members?

- Are computerization projects going forward in what seems to be an effective fashion? In other words, does it appear that computers are helping the membership to do its work?

Even at such an early stage, supervision of volunteers, who have computer-related duties, is important. However, the task must be approached with tact and discretion. It often happens that one individual is given the impression that he or she has a free hand with technology. This is especially common when other group members are ignorant of the role that computers will eventually play in their organization. If a volunteer is first told that he or she is in charge of computers and then informed of multiple requirements and restrictions, you can readily understand the resulting anger.

Reassigning Technical Responsibilities

This list is intended to help you decide whether your situation is acceptable for the time being or in immediate need of reorganization. The problems inherent in entrusting technology to one individual are too numerous to allow the situation to long continue. However, if things are going along reasonably well, you may want to make changes gradually or wait until your own "lone ranger" decides voluntarily to give up the role. He or she may move away or simply find it impossible to continue to devote so much time to this volunteer job. It would be well for the board to evaluate the situation and make some tentative decisions. Is it possible to loosen the technology volunteer's grip on his or her territory without creating excessive conflict?

If you decide that your technical guru is providing a valuable service and is at least somewhat open to working with other members of the organization, it may be possible to redistribute technical responsibilities gradually. The following are some ways to broaden responsibility:

- Make sure that your technology plan is in place and discussed regularly. Your technology guru should be a participant in the development of the plan but should function more as a facilitator than a decision maker.

- Ask your technology volunteer to make regular progress reports at board meetings.

- Schedule regular meetings between the technology volunteer and group members to identify their needs and find ways in which technology can support their work.

- Ask your guru to fully train another volunteer to serve as his or her back-up. When the guru is unavailable, the backup volunteer should be able to provide technical assistance and deal with emergencies.

Firing Your Guru

If, however, the iron grip of the technology volunteer is impeding technology planning and implementation, thus affecting the organization's effectiveness, it may be time to "fire" your guru. This is always a painful experience and boards often try to find other positions within the organization where the technical volunteer can presumably do less damage. This is the technique usually referred to as "kicking someone upstairs." It sometimes works but if you are dealing with a highly territorial personality, you must be prepared to lose a talented volunteer.

Once the board is in a position to reorganize the technology program and is able to appoint new technology volunteers, make expectations clear from the beginning. Outline the process for making decisions. Most important, provide supervisory oversight for these new volunteers. This can be done without being bossy or appearing to be constantly looking over their shoulders. When supervising these newly appointed technical volunteers, the focus must be on communication. Although everyone is, in a sense, equal, no one can work in isolation. Therefore, the most important role of the supervisor is serving as an information conduit, keeping technical volunteers abreast of new developments and communicating technical needs to the nonprofit's decision makers.

Supervising Technical Staff Members

If all is going well and the organization is growing, a small staff will gradually begin to take over some of the functions that have been performed by volunteers. Changes in technology roles tend to occur as the workload increases. Some administrators say that at the point when maintaining computer equipment, installing software, and troubleshooting computer-related problems require 10 hours a week or more, a volunteer-driven technology program tends to flounder.

Sometimes the answer is to recruit more technology volunteers. However, this can be cumbersome and so gradually responsibility is transferred to staff members. For example, the tech team may initially become concerned that there will not be enough volunteers available during the summer months. If some are planning extended vacations, a staff member may be asked to fill in, performing routine maintenance tasks. Bookkeeping may become part of an administrative assistant position and gradually technology ceases to be a volunteer responsibility.

Differences between Technical Volunteers and Technical Staff

While a technical volunteer may have no other responsibilities than tending to the computer system, a staff member in a small organization usually has a wide variety of responsibilities. This new phase is accompanied by new supervisory issues. In one sense, it is easier to supervise a staff position. Although one hopes that a staff member will feel a personal commitment to the organization, he or she is also working to earn a salary. It is, therefore, somewhat easier to assign responsibilities and require that they be performed efficiently.

However, a staff member is, in a sense, an outsider and may view the organization very differently from group members who became involved because of a sense of personal commitment. Newly arrived staff members will be unable to establish priorities or function effectively without support from the nonprofit's insiders. Perhaps the most important responsibility of the supervisor is, therefore, to educate the staff member about the organization's goals and clarify the relationship that exists between technology development and mission. Otherwise, a staff member might be spending his or her time in ways that will have little impact on the nonprofit's success.

Because technology usually begins as a volunteer responsibility, a staff member may not view it as real work. In many nonprofits, there tends to be an unfortunate belief among staff members that the work of volunteers is just fluff. To take this misconception one step further, there may be an unspoken assumption that the real work of the organization is done by its staff, and volunteers are there to be humored. As technology responsibilities are transferred to staff, they too can be viewed as fluff.

If the supervisor does not view technical responsibilities as having a high priority, then a staff member will have further reason to take them lightly. For this reason, it is vital that the tech team occupy a position of respect in the organization and that it remain active. Communication between staff and tech team is essential. Whether technical responsibilities are performed by staff or by volunteers should not affect the tech team's central role. Unless they continue to provide guidance in technical matters, technology may suffer when responsibilities are taken over by staff. However, as the nonprofit acquires a paid staff, one or more staff members should become tech team members.

Developing Good Managers

The ability to manage the work of other people is both a gift and a learned skill. Some individuals seem to have a natural aptitude but no one is born with the skills that are needed to become a good supervisor. Such expertise must be learned. Managing nonprofits is similar in many ways to managing business organizations. Although the goals of the organizations are different, interpersonal interactions are quite similar. Therefore, it is very helpful for supervisors to become familiar with the discipline of business management.

This is a field of study that has developed in recent years and has provided many valuable insights into managing both resources and people. Even though the word "nonprofit" may not appear in your local community college's catalog of classes, you will discover a variety of valuable courses in the business management curriculum. New supervisors might be encouraged to take one or more of these courses to improve their skills. College faculty may also be available to facilitate management workshops for all supervisory staff and volunteers. If neither of these options is appropriate, a wealth of insightful literature is available at your local public library. Well-known authors like Peter Drucker have written literally millions of words on management theory and practice that can be both entertaining and enlightening.

The Nature of Computer Responsibilities

Like all other staff members, the people assigned technology responsibilities must develop good work habits. Because computer maintenance may be only one of

LEARN MORE ABOUT

Management Theory and Practice

- Investigate the Management Center at www.tmcenter.org.

- Take a look at the Management Assistance Program for nonprofits at www.mapnp.org.

- Also check out the Nonprofit and Public Management Center of the University of Michigan at www.umich.edu/~nonproft/

- Visit the Free Management Library (www.managementhelp.org/topics. htm) to discover a complete library of resources for nonprofit *and* for-profit businesses.

- Search the Database of Nonprofit Management Education Programs at http://tltc.shu.edu/npo.

- Discover the "Tools" section on the Idealist site at www.idealist.org/tools.html.

several responsibilities, work must be scheduled efficiently and less enjoyable tasks cannot be left on the back burner while pleasanter ones get attention.

Computer crises tend to occur when routine maintenance gets behind; Windows updates are not installed; hard drives are not scanned for viruses. Everyone likes certain aspects of a job more than others. It requires maturity and self-discipline to allocate one's time, based on the needs of the organization rather than personal preference. This means that a staff member needs to understand that technology is a real part of his or her job. To make this clearer, include it specifically in the job description. Supervisory conferences can also serve to emphasize that technology is not a small extra duty that can wait for a time when nothing else of importance is pending. The staff member's evaluation should give as much weight to technology as to other responsibilities.

Staff Members with Multiple Responsibilities

A staff member may first be hired to perform various duties unrelated to technology. Then, in time, computer responsibilities are gradually added. When this staff member leaves the organization and a new person is being sought for the position, new problems arise. Administrators and search committees may wonder which applicant will be the best fit for the job. After all, the qualifications needed to perform secretarial duties or maintain financial records are different from those required to manage a computer system. Almost no one possesses all these talents in equal amounts.

Maybe one applicant has superior office management skills; another is better with computers. Which should be chosen? Possibly, the most important determinant in making the decision is personal fit. How will this applicant work with other group members? If the applicant has some technical aptitude and has a good working relationship with the rest of the group, the foundation will be laid for success. Is he or she able to make good decisions? This is especially important in a staff position that may involve conflicting demands. Which task comes first and which can wait?

In addition, there needs to be some indication that the applicant has the potential to be successful at all the responsibilities listed in the job description. Specific skills can be acquired later, but aptitudes should be there right from the start. An applicant who has never been interested enough in computers to progress beyond email will not suddenly discover a knack for technology. A technically oriented individual who cannot spell or produce a grammatically correct sentence probably does not have the potential to succeed in a position that requires verbal skills. Finally, a history of successful work experiences can tip the balance toward one applicant or another.

Assigning Supervisory Responsibilities

As a young nonprofit is making the transition from an all-volunteer organization to one that includes both volunteers and paid staff, supervisory responsibilities are often nebulous. An axiom frequently found in management texts states that each staff member should have only one supervisor. Imagine a group that has only recently acquired a paid director. Since board members and other leaders are accustomed to speaking their minds freely, they will do so to the new director. Are these instructions or merely opinions? It is important that the board give a lot of thought not only to responsibilities, but also to authority and reporting lines. Once these decisions have been made, board members must abide by them.

The director usually reports to the board. Accustomed to doing much of the director's job themselves, some boards may authorize their directors to make certain decisions and then overrule them. This not only increases the board's workload but also interferes with the ability of the director to do the job. Technology decision making is especially vulnerable to such conflicts since computer issues require considerable research and investigation. When repeatedly thwarted, directors will either seek new employment or mentally step away from responsibility. In other words, directors might say something like this to themselves: "I'm really not in charge here. If I cannot fix problems without interference from the board, why should I waste my energy trying? If they want to make the decisions, let them." The result is an organization in which no one really accepts responsibility. When something goes wrong, everyone points fingers at everyone else.

Enlarging the Staff

When a second staff member is hired, director and board usually work together to create a job description. The job description should state that the person occupying the new position will report to the director. Board members usually understand the wisdom of this decision but may have difficulty implementing it. Let's assume that a small nonprofit has a board, a tech team, and a director. They have just hired a new administrative assistant who has several technology responsibilities in her job description. All of these people quite naturally have an interest in the way the administrative assistant performs her job. This means that possibly 10 people might be tempted to give her instructions.

Establishing Lines of Authority

Considering the nature of the work and the low salaries that most nonprofits pay, the applicants for such positions may perform at or slightly above entry level. They may be young people with limited experience and may never have held a full-time job or worked in an office. To be effective, they will need considerable training and a lot of guidance from their supervisors. Until they are fully trained and have some familiarity with their organizations, they are not ready to make independent decisions.

Now imagine a board member giving such a staff member instructions and a tech team member insisting that he or she immediately perform some other task. The director, the actual supervisor, has already planned their day so the inexperienced staff member must try to make sense of three conflicting demands. It just does not work. Everyone, especially the newly arrived staff member, will end up feeling angry and frustrated and dissatisfied.

Going through Channels

When members of the organization need the services of a staff member, they must accustom themselves to channeling their requests through the supervisor. This does not mean that a volunteer cannot call Betty to get a phone number or ask a brief question. It does mean, however, that the supervisor, in most cases the director, must be the one who makes decisions about the staff member's duties and priorities. When evaluation time comes around, supervisors must be able to hold staff members accountable for the work assigned.

When goals are not met and responsibilities are forgotten, is the staff member to blame or is the real problem multiple, conflicting expectations? You can hardly blame a staff member for taking advantage of such a situation. If administrative assistant Betty does not like a job or a decision, maybe board member Sandra will agree. "But Sandra told me to" becomes an excuse to which there is no response. Everybody loses in such a scenario, but the biggest loser is the nonprofit.

Coping with Disruptive Power Seekers

Occasionally, it is just one power-seeking individual, usually a board member, who takes command. He or she is able to acquire power because other board members are unwilling to get involved. In every organization, there are board and committee members who enjoy the social aspect of their assignments but who do not have the time or the sense of commitment required. In such situations, it is easy for power seekers to effectively supervise staff, and make major decisions, thus supplanting the nonprofit's organizational structure and substituting personal goals for mission.

If these individuals are not interested in technology, they may withhold needed funds. If they view themselves as authorities, they may ignore the technology plan and completely redirect the technology program. Such individuals exert a negative impact on every aspect of an organization, but technology is especially vulnerable. Lazy decision makers may be unwilling to make an effort to understand technology issues. Rather than reveal their ignorance, they may agree to whatever is proposed. Successful organizations have unambiguous, written guidelines that clarify reporting lines and decision-making authority. They also have dedicated leaders who accept their responsibilities and actively discourage power seekers.

Setting Work Schedules

While some group members seek power, others use a nonprofit to wile away a few free hours. Small volunteer-dominated nonprofits have a hard time pinning their members down to a regular work schedule. Once they commit themselves to providing a service, however, regular schedules become essential. While it may not be catastrophic if someone fails to attend a meeting, a failure to open the food pantry or meet with a client must be taken seriously. Similarly, failure to renew the antivirus program cannot be viewed as a minor omission. Most organizations have some members who view their participation as a series of social outings, opportunities to meet with friends, and maybe do a little work.

Although social interactions help to make volunteer work more enjoyable, they cannot be the main reason for involvement. Peer pressure placed on forgetful volunteers can help instill good work habits, but if this does not work, they need to be replaced with more reliable workers. There are always roles in nonprofits for less committed volunteers, but there must be a core who arrive on time, do the work assigned, and do not allow their busy social calendars to interfere with their work.

As an organization begins hiring paid staff, it becomes somewhat easier to demand regular work habits. Work schedules can be assigned but in actual practice, it may be difficult to transform an informal organization of volunteers into a professional one in which staff and volunteers work set schedules, Susan will always need to leave early on Thursdays to take her son to his violin lesson, and others will have similar personal errands. A nonprofit organization does not change overnight, and it is important that, as an employer, it try accommodate the needs of its members.

Implementing Flextime Fairly and Effectively

In recent years, many employees have been offered the opportunity to adjust their work schedules to meet their personal needs. Called "flextime," this practice provides time for personal business and family responsibilities, but the time is always made up. For flextime to be successful, these personal plans must be made in advance and incorporated into work schedules. Only in a genuine emergency should staff members be able to come and go without advance planning. This means getting approval from their supervisors and letting other staff members and volunteers know when they will not be available. Such notification can be done by email or even on a bulletin board that everyone checks when they arrive at work. Of course, volunteers cannot be held to quite the same punctuality standards as paid staff, but their schedule changes can create just as many problems. Volunteers might post their schedules on a bulletin board like the one above but they should do so at least once a week, not simply post it once and forget it.

Limiting Pager Use

The discussion of work schedules brings up another issue that can have a big impact on staff morale. It is the practice in some nonprofits of asking staff members and/or volunteers to carry pagers, even when they are off-duty. Medical and counseling organizations usually know how to use pagers in such a way that they are not unduly intrusive. Certain individuals are designated as being on-call nights and weekends to respond to emergencies. A roster is made up and everyone qualified to respond to calls takes a turn carrying the pager. The only problem is getting them to remember to pick up the pager for their assignments. The practice of carrying pagers, however, has been spreading rapidly and pagers are beginning to intrude into the personal lives of many nonprofit staff members.

There is an enormous difference between a suicidal client being able to call a counselor and a computer-challenged volunteer being able to interrupt the home life of a technician. Yet it is not uncommon for technical staff to be asked to carry pagers. For example, the pager may be purchased for the phon-a-thon. Since staff and volunteers will be making phone calls to solicit donations outside normal working

IN THE REAL WORLD

Empowering Staff and Volunteers to Solve Their Own Problems

The following is a copy of a card that one nonprofit distributes to its staff and volunteers. Copies of the card are often found taped to computer monitors, and one volunteer said she wishes she could tape it to her brain. It is an example of the many ways in which even inexperienced staff and volunteers can resolve some of their own crises without constantly running to the technician for help.

What to Do If Your Computer Freezes

Try to close the program by pressing Alt + F4.

If this doesn't work, press Ctrl + Alt + Delete all at the same time.

If this works, a box will appear. Choose "End Task."

If this doesn't work, close the program, and then press Ctrl + Alt + Delete again. When a box appears, click on the "Users" tab at the top of the box. Click on "Logoff."

If this doesn't take you to another screen, click "Shut Down" on the menu at the top of the box.

If you don't see a box (if you pressed Ctrl + Alt + Delete and nothing happened) press Ctrl + Alt + Delete again. You may have to do this twice but it should shut down the computer.

When the computer shuts down, wait 30 seconds and then press the power button to turn the computer on again.

If Ctrl + Alt + Delete doesn't work, try the Power button. Hold down the power button on the front of the computer for 5 seconds. After the computer shuts down, wait 30 seconds before turning it back on.

If this does not work, flip the switch on the surge protector box. This will work!

hours, they need to be assured that the computer system will not fail them. The staff member with technical responsibilities agrees to remain available in case an emergency occurs. Then perhaps he is asked to carry the pager during his lunch hour. Since even small computer crises can bring some jobs to a standstill, the technician is gradually asked to carry the pager more and more frequently. Although an administrative assistant may occasionally be asked to do the same, it is more often the technical staff whose privacy is invaded on a regular basis. Although a young man or woman, unencumbered by domestic concerns, may initially feel that being on-call carries with it a sense of importance, you can be quite sure that he or she will soon tire of it. He or she will quickly find another job at which he or she can call his or her life his or her own.

It is certainly true that as an organization becomes more dependent on computers, it becomes more dependent on support staff. However, this does not mean that they have any obligation to sacrifice their personal lives. Everyone who uses a computer should be able to cope with common crises. What do you do when the network goes down? How can you retrieve records that have seemingly disappeared into the ether? It is the technician's responsibility to prepare staff and volunteers to handle such emergencies but not to be always available to deal with them personally. Training workshops may be useful, but it must also be recognized that some problems will simply have to wait until the next day when the staff member is available.

Supervising Technicians

As an organization grows, it hires additional staff and expands its computer capabilities. Eventually, it is necessary to hire someone who possesses specialized computer expertise and whose responsibilities are almost exclusively focused on managing the computer system. In the last chapters, we discussed hiring and training technical staff. Once hired and trained, technical staff must be fully integrated into their organization, since they will play an important role in achieving its goals. Technical support staff must be supervised and evaluated just as other staff are supervised and evaluated. However, their relationship with their supervisor is somewhat different. Technicians usually possess highly specialized skills but little experience. Supervisors may have lots of experience but almost no technical skills.

Young Technicians: Long on Skills, Short on Experience

Unlike other positions in which skill and experience usually go together, technical positions place an unusual burden on the supervisor. Since nonprofit salaries are not commensurate with those in the computer industry, it is likely that you have hired a young man who will need a few years experience under his belt to command a higher wage. On one hand, the technician has acquired proficiencies and speaks a language that the supervisor may not understand. On the other hand, the supervisor understands the needs of the organization far better than the inexperienced technician. Together, they have what it takes to build a successful technology program but both must learn to communicate with one another.

If computer projects are to reap rewards for the organization, they must be the result of a team effort. Supervisor and technician must share their knowledge, both becoming teachers and both accepting the role of learners. Of course, all good supervisors know that there is much to be learned from their subordinates, but the technician's combination of knowledge and ignorance is unique. How, the supervisor may wonder, can this young man who cannot even remember to set his alarm clock be trusted to manage equipment valued at thousands of dollars? Of course, nonprofits sometimes hire mature technicians, but bridging the generation gap is often the real key to successful supervision.

Introducing Technical Staff to Your World

Since your group did such a good job of selecting a qualified applicant and providing thorough training, let's assume that your young technician has the skills, intelligence, and other personal attributes needed. Such a person is entitled to be treated with respect. Youth is not an acceptable reason to dismiss the opinions and judgment of any staff member.

When your new technician arrives, he will want to talk about your computer system, assessing its strengths and weaknesses. It would work better, he tells you, if he changed this and purchased that. Of course, such concerns are important, but it is essential to shift the focus of discussion, especially in those first few weeks, away

TIPS & TECHNIQUES

The Committed Technician

Like every volunteer and staff member, your technician will enjoy his job more and possibly remain on the job longer if he believes that what he's doing is important. The problem is that he rarely sees the fruits of his labors. He has no contact with the many people whose lives are made happier or healthier as a result of the work of your nonprofit. Give your technician opportunities to see your work up close.

- Invite him to group get-togethers.

- Ask him to tell the children in daycare a story, teach them a game, or help them with homework.

- Ask him to attend planning meetings.

- Request his help with a fundraiser.

- Encourage him to share his ideas for making activities better.

- Choose opportunities for participation that do not take a lot of time from his work but make him feel like part of the team.

from hardware and software and toward the organization's goals. Although the two may go hand-in-hand, the productivity of staff and volunteers takes precedence over the speed and power of the computer system. How will the technician make it possible for staff and volunteers to be more successful in their work? What are the problems they are experiencing and how can computers help to solve them? In other words, the emphasis during this period should be on bringing the technician into your world. Help him understand the real definition of computer support, that is, supporting not computers but the people who use them. Accustom him to making decisions and choosing priorities with this focus clearly in mind.

Practicing User-Focused Decision Making

Let us say, the technician requests permission to purchase a new piece of equipment. What changes will it have on the way group members do their work? Use the discussion as an opportunity to encourage him to think out the connections between the purchase and the individuals. Maybe the purchase will speed up the system. Are staff now experiencing problems with speed? Is the amount of work they can perform dependent on the speed of the computer or on other factors? If the reason for the purchase is to be able to run new applications, consider whether they are needed. How would group members do their jobs differently if they had access to these new applications? Be careful not to seem like a wet blanket. Your goal is not to dissuade him from the proposed purchase but to help him think it through more clearly.

One of the biggest advantages of hiring young people is that they learn quickly. They have not had time to become set in their ways and are accustomed to absorbing new information and new ways of doing things from parents, teachers, coaches, and other older adults. If you **are** consistent in the way you approach proposed changes and purchases, the technician will soon be thinking through these connections with a little encouragement from you. It is only when this process is automatic, when he understands the work of the organization and views the computer system in that context, that he is ready to make independent decisions.

Computers Are Not Toys

You may notice that your technician repeatedly requests upgrades for his own computer workstation, while he appears to be less interested in the computers assigned to other staff members. Sometimes these requests are made for a good reason, but your young computer enthusiast's behavior might also be viewed in the same vein as asking Santa for more toys. While it is true that the technician will usually need a somewhat more powerful computer than other staff members, your system is only as fast and powerful as the oldest computer on the network. You might think of a good technician as resembling the shepherd in the Biblical story of the "good shepherd." He should be concerned about every computer on the network, even the least interesting.

Goal Setting Comes First

Everyone in an organization needs clear goals to be productive, and in no case is this more important than with technical support staff. Because of their inexperience, young technicians may not really understand how much time a project requires. They may imagine that they will get to an assignment "just as soon as. . ." It takes maturity to realize that you cannot do all the things you want to do. Following up on sudden inspirations can significantly delay the accomplishment of more important tasks. Establishing clearly defined, measurable goals, accompanied by a reasonable timeline, can help an inexperienced staff member plan his work schedule more realistically. Interim deadlines can alert both technician and supervisor to problems before they become crises. Goal setting is only effective, however, when goals are reviewed often. They serve as a good starting point for regular meetings between supervisor and technician.

Emphasizing People over Machines

In the chapter on hiring technical staff, it was emphasized that your technician must be a "people person." He need not be an extrovert, but he must like being with people as much as he enjoys spending time with computer equipment. However, staff and volunteers must do their part as well. To feel happy and satisfied with his job, your technician must be able to find friends or at least warm acquaintances within the organization. When he enters the break room, the room must not fall silent. Instead, he should be welcomed to informal gatherings, committees, meetings, and even party-planning groups. Supervisors can make a big difference in the way a young technician is received by the group. Inevitably, he will have to endure the complaints of frustrated computer users. However, a supervisor can use his or her influence to make sure that the technician becomes known as a colleague before he is seen as the perpetrator of annoying computer changes.

Preparing for Turnover

A colleague who directs a sister nonprofit is feeling increasingly anxious. For the past year, he and his organization have enjoyed the services of an outstanding young technician. Although the young man had almost no previous experience, he learned quickly and gradually took on a central role in the organization. My colleague tells me that he is becoming paranoid, imagining that colleagues are plotting to hire away the young technician. Having lost other talented young staff members in the past, his fears are not really unfounded. Competent technical support staff are hard to find and the competition for their services is sometimes intense.

Bits, Bites, and Brownies

In one nonprofit, it appeared that integrating the new technician into the organization was going to be an uphill struggle. Not only was the group almost entirely female but most staff members and volunteers were also over the age of 50. What could they possibly have in common with a 22-year-old member of a heavy metal rock band? On his first day of work, however, an especially computer-challenged volunteer encountered him in the hallway and begged him to fix her computer.

It happened that it was not the computer but the computer operator that needed help. On extra good behavior since this was his first day on the job, the young man very tactfully explained the problem. He also showed her some simple keystrokes that she viewed as nothing short of magic. Being one of the more talkative volunteers, she quickly spread the word about the young genius. The next day, he was besieged by admirers, seeking his help. Soon, the supervisor had to place limits on the time he could spend on personal hand-holding, but by then his reputation was secure. Although rather shy, the young technician enjoyed the fuss that was being made over him. He had never been wonderful before, and he especially enjoyed the home baked treats with which his labors were frequently rewarded.

Had the technician looked on that first volunteer as an unwanted interruption, the story would have been quite different. Too often, we assume that computer skills are the sole property of stereotypical "geeks" who spend their free time alone in their rooms with only their computers for company. This is yet another evidence of the cultural divide that separates computer users from nonusers. Fortunately, in this case the selection committee was smart enough to view his band member status as an evidence of sociability and did not allow their personal feelings about contemporary music to influence their decision.

It is a good idea to assume that most young technical staff members will leave your organization within a year or two. Of course, many nonprofits have retained their technicians for considerably longer, but it is unwise to count on longevity. In fact, it is a good idea to be prepared for somewhat sudden leave-takings. Most staff members, encumbered as they are with families, mortgages, and golden retrievers, cannot simply pull up stakes and leave. When a young man waits until the last minute to enroll in grad school or has an opportunity to hitchhike across Europe, he may disappear with hardly any advance warning.

Of course, any leave-taking will be difficult for your nonprofit, but there are some things that you can do to make the transition as painless as possible. For example, other staff members need to know where instruction manuals, spare parts, and printer supplies are kept. They need to know how to perform basic maintenance tasks that, if not done regularly, can bring down your network. Changes made to the system should be put in writing and should be easy to find when the need arises. Network supervisor passwords should be readily available. If you have done your job well, your technician has been working closely with other staff members so the network is not a black hole. Someone was able to pinch-hit last winter when the technician came down with the flu. Someone else kept the network going while he was on vacation. Sure it will be tough to manage without him, but it does not have to be the end of the world.

Summing It Up

Many nonprofit supervisors feel they are unprepared for the job of supervising technical staff members. It is not necessary, however, to possess sophisticated computer skills to be an effective supervisor. Good management skills are the secret to supervising both volunteers and staff members, no matter what their area of specialization. While it is true that supervisors must possess enough basic technology knowledge to understand their young technicians' plans and problems, technicians can also be taught to communicate more effectively, expressing themselves without the aid of computer jargon. Technical staff share most of the same strengths and weaknesses as other young people who are recent arrivals to the workplace. It is the manager's task to harness their energy, enthusiasm, and technical expertise while imbuing good work habits and team spirit.

CHAPTER 9

Safeguarding Essential Information

After reading this chapter, you will be able to:

- Understand the importance of computer security to your organization.
- Balance protection with convenience.
- Avoid computer predators.
- Safeguard essential data.
- Implement a disaster preparedness plan.
- Safeguard the privacy of your members and clients.

Why Security Matters

As we have discussed different technology issues, the subject of security has arisen again and again. The reason is that it touches on every aspect of computerization including staffing. You can be quite sure that within the next month, some crisis will threaten the safety of the technical side of your organization, and thus your organization itself. There is always the possibility that absolutely essential information will be lost. Although this point cannot be emphasized too strongly, it does not mean that you should abandon modern technology; it is almost impossible in today's world to compete successfully without it. Nevertheless, security precautions must become an integral part of every automation project.

Small organizations that depend almost entirely on volunteers are not the only ones that experience security crises. Even fully trained technicians, no matter how experienced, quite naturally focus their attention on the hardware and software they maintain, sometimes forgetting that technology is merely a means to an end. It is the information that the computer system stores that really matters. The technician, who is concerned with the health of the system, may not view the loss of data as the crisis it really is.

Security Is a Management Issue

For this reason, security must be seen as a management issue. It is the responsibility of the board, director, and other administrators and supervisors to make computer security part of the organizational culture. What is needed is a unified strategy that involves not only the technical staff, but every member of the organization. Such a strategy must balance protection with convenience. Before we discuss these management concerns, however, it would be wise to better understand the technical issues involved. Exactly what are the dangers that threaten our computers? Who creates them and for what reason? How do intruders accomplish their goals? To begin to answer these questions, let's start with some simple definitions.

Computer Viruses and Their Near Relations

To most people who watch the evening news or read the morning newspaper, computer viruses seem a lot like evil monsters that invade homes and offices. Everyone seems to have a slightly different mental picture of computer viruses, but many respond to the biological analogy by imagining tiny bugs eating away at their computers. In actuality, viruses are malicious mini-programs that are intended to alter the way a computer functions. Like the germy type of virus, they can duplicate and reduplicate themselves a nearly infinite number of times, often replacing a computer's executable files with copies of the infected file. Each copy of the mini-program is capable of performing unwanted or even disastrous activities on the computer it inhabits.

How Viruses Spread

Until recently, viruses were most often spread by email attachments. However, it is now possible to insert them into almost any type of file, and so they can be found on websites or even in word processing files. Specifically, what are some of the things you might expect a virus to do to your computers? Some are programmed to damage the computer by corrupting programs, deleting files, or reformatting the hard disk. Not all viruses are really malicious; some are intended merely to announce to the computer user that they are present and give their creator a sense of power. However, even these viruses can create inadvertent problems, causing erratic behavior and even system crashes.

Viruses are often included in tempting freeware offerings like games, music, or other files that are downloadable from websites. Sometimes, the virus is even stored in a message alerting you to beware a new virus and encouraging you to pass the alert along to your friends. Some of these messages even provide instructions for renaming or deleting a file so as to open your computer up to the intruder.

Computer Worms

Although it is probably not really productive to describe the technical differences between garden-variety viruses and worms, which are really viruses too, it is important to understand what worms do. Usually hidden inside other files like MS-Word and Excel documents, worms like the famous "Mydoom" can delete files from your system, send out thousands of emails without your consent, and create a "back door that allows a hacker to turn your computer into a "zombie" under his own malicious control. Worms are particularly difficult to combat because although they hide in other files, they are self-contained and do not need to be part of another program to propagate themselves.

Trojan Horses

Named, of course, for the hollow, wooden horse in which, according to Virgil, the ancient Greeks hid themselves and, thus, entered the city of Troy unobserved, Trojan viruses are applications that hide in your computer system. At first they appear harmless and may go unnoticed until they are triggered to "go off." When this happens, they activate themselves to perform some action. When the designated time arrives, they instruct your computer system to do something and that "something" is always an action you wish you could have avoided.

Many Trojans are programmed to request data from a specific website. At the designated time, computers all around the world, which have acquired the virus and inadvertently sent it to other computers, suddenly activate and attempt to reach the chosen site. The website under attack receives so much traffic that it cannot function; it slows down, and may even shut down. This is called a denial of service attack. In the case of a large online business, this can mean millions of dollars in lost revenue. A different type of Trojan initially remains quietly in a computer system "listening" for a particular outside user (usually the creator of the Trojan virus) to come "knocking" at the system door. It then opens its virtual doors wide and lets this intruder take over the computer or network.

Phishing

Unlike computer viruses, phishing is really a computer-age variation on a very old practice of con artists'—the swindle. If you use email, you have most likely been targeted by some sort of "phishing" scam. The anonymity of the Internet makes it possible for the criminally minded to use a legitimate company's name and/or logo to obtain personal information about you. Phishing is the basis of much of the identity theft that is currently plaguing the law enforcement world.

Have you ever received an email message from your bank or insurance company that asked you to respond by supplying personal information such as your Social Security number? In all probability, this was a phishing expedition. Legitimate businesses are fully aware of the dangers of sharing personal information online, and so it is most unlikely that this was a legitimate request. Sometimes, you are asked to go to a specified website and log in. You are also given the helpful hint that if your assigned password does not work, you can just use your Social Security number. Scammers who pretend to be representing your bank may tell you that you are overdrawn or your account is about to be closed. One of the most frustrating things about these scams is that they can look so legitimate. The web page you are directed to may look exactly like Wells Fargo or Citibank because the real pages have actually been copied.

A variant of the phishing scam is "pharming." Malicious software is planted in a user's computer (like the bad seed). In some cases it is planted in large servers. In either case, even if you type a known and trusted website address, the software will intervene and send you to a bogus one.

Adware

So far, we have been describing dangerous threats to personal and computer safety. Adware is more an annoyance than a threat. It is sometimes defined as "a program that delivers unsolicited advertisements to your computer." These programs are usually not dangerous, but they represent an invasion of your computer system nonetheless. Adware is responsible for many but not all of those annoying pop-up screens. Although many are generated by websites and appear as advertisements when you visit the website, adware pop-ups can appear anytime you use your web browser, no matter which site you are visiting at the time. This is possible because you have inadvertently downloaded software to your computer when you clicked on a link, either in an email message or advertisement on a web page.

Adware more broadly defined includes the "cookies" or small files that are automatically downloaded to your computer and that keep track of your visits to a website and relay this information to that site. When such a file also keeps track of your visits to other sites and communicates information about your surfing habits, it has crossed the boundary into spyware.

Spyware

Although Adware is usually just a commercial ploy to get your attention, Spyware is a more serious threat to personal privacy. It is a term used for programs that collect information from your computer without your knowledge and send it to a third party. Spyware programs may perform relatively harmless functions such as anonymously reporting which websites you visit. However, they can also capture user names, passwords, and email content, sending this data back to someone who may sell it or use it to take on your identity. Because the Internet is such a recent development, ethical standards have not been fully developed or backed up with legislation. Thus, spyware is often packaged with popular, mainstream software. More malicious spyware may be buried in the Trojan horse viruses described above and collect bank account numbers, passwords, Social Security numbers, and other highly sensitive information.

Hacking

"Hacking" is a general term for attempting to gain access to a computer system without authorization to do so. The goal of hackers (or crackers as they are often called) is to "get inside," whether simply for the fun of it, to find personal information such as passwords and credit cards numbers, or to take control of the system. Hackers may also gain entrance in order to use your Internet connection to transit their own material, often pornographic or otherwise illegal.

Because the term "hacking" is used so often and with such very different intentions, it is useful to be more specific in describing the activities. The following types of hacking behavior range from innocuous to disastrous.

- **The probe:** Probes have been called the electronic equivalent of testing doorknobs to find an unlocked door. A probe may be relatively harmless or can lead to future intrusions.

- **The scan:** Scans are actually large numbers of probes that together provide a lot of information about a computer system. Most interesting to hackers is the information generated about weaknesses and vulnerabilities.

- **The account compromise:** This is an unauthorized entry that does not involve system-level or root-level privileges (administrator privileges). Damage is limited to individual user accounts and so cannot compromise the whole system.

- **The root compromise:** This involves unauthorized entry at the root or system level. Once such an entry is achieved, the hacker has almost total power of the system and can hide all traces of the intrusion.

- **Packet sniffing:** Information is sent over networks in small packets, so a packet sniffer is a program that captures data from information packets as they travel. If the "sniffer" is able to capture passwords from the packets, a hacker can gain immediate access to the system.

- **Exploitation of trust:** This is a term used for attacks that involve forging a computer identity and appearing to other computers on a network as one of their own trusted group.

- **Internet infrastructure attacks:** These are not personal attacks but rather attacks intended to damage the Internet itself and to slow or halt Net traffic.

Other Threats to Personal and Computer Safety

Bear in mind that one need not be a computer expert to use computers for illegal or unethical purposes. The nature of the Internet shelters and disguises criminals, and blurs the lines between acceptable and unethical behavior.

Fraud

Even in nonprofit organizations, an occasional staff member or volunteer may use the computer system for his or her own purposes. Although it may be simply an issue of someone using the system for recreation or personal business, there have been instances of individuals defrauding or "booby-trapping" an organization. For example, it is possible to use a computer to skim small amounts of money from financial accounts. Computer banking and automatic bill paying services may facilitate such activities. When an organization has multiple bank accounts and vendors, it becomes difficult to trace repeated misdirection of small sums. Employees have also been known to use nonprofit computers to:

- Increase their hourly wage.

- Decrease someone else's pay.

- Give themselves additional vacation time.

IN THE REAL WORLD

Beware the Disgruntled Employee

John, a technician who worked for a small museum, had a drinking problem and repeatedly failed to show up for work. When he was fired, he immediately changed all passwords, disabled the antivirus program, and changed the language of the computer system to Swedish. Angry employees who feel they have been wronged or mistreated sometimes sabotage a system for revenge. Nonprofits may be vulnerable when they must lay off staff due to funding shortfalls. The following are some of the things a disgruntled individual might do to cause trouble:

Delete files

Change data or enter it incorrectly

Change administrator passwords

Delete user accounts of staff and volunteers

Destroy programs

Crash systems

Hold data hostage

- Alter inventory records to conceal the absence of stolen items.

- Alter long distance telephone records.

Personal Privacy

While nonprofits may have somewhat fewer worries about fraud and computer sabotage than business organizations, they are sometimes more at risk when it comes to threats to personal privacy. Nonprofits maintain some of the most highly confidential personal records, including medical histories and psychologists' notes, as well as information about their clients' credit and other financial problems. These are records that could do a great deal of harm if they fell into the wrong hands.

A lucrative market exists for such information. It can be sold to businesses that maintain huge databases of personal data. Called data mining, the practice involves collecting medical records, information about personal habits, travel, grocery purchases, hotel reservations, and credit histories, then linking them all together to provide highly revealing personal profiles that can be sold at premium prices. In addition, private investigators are not always ethical in the ways they obtain information and may attempt to bribe staff members. Occasionally, threats to privacy come simply from nosy staff and volunteers who enjoy browsing through records, discovering bits of potential gossip about their friends and neighbors.

Errors and Omissions

No list of computer threats would be complete without including ordinary, well-meaning people who simply do not know what they are doing. Recent computer programs are much more user-friendly than their predecessors, and it is no longer possible to accidentally reformat a hard disk or make other similarly devastating errors. However, it is still possible to inadvertently lose weeks or months of work. Warning messages and help screens continue to be written in language that is all but unintelligible to many users. When novices are shown a warning each time they attempt to make a small change, they may ignore warnings intended to avert catastrophes. Carelessness, too, can destroy the value of computer-generated information. The cliché "garbage in, garbage out" is all too true. The widespread use of volunteers to perform tasks that really require the expertise of a computer technician further contributes to the problem.

Security Management Practices

It is time to go back and visit our colleagues at the Pleasantville Family Advocacy Association. As we learned earlier, they are doing very well. They now have a building of their own and a small staff that includes a systems administrator. Fresh from a Microsoft certification program, the systems administrator has been imbued with the importance of security. He understands that networks are vulnerable to a variety of intruders. He not only understands how careless users can leave the system open to attack, but he also worries constantly about the many security breaches he has discovered.

When Security Is a One-Person Crusade

Something must be done, the diligent young systems administrator concludes. He decides that he will make the system more secure without consulting his supervisor or other members of the organization. They would not understand, he reasons. They are all continuing to use the same passwords they were issued when the system was first installed; he will change that. Users chose passwords that were too easy to discover, like their birthdays and the names of their pets; he will change that too.

In fact, as he thinks about all those members of the organization with their unsophisticated computer skills and careless behavior, he decides that they have entirely too much access to the system. He will take advantage of the feature in the server software that allows him to set specific rights for each user. Inspired by his security plan, he works late one evening resetting passwords and deciding what rights each user will have on the system.

Communication Is Essential to Security

Since the technician worked late the night before, he arranged to arrive late next morning. When he walked in the door, he was greeted by absolute chaos. Why, he wondered, was everyone upset? After all, he had left notes for everyone, informing them of their new passwords. Well yes, but only some of the staff managed to decipher his penmanship and even some of these talented cryptographers could not manage the long and complicated passwords with upper and lower case letters, numbers and symbols.

Once passwords were mastered, staff and volunteers had another unpleasant surprise waiting for them. Many discovered that they could no longer get to the records they needed to do their work. Some could see the records but could not make necessary changes. Since the technician did not really understand the work that each staff member and volunteer did, he made his decisions based on what he saw as their level of computer competence.

Security Must Be Everyone's Concern

It was inevitable that these unilateral decisions started a war between the system administrator and the rest of the group. On his part, he felt hurt and misunderstood.

Why could they not understand that he had just been protecting the system? They, on the other hand, continued to be irate. It took some time for all the problems to be corrected, so for a week or more, counselors would arrive, only to discover that they could not access their clients' records, the bookkeeper could not use some features of the accounting program, and it appeared to some users that the membership database had completely disappeared.

After such experiences, you cannot blame computer users for viewing security as a "bee in the bonnet" of their systems administrator. To them, security meant doing their work less efficiently and with more hassles. Naturally, they found ways to get around at least some of his decrees. When he was reprimanded by the executive director for his troubles, he made matters worse by restoring some rights that users really did not need. Overall, the experience set the stage for a major security crisis.

Is There a Better Way?

Over lunch, the director poured out this horror story to her colleague, the executive director of the Taylor Teen Center. Even less knowledgeable about computers than she, he wondered how he could prevent a similar crisis at his organization. The new Teen Center building would soon open, and in addition to staff computers, there would be eight PCs for teen use. Since teen websites are often the ones most vulnerable to attackers, he wondered how he could safeguard their fledgling network. When he returned to work, he went immediately to the server room to repeat the story to the Teen Center's own young technician. Recently hired, the technician was still becoming familiar with the eccentricities of the computer system and had not really gotten around to giving much thought to security.

Developing an Effective Computer Security Program

As they talked, both director and technician remembered other security horror stories, and for the first time both considered what it would really be like when all the new computers were in operation. Members of the tech team were called together, and gradually, panic gave way to reason. What was needed was a comprehensive security plan. With the experience of the Pleasantville group serving as an example of what not to do, it was decided that this would not be a "top-down" plan.

Everyone would need to be involved and that meant extensive training. If computer users did not understand the dangers, they would not remember to take precautions. A series of training sessions was organized, some for inexperienced computer users and some for more advanced users.

Planning for Security

No one, no matter how unskilled, would be given orders or made to feel incompetent. It was essential that both staff and volunteers improve their computer skills and become more comfortable with computers. Being told that they were foolishly allowing malicious predators to attack the system would certainly not improve their self-confidence. Neither would anyone arbitrarily take away needed rights on the system. However, the technician would learn more about the work of the organization so that he could intelligently determine which jobs needed higher-level access to the system.

Password Security

After much discussion, it was decided to begin with password security. If staff, volunteers, and teens all understood how intruders get hold of passwords and use them to invade computer systems, they would be more than willing to protect them (see Exhibit 9.1). This is a good topic for a first security-focused workshop. Issues are not difficult to understand, and it is easy to make a connection between personal habits and disastrous experiences.

Next Steps

Once that first workshop was held, neither the technician nor the director was quite sure how to proceed. What else were they doing wrong? They agreed that it was important not to go overboard. Keeping the trust and support of staff and volunteers was perhaps the most important goal of the project. Without their buy-in, little progress could be made so they would not impose volumes of new regulations. Instead, they would analyze their security weaknesses to identify their most serious problems (see Exhibit 9.2). New security measures could then be focused on just their most urgent needs. Later when computer users were better prepared, other problems could be addressed.

EXHIBIT 9.1

Password Safety for Computer Users

Both staff and volunteers should understand that if hackers can gain access to passwords, they can endanger the whole organization. Here are some basic questions to consider about password safety:

- Do staff and volunteers understand that under no circumstances can anyone else use their computer account or password?

- Is the list of user accounts and names kept secure?

- Are accounts terminated when staff and volunteers leave the organization?

- Must all users authenticate themselves to use any part of the network?

- Are staff and volunteers taught how to create passwords that are hard to hack? Do they understand that names, dates, and other commonly anticipated passwords should be avoided?

- Are they asked to use a mix of letters, numbers, and symbols when creating a password?

- Has the system administrator changed all preset and packaged passwords (such as the default password) that is assigned when a new user account is created?

- Are staff and volunteers required to change passwords at regular intervals?

- Have users been warned to never send their password as a part of an email message?

- Have users been warned not to type their passwords when someone may be watching?

- Are passwords masked on display screens?

- Are users advised to change their passwords immediately if for any reason they think they may have inadvertently shared their password.

- Is there a limit to the number of times a user can attempt to log in incorrectly?

- Are staff and volunteers asked to log out of their accounts when they finish using computers?

EXHIBIT 9.2

A Security Checklist for Keeping Computers and Computer Users Safe

If your nonprofit maintains a local area network, meet with your systems administrator to learn what is being done to maximize computer safety. Here are some questions to get you started:

- Does your network have an opening screen that users must visit before accessing the system? Does the screen reinforce good security practices and keep out unwanted visitors?

- Has careful thought been given to the information users really need to do their jobs and has access been limited accordingly?

- Is account activity monitored? Would your systems administrator be aware of predators hacking your system? Are logs checked regularly?

- Are accounts terminated when staff and volunteers leave the organization?

- If a user forgets to log out, will he or she be automatically logged out after a reasonable amount of time?

- Is preapproval required for remote access capability?

- Are staff and volunteers aware that they should not send confidential information over public lines unless the files are first encrypted (usually indicated by the padlock on the browser screen)?

- If your organization routinely connects to another network that's outside your control, is your systems administrator aware of the security features in use? Are they acceptable?

- Are firewalls in use as needed?

- Are dial-in communication numbers protected from outsiders?

- Are modems disabled when not in use or kept off automatic answer modes?

The Systems Administrator's Responsibility

As the teen center technician was considering ways to instill good security habits in others, it occurred to him that maybe his own actions left some room for improvement. Your own systems administrator may also be guilty of carelessness when it comes to routine security procedures. He may also threaten the security of the system by failing to maintain the system properly and repairing equipment in a slapdash way. Whether your system is being maintained by a technician or by a group of volunteers, you might ask the following questions:

- Are computers checked regularly to be sure updates to the Windows operating system and antivirus programs have been downloaded and installed on schedule? Computers can be set to do this automatically but someone must make sure it is really happening.

- Is the entire system backed up daily? More frequent backups may be needed during busy times like fundraising campaigns.

- Does any confusion exist about who is responsible for making backups?

- Are backups taken off-site to a designated location? (Imagine that your server is destroyed by fire or flood. If backups are stored on-site, they will be lost as well.)

- Is there a system in place for keeping antivirus subscriptions current? Is there a written record showing when each subscription expires?

- Are virus scans scheduled to run automatically at times when computers will really be logged in? It does no good to schedule them in the middle of the night if computers are turned off.

- Are your computers equipped with anti-spyware programs?

- Has your systems administrator alerted staff and volunteers to the dangers of spyware? Do all your computer users understand that software can be downloaded without their being aware of it?

- Is a firewall in place? Are firewall updates downloaded and installed automatically?

- Does your organization have a written technology disaster plan in place?

- If the network server's hard drive crashed tomorrow, how much data would you lose? How long would it take for the network to be fully functional again?

- What plans are in place for repairing or replacing computer equipment including hubs, switches, and even your network server? How quickly could the systems administrator bring the network back up if an essential piece of equipment failed?

- Have you identified and limited access to confidential information like client records and contributor information?

- Is a plan in place for cleaning computer equipment regularly?

- Are your systems administrator and others who regularly work with computers trained to take safety precautions with high voltage equipment? Are they aware of the potential dangers from laser printers like burns from the fuser assembly and eye damage from the laser itself?

- Are your technician and other staff members aware of federal, state, and local government disposal regulations for batteries, toner cartridges, ozone filters, and CRTs?

- Are precautions taken against electrostatic discharge (ESD)? This is particularly important in dry climates with less than 70 percent humidity. Small electronic components, such as microchips, are especially susceptible to electric shocks.

There's No Need to Panic

As the Teen Center director and the technician talked, each kept remembering more and more horror stories. Coping with security began to seem like an overwhelming job. How could they possibly secure their computer system when so many others had failed? It is understandable that small nonprofits feel somewhat intimidated when confronted by professional hackers who know far more about computers than they do.

However, they are forgetting that the very best weapons are available to them (see Exhibit 9.3). By conscientiously following routine safety procedures, they can effectively thwart most attackers. Of course, hackers know a lot about computers, but even computer professionals depend on these same routine procedures and even professionals are attacked when they get careless.

Multiple Layers of Protection

Another excellent way of protecting a computer system is to use several layers of protection; if one layer fails, the other layers will continue to protect the system. In other words, do not rely on one antivirus program. Keep at least two programs updated. Services like "HouseCall," which is available on the Internet, scans your computers at no cost, so even small nonprofits on tight budgets can maintain a high level of protection. If you install two anti-spyware programs, you will discover that each will catch problems that the other misses. By using both, you significantly increase protection. Hackers are successful largely because of the carelessness of computer users, and it does not take a computer genius to remember to update the firewall or spyware program and make a note on the log.

Website Protection

Soon after the teen center opens, a group of volunteers is planning to create a website that will advertise its activities and solicit funds. However, a website is perhaps the easiest target for an intruder. Because websites communicate with outsiders over unsecured lines, there is really no way to make a website as secure as a computer or computer network. For this reason, it is a good idea to keep your website off your network. This is most often done by contracting with a hosting service to load the website on its own computers. The hosting service is far more experienced with hacking tactics and is in a better position to protect all the websites it hosts.

EXHIBIT 9.3

List of Basic Security Precautions

- Update your operating system often.

- Consider replacing your Microsoft Internet Explorer browser with one that is less often the target of viruses such as Firefox.

- Consider replacing your Microsoft Outlook or Outlook Express email program for the same reason.

- Install a firewall.

- Install more than one active antivirus program.

- Install both an active and passive anti-Trojan program.

- Install at least two anti-spyware and anti-adware programs.

- Install an intrusion prevention and detection program.

- Run regularly scheduled tests to be sure your system is secure.

- Back up your files.

- Update all your security programs on a regular schedule.

- Use layered protection. This means running multiple security products so that if one layer fails, another will still be in place.

Each time you modify your website, you will upload the edited pages to your host's server. To do so, you will be given a password. Remember the packet sniffers described above. Passwords sent in plain-text mode are subject to line sniffing and so should never be shared through email or online messaging. Be sure that when you are uploading updates to your website, you do so over a secure connection (usually indicated by the padlock icon in the lower right corner of your browser).

Public Computers

Since computers empower people, the absence of computer access conversely interferes with their ability to live happy and successful lives. Many nonprofit organizations, therefore, consider it part of their mission to provide computers for the many who do not own their own PCs. Money is not the only reason why people may not have their own computers. Some lack the needed skills to set up and troubleshoot their own equipment. Others need continuing assistance to perform basic computer tasks.

Food and Drink in Computer Labs

Many public computer lab managers express frustration at the food and drink that users bring with them. Most have rules prohibiting food, but becoming an agent of the food police is a thankless job. Keyboards are most in danger since spilled Coca-Cola can mean the end of their useful lives. Fortunately, however, keyboards are relatively inexpensive and can be covered with thin plastic membrane covers. Aerosol "canned air" is useful to remove potato chip crumbs but care is needed not to blast them deeper into keyboards. Purchasing computer desks with keyboard trays that move in and out also protects keyboards when they are not in use. These are great for staff and volunteers but may be too flimsy for constant public use.

Keeping Public Computers Healthy

Cigarettes should definitely be prohibited from computer labs since both the smoke and ashes can damage computers, to say nothing of the fire danger they pose. Since most public buildings are now smoke-free, this is not usually difficult to enforce in public computer labs (although administrators with private offices are sometimes the ones who violate the rule).

While teenagers often accompany their surfing with music, it is important that they not keep time with drumming fingers, slamming hands, or tapping feet since vibrations can damage hard drives. Magnets can also destroy hardware and erase data (remember that computer data is composed of magnetic impulses), but again, it is more likely to be staff and volunteers who attach notes to computers with magnets.

Placing Public Computers on a Separate Network

As you may remember, the teen center planned to open with a small computer lab so teens could surf the Internet. Many teenagers are devotees of chat rooms and messaging programs that pose special dangers to computer networks. Teen-oriented websites are probably the ones most prone to virus attacks. Many computers have been compromised by users who download files that appear innocent, like music and graphics files, but are later discovered to contain very malignant viruses. Public computers therefore require special precautions.

One of the first precautions the teen center technician decided to take to discourage hackers was to create a separate virtual wireless network just for the teen computers. Remember that when your computers can communicate with one another over a local area network, one computer can download a virus capable of crashing the entire network.

Since there were many teen users and no way to fully inform them about security measures, it made sense to give them their own network. If the public network were attacked by hackers, the administrative side of the organization could continue to do its work. Staff and volunteers accessed one network when they were attending to the organization's business, effectively separated by a firewall from the public network. Although this may sound like a complicated solution, it is usually simply a matter of changing some settings. If yours is already a wireless configuration it is especially easy to do.

Software Programs for Public Computers

Perhaps the most difficult challenge that systems administrators face when it comes to public computers is keeping them exactly as they were when they were originally set up. That means that operating system and programs remain unchanged and no unwanted "extras" like malicious viruses make their way into the system. Essentially, there are two ways this goal can be achieved. The first and preferred way is to keep intruders out. This means placing both physical and virtual barriers between the intruder and the computer system.

If this does not work, a second line of defense is needed. Whatever changes an intruder is able to accomplish must be undone. The system must be returned to its former state; in other words as it was before it was attacked. One software utility that is intended to return computers to their original state is Roxio's "GoBack." GoBack, which sells for about $50.00, literally takes computers back in time, to the moment when they were functioning normally. It will also recover files that were

TIPS & TECHNIQUES

Six Security Tips from the Pros

- Change passwords often. Make them complicated and never share.

- Assume the worst. If you do not know the sender of an email or something about a web page looks odd, do not trust it.

- Keep antivirus and firewall software up to date.

- Use a spam blocker to limit unwanted and potentially dangerous email.

- Never provide personal information at websites if you can avoid it. You never know who's collecting the information.

- Use different usernames and passwords for work, personal business, and recreational surfing.

accidentally deleted or changed. The program keeps a record of every change that is made to the hard disk, whether to Windows system files or to software applications. Even before Windows loads, GoBack begins logging each change to the hard disk. This means that GoBack is not a substitute for making regular backups since the log will be lost if the hard drive fails.

Imagine that a public user opens an email attachment, triggering a barrage of outgoing messages and at the same time damaging your operating system and programs. With GoBack, it is easy to choose a time before the computer was invaded and return the computer to that moment. This works well not only for viruses but for legitimate programs that accidentally crash your system. Note that new software solutions will be arriving on the market constantly. Keep abreast of recent software reviews to find out which programs are most appropriate to your needs.

Summing It Up

No issue is more vital to the success of your technology program and, in some ways, to the success of your organization, than reliable computer security. Although most Internet users are responsible people, the cyberspace environment has become home to predators who use the unique opportunities it offers to prey upon the unsuspecting. Although the specific activities that threaten nonprofits are highly technical in nature, there is no need to possess sophisticated technical skills to deal with them successfully. Once again, it is effective management skills that can thwart all but the most determined attackers. Regular attention to standard security precautions, like installing antivirus and firewall program updates on schedule, can mean the difference between success and failure.

At the heart of this book is the belief that sound management skills can empower committed nonprofit groups to partner with technology to achieve their goals. Conversely, ignorance, absence of planning, erratic maintenance, and disruptive interpersonal behaviors all contribute to failure. Leaders of mission–based organizations must assume responsibility for technology, and they can do it effectively without specialized technical expertise. It has been their sense of commitment and their ability to effectively coordinate the activities of diverse individuals that have made them leaders. These same qualities can make them technology leaders as well. By helping their members understand both technology's strengths and pitfalls, they can build organizations that that are empowered, not endangered by technology.

Index

software use, 43, 45
trainers, 183
volunteers, 6, 8, 43, 45, 191, 192, 209
Windows, 25

U

URL, 99
publicizing, 100

V

Vendors
local versus national, 63, 64
references, checking, 67, 69
salespeople, dealing with, 69, 71, 73
selecting, 73, 74
as source of information, 57, 58
ViaVoice, 112
Viruses
antivirus programs, 48, 49, 89–91
denial of service attack, 240
described, 238
methods of spreading, 239
and teenagers, 255, 256
Trojan, 239, 240, 242
and use of home computers, 48
worms, 239
Volunteers
computer literacy, 57
computer use policy, 217
conscripted, 216
errors, 245
expertise, 4, 8, 38, 40, 41, 45, 204–208
"firing," 220
home computers, use of, 47, 48
leaders, 8
older volunteers
and computer literacy, 209
and computer use, 179, 181
short-term memory limitations, 209, 211
sources of information on, 210
and paid staff and management structure, 83, 84
personnel policies, 8–12
problems with, 204, 205

responsibilities, 3, 8–12, 218–220
skills and interests, 6
stability and security considerations, 56
staff versus volunteers, 221, 222
strengths and weaknesses, 8
supervising, 214–220
supervision, 203–205, 214–220
teens and college students, 45, 46
time constraints, 204, 205
training, 6, 8, 43, 45, 191, 192, 209. *See also* Training
virtual, 211–214
website design and maintenance, 97–99
work schedules, 227

W

Webmaster, selecting, 97–99
Websites
accessibility, 101, 102
addresses (URLs), 99, 100
advertising staff positions, 158
Chronicle of Philanthropy Careers, 158
Dell Computer, 66
discounts for nonprofits, 70
free browsers, 87
grants, 35
GrantStation PRO, 90
hosting services, 103–105, 253, 254
links, use of, 99
management theory and practice, 223
McAfee, 122
Microsoft, 122
Monster.com, 159
Mozilla, 87
Nonprofit Organizational Assessment Tool, 6
Nonprofit Times Jobs, 158
nonprofit website, design and maintenance of, 97–105, 253, 254
Norton Anti-Virus, 122
Npower, 6
online technical support, 123
Opera, 87
protection, 253, 254
resources for board members, 24
reviews of computers, 67